T0203215

Static Analysis of Software

Static Analysis of Software

of Software

The Abstract Interpretation

Edited by
Jean-Louis Boulanger

ISTE Ltd
27-37 St George's Road
London SW19 4EU
UK

www.iste.co.uk

John Wiley & Sons, Inc.
111 River Street
Hoboken, NJ 07030
USA

www.wiley.com

© ISTE Ltd 2012

Library of Congress Cataloging-in-Publication Data

Static analysis of software : the abstract interpretation / edited by Jean-Louis Boulanger.
p. cm.
Includes bibliographical references and index.
 ISBN 978-1-84821-320-3
 1. Computer software--Testing. 2. Debugging in computer science. 3. Computer software--Quality control. I. Boulanger, Jean-Louis.
 QA76.76.T48S75 2011
 005.1'4--dc23
                                                                                      2011039611

British Library Cataloguing-in-Publication Data
A CIP record for this book is available from the British Library
ISBN: 978-1-84821-320-3

Printed and bound in Great Britain by CPI Group (UK) Ltd., Croydon, Surrey CR0 4YY

Table of Contents

Introduction

Context

Although formal program analysis techniques (see works by Hoare [HOA 69] and Dijkstra [DIJ 75]) are quite old, the implementation of formal methods goes back to the 1980s. These techniques enable us to analyze the behavior of a software application described in programming language. Program correction (good behavior, program stop, etc.) is then demonstrated by program proof based on the calculation of the weakest precondition [DIJ 76].

It was not until the end of the 1990s that formal methods (Z [SPI 89], VDM [JON 90]) and the B method [ABR 96, ARA 97] were used in industrial applications and could be applied in an industrial context. One of the obstacles to their use was how they could be implemented in an industrial application (large application, time and cost constraints, etc.). They could only be implemented using tools that were mature enough and had sufficient performance.

It is worth noting that in the context of critical applications, at least two formal methods have a recognized and commonly used design environment that covers part of the realization of the code specification process while integrating one or several verification processes, that is to say the B method [ABR 96] and Lustre language [HAL 91, ARA 97] and its graphic version, called SCADE® [DOR 08]. The B method and SCADE® environment are associated with proven industrial tools. For example, AtelierB and Btoolkit, commercially produced by Clearsy and Bcore, respectively, are tools that completely cover the B method development cycle (specification, refinement, code generation and proof).

Introduction written by Jean-Louis BOULANGER.

Formal methods are based on different formal verification techniques, such as proof, *model checking* [BAI 08] and/or simulation.

The use of formal methods, though in full expansion, is still marginal compared to the number of code lines. Indeed, there are currently many more lines of Ada [ANS 83], C and C++ code that have been manually produced via a formal process only. For this reason other formal techniques have been implemented to verify the behavior of a software application written in a programming language such as C or Ada. The main technique, called *abstract program interpretation* [COU 00], enables us to evaluate the set of behaviors of a software application using static analysis. In the past few years, this type of technique has given rise to several tools, such as Polyspace[®1], Caveat[2], Absint[3], Frama-C[4] and/or Astrée[5].

The efficiency of these static program analysis techniques has greatly progressed with the increase in the power of office equipment. It is worth noting that these techniques generally require the integration of complementary information into the manual code, such as pre-conditions, invariants and/or post-conditions.

SPARK Ada[6] is an approach where Ada has been extended [BAR 03] in order to introduce additional elements (pre, post and invariant) and a sequence of adapted tools has been defined.

Objective

In [BOW 95] and [ARA 97], we have the first feedback from industrialists regarding formal techniques, and in particular feedback on the B method, Lustre language [HAL 91, ARA 97] and SAO+ (SCADE[®]'s predecessor). Other works, such as [MON 00, MON 02, HAD 06] provide an overview of formal methods from a scientific point of view.

With regards to the presentation of context and the state of the literature, our objective is to present concrete examples of the industrial uses of formal techniques. By formal techniques, we mean different approaches based on mathematics, which enable us to demonstrate that a software application respects a certain number of properties.

---

1 See www.mathworks.com/ products/polyspace/.
2 See www-list.cea.fr/labos/fr/LSL/caveat/ index.html.
3 See web www.absint.com.
4 To find out more, see web frama-c.com.
5 See www.astree.ens.fr.
6 See www.altran-praxis.com/spark.aspx contains additional information about SPARK Ada.

It is worth noting that the standard use of formal techniques consists of running specification and/or design models. Increasingly, however, formal techniques are seen as a way of carrying out verification (static code analysis, proof that the property is respected, proper management of floater calculation, etc.).

This book is part of a series that covers four different aspects:

– this first volume concerns industrial examples of the implementation of formal techniques based on static analysis, such as abstract interpretation: there are examples of the use of Astrée (Chapter 2), Caveat (Chapter 2), CodePeer (Chapter 5), Frama-C (Chapters 2 and 6) and Polsypace® (Chapters 3 and 4) tools;

– the second volume gives industrial examples of B method implementation [ABR 96];

– the third volume is dedicated to the presentation of different modeling techniques, such as SCADE® 7 [DOR 08], ControlBuild[8] and MaTeLo[9].

– the fourth volume is dedicated to the presentation of the railway sector's application of formal technics.

In conclusion to this introduction, I would like to thank all the industrialists who have given their own time to write these chapters, each one being even more interesting than the next.

Bibliography

[ABR 96] ABRIAL Jr., *The B Book – Assigning Programs to Meanings*, Cambridge University Press, Cambridge, August 1996.

[ANS 83] ANSI, ANSI/MIL-STD-1815A-1983 Standard, ADA Programming Language, ANSI, 1983.

[BAI 08] BAIER C., KATOEN J.P., *Principles of Model Checking*, MIT Press, London, 2008.

[BAR 03] BARNES J., *High Integrity Software: The SPARK Approach to Safety and Security*, Addison-Wesley, London, 2003.

[BOW 95] BOWEN J.P., HINCHEY M.G., *Applications of Formal Methods*, Prentice Hall, Upper Saddle River, 1995.

---

7 SCADE® is distributed by Esterel-Technologies, see www.esterel-technologies.com.
8 To find out more about the ControlBuild tool, see www.geensoft.com/en/article/controlbuild.
9 To find out more about MaTeLo, see www.all4tec.net/index.php/All4tec/matelo-product.html.

[COU 00] COUSOT P., "Interprétation abstraite ", *Technique et Science Informatique*, vol. 19, p. 155-164, no. 1-2-3, Hermès, Paris, 2000.

[DIJ 75] DIJKSTRA E.W., "Guarded commands, nondeterminacy and formal derivation of programs", *Communications of the ACM*, vol.18, no. 8, pp. 453-457, 1975.

[DIJ 76] DIJKSTRA E.W., *A Discipline of Programming*, Prentice Hall, Engelwood Cliffs, 1976.

[DOR 08] DORMOY F.X., "Scade 6 a model based solution for safety critical software development", *Embedded Real-Time Systems Conference*, Toulouse, France, 2008.

[HAD 06] HADDAD S. (ed.), KORDON F., PETRUCCI L., *Méthodes Formelles pour les Systèmes Répartis et Coopératifs*, Hermès Lavoisier, Paris, 2006.

[HAL 91] HALBWACHS N., CASPI P., RAYMOND P., PILAUD D., "The synchronous dataflow programming language Lustre", *Proceedings of the IEEE*, no. 9, vol. 79, pp. 1305-1320, 1991.

[HOA 69] HOARE CAR, "An axiomatic basis for computer programming", *Communications of the ACM*, vol. 12, no. 10, pp. 576-583, 1969.

[JON 90] JONES C.B., *Systematic Software Development using VDM*, (2nd edition), Prentice Hall, Engelwood Cliffs, 1990.

[MON 00] MONIN J.F., *Introduction aux Méthodes Formelles*, Hermès, Paris, 2000.

[MON 02] MONIN J.F., *Understanding Formal Methods*, Springer Verlag, Heidelberg, 2002.

[OFT 97] OBSERVATOIRE FRANÇAIS des TECHNIQUES AVANCEES (OFTA), *Applications des Méthodes Formelles au Logiciel*, vol. 20, Arago, Masson, Paris, June 1997.

[SPI 89] SPIVEY J.M., *The Z Notation – a Reference Manual*, Prentice Hall, Engelwood Cliffs, 1989.

Chapter 1

Formal Techniques for Verification and Validation

1.1. Introduction

The aim of this chapter is to recall concepts and techniques that are implemented in order to verify and validate software based systems.

Verification and validation (V&V) activities are essential if we are to build a software application that reaches a specific confidence level. V&V encompasses a set of activities that extend over the entire realization cycle.

Within this relationship, we place ourselves in the context of a process of software realization that is based on a V-cycle, as the standards applicable to dependable systems recommend (generic, CEI/IEC 61508 [IEC 98], rail, CENELEC EN 50128 [CEN 01], aeronautical, DO178 [RTA 92], nuclear [IEC 06] and automotive ISO 26262 [ISO 09]).

1.2. Realization of a software application

It is worth noting that we are talking about the *realization* of a software application and not the *development* of a software application. The realization of a software application includes development activities but also activities of verification, validation, production, installation and maintenance.

Chapter written by Jean-Louis BOULANGER.

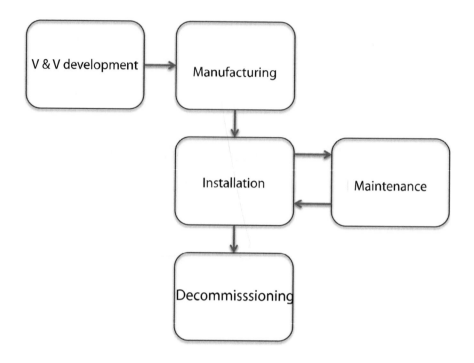

Figure 1.1. *Realization of a software application*

V&V activities are important and will be more or less developed depending on the required safety level. The production activities of the final application and the installation are crucial, and require the implementation of specific processes. The decommissioning of a software application is mentioned but is of no concern, in contrast to the decommissioning of a complex system, such as the decommissioning of a nuclear plant or a rail installation.

Maintenance of the software application is a very difficult activity. Indeed, after evolution it is necessary to uphold the safety level while controlling the cost of the evolution and minimizing the impact on the system in service.

A software application is faced with a problem when it comes to maintenance: its lifespan. For rail, the lifespan is 40 to 50 years, for aeronautics it is 40 years, for nuclear power 50 years and for the automotive industry it is 15 years. In view of these lifespans it is necessary to take measures in order to guarantee the maintenance of the service and the software application.

1.3. Characteristics of a software application

It is possible to characterize a software application according to the following properties:

– visible *but* intangible: anyone is capable of implementing a software application and identifying its behaviors but an application remains a series of bits copied into a memory, the alteration of which produces another application;

– used *but* does not wear out: a software application has so-called *systematic* faults but the wear due to time does not degrade the software application; we say that it is aging, in the sense that its performances become degraded (for example during changes in versions of the operating system), it no longer corresponds to the standard and the behaviors on the new architecture are no longer the same;

– does *not* deteriorate from the effects of testing: indeed planting of the software application does not lead to its loss and or induce any costs, which the implementation of a *crash-test* in the automotive domain can, for example;

– *always* and *still* traditionally made: man remains the main player in the realization cycle of a software application. The implementation of code-generating tools remains to be developed and is based on complex tools that are once again developed in a traditional manner, hence the problems mentioned regarding tool qualification;

– (too?) *easily* reproducible: the ease with which a software application can be reproduced leads to having n versions of the same software application on m media;

– (too?) *easy* to modify: a simple hexadecimal editor enables the program in the memory to be modified, an EMC (electromagnetic compatibility) problem and/or a particle are capable of making a bit in the memory evolve, thus making the program or associated data evolve, etc;

– of great complexity and therefore very *high* (too high?) cost: the size of software applications has gone from several tens of thousands of lines to several hundreds of thousands of lines of code and the question of how to manage this complexity thus arises;

– etc.

This list of characteristics reminds us that a software application is not a simple object but is an object that must be managed from its realization to its installation, without forgetting its maintenance. Management implies the implementation of a set of rules that must take into account the control of actions carried out via verification activities.

1.4. Realization cycle

As previously stated, the realization of a software application is broken down into stages (specification, design, coding, tests, etc.). This is called the lifecycle. The lifecycle is necessary to describe the dependencies and sequences between the activities. The lifecycle must take into account the progressive refinement aspect of the development as well as possible iterations. In this section, we will present the lifecycle that is used to build a certifiable software application.

DEFINITION 1.1. – *Certifiable application.* A certifiable software application is a software application that has been built in such a way that it can be certified.

The notion of a certifiable software application is linked to the notion of certification. Certification is an activity that is based on the ability to demonstrate the safety of an application, the ability to evaluate the safety of the application and the certification itself, which aims to rule on the conformity of a product in relation to a frame of reference.

DEFINITION 1.2. – *Certification.* Certification consists in obtaining a certificate, which is a commitment to the fact that the product respects a set of standards frame of reference. Certification is based on the results of an evaluation and on the production of a certificate.

From definition 1.2, it is only necessary that the certification of a software application must include two elements:

– a frame of reference (standards, trade documents, *de facto* standards, etc.);

– all the elements produced (documents, code, production environment, trial scenarios, trial results, etc.) during the realization of the software application.

Certification is split into two stages: the analysis of conformity via an *assessment*; and the achievement of a certificate.

DEFINITION 1.3. – *Assessment.* The assessment of a software application consists of carrying out an analysis of the conformity of a product with regards to a frame of reference (law, standard, state of art, customer needs, etc.). The analysis of conformity follows a predefined process.

1.4.1. *Cycle in V and other realization cycles*

As Figure 1.2 shows, there are several cycles: (a) cycle in V, (b) cycle in a cascade, (c) cycle in a spiral, etc., for the realization of a software application. The cycle recommended by the different standards (CENELEC EN 50128 [CEN 01a],

DO 178 [ARI 92], CEI/IEC 61508 [IEC 98], CEI/IEC 61880 [IEC 06], ISO 26262 [ISO 09]), however, remains the cycle in V.

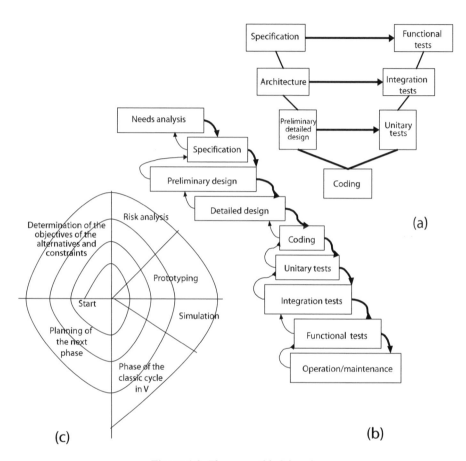

Figure 1.2. *Three possible lifecycles*

Figure 1.3 shows the cycle in V as it is generally presented. The objective of the analysis of needs is to verify the appropriateness of the expectations of the client and the technological feasibility. The specification phase has the objective of describing what the software must do (and not how it will do it). In the context of the architectural definition, we are seeking to carry out a hierarchical decomposition of the software application in a module/component and identifying the interfaces between these elements.

The description of each module/component (data, algorithms, etc.) is carried out in the context of design. Often the design phase is separated into two stages. The first stage, called *preliminary design*, aims to identify the data handled and the necessary services. The second stage, called *detailed design*, aims to describe all the services through their algorithms. The design phase then gives rise to the *coding phase*.

Figure 1.3 shows that there are different test phases: unitary tests (focused on the lowest level components); integration tests (focused on software and/or material interfaces); and functional tests (sometimes also called *validation tests*), which aim to show that the product conforms to its specification.

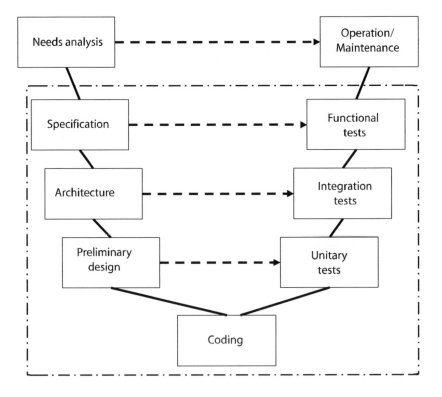

Figure 1.3. *The V-cycle*

The operating/maintenance phase concerns the operational life and the mastering of possible evolutions.

It must be noted that there is a horizontal correspondence (dotted arrow) between the specification and design activities and the test activities (see section 1.5.2). The V-cycle is therefore broken down into two phases: the descending phase and the ascending phase. The activities of the ascending phase need to be prepared during the descending phase. Figure 1.4 is thus closer to the recommended V-cycle.

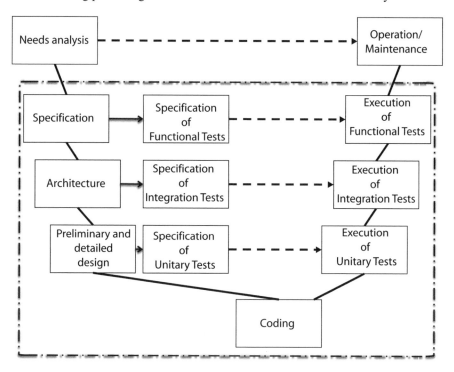

Figure 1.4. *V-cycle including the test specifications*

1.4.2. *Quality control (the impact of ISO standard 9001)*

It must be remembered that the term *quality assurance* will be used most of the time. Quality assurance consists of implementing appropriate pre-established and systematic layouts that are meant to inspire the confidence necessary to achieve a required quality.

The general layout adopted by a company to obtain the required quality of its products or services are described in the company's *quality assurance manual* (QAM). Each layout (specification, test, etc.) is defined within a "procedure".

In the context of the complex layout, a guide describing the implementation may be available. Each procedure associated with a layout will identify the input and output documents. Standard plans describing the format of documents will also be available.

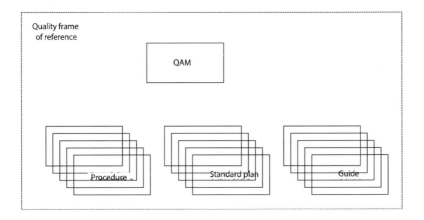

Figure 1.5. *Quality frame of reference*

A company's quality frame of reference is therefore made up of a QAM, set procedures, guidelines and a set of standard plans that characterize the documents to be produced.

For a given project, the quality objectives and procedures implemented to make the product and the realization conditions must then be identified. To do this, each project must carry out a *quality assurance plan* (QAP). The QAP is a document describing the specific layouts implemented by a company to obtain the quality of the considered product or service. The mastering of the quality of the software application will include the implementation of a *software quality assurance plan* (SQAP).

ISO 9000 is a group of standards for quality management that are applicable to several domains (manufacturing, service, etc.). To satisfy ISO 9000, it is necessary to demonstrate the ability of an organization to produce goods and services. This demonstration includes certification by an independent organization.

The spirit of the ISO 9000 group of standards is "Do what you say, say what you do, and show that you have done it".

More specifically, ISO 9000 is broken down into:

– standard ISO 9000: a document describing the guidelines for the selection and use of standards;

– standard ISO 9001: provides a model for quality assurance in the context of design, realization, installation and after-sales service;

– standard ISO 9002: provides a model for quality assurance in the context of production and installation;

– standard ISO 9003: constitutes a model for quality assurance in the context of controls and final trials;

– standard ISO 9004: with the help of directives common to all companies, completes the three previous standards that concern the external assurance of quality in contractual situations.

Regarding the realization of a software application, standard ISO 9001 [ISO 08] remains the most relevant, but it is necessary to associate it with standard ISO 90003 [ISO 04], which is an interpretation guide of ISO 9001:2000 for the software.

1.4.3. *Verification and validation*

The realization of a software application must take into account the design of the application but also the activities that enable the demonstration that the software application has achieved a certain level of quality. Achieving a level of quality includes the demonstration that no fault has been introduced during the design and that the product corresponds to the needs that have been identified.

Above all, it is necessary to recall what V&V are.

DEFINITION 1.4. – *Verification*: confirmation by tangible proof that the specified requirements have been met at each stage of the realization process.

DEFINITION 1.5. – *Validation*: confirmation by tangible proof that the requirements for a specific use or an anticipated application have been met.

The two previous definitions are taken from the ISO 9000:2000 standard [ISO 00]. They introduce the notions of requirements and evidence. In order to be more specific, we can return to the presentation made by I. Sommerville [SOM 07]. He cites Boehm, who in 1979 stated that:

– verification ensures that the product conforms to its specification; and

– validation ensures that the system that is implemented corresponds to the expectations of the future user.

According to its definition, validation therefore aims to demonstrate the adequacy of the product with regards to the initial need.

Figure 1.6 represents the main problematic in the realization of a software application. Indeed, there is a need to be realized and there is a realization: verification is there to show that all the needs are taken into account by the realization and that there are no unexpected elements. The development team will always have a good reason for introducing undesired pieces of code (functions to be reused, addition of a service, etc.) and taking into account all the needs (technical difficulty, omissions, etc.).

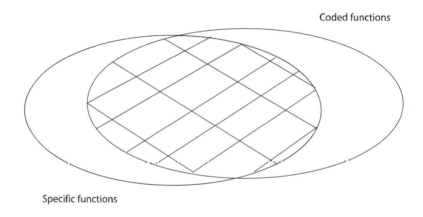

Coded functions

Specific functions

Figure 1.6. *The software development problematic*

In view of these definitions, we can conclude (see Figure 1.7) that verification applies to all stages of the V-cycle and that validation is an activity that aims to show that the specification is respected by the final product: this activity concerns functional tests, also called validation tests.

As Figure 1.7 shows, verification concerns the search for faults within the V-cycle and validation concerns the demonstration that the product corresponds to its need, hence its localization in the upper level of the V-cycle. Verification covers validation.

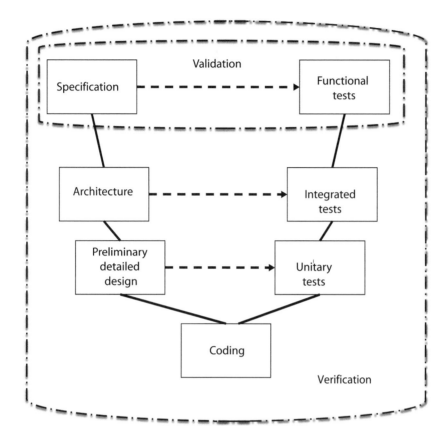

Figure 1.7. *V&V on the V-cycle*

1.4.3.1. *Verification*

In the context of standard CEI/IEC 61508 [IEC 98], *verification* is the activity that requires each phase of the lifecycle (general, material and software) to be demonstrated by analysis and/or trial, which for the specific entries, the deliverable elements fulfill the fixed objectives and prescriptions (requirements) for the phase on every account. Here is a non-exhaustive list of verification activities:

– the reviews relative to the outputs of a phase (documents concerning all the phases of the safety lifecycle) destined to ensure the conformity with objectives and prescriptions of the phase, and taking into account the entries that are specific to that phase;

– the design reviews;

– tests carried out on finalized products in order to ensure that their functioning conforms to their specification;

– integration tests carried out during the element-by-element assembly of the different parts of a system, based on environment trials in order to ensure that all parts function correctly with one another and conform to specifications;

– etc.

Verification is a process that deals with realization phases and concerns:

– the system structure, how it is made, in reference to standards and the properties to be satisfied (verify the product);

– the means implemented and the production process with reference to rules about the work method, how one must proceed (verify the process).

Verification aims to show that the product is properly built. The notion of a "properly built product" means that no fault has been introduced during the phases associated with realization.

There are two types of verification:

– *static verification*, which does not demand the execution of all or part of the system being analyzed;

– *dynamic verification*, which is based on the execution of all or part of the system being analyzed.

In addition to product verification, it is important we do not forget the *verification of the quality of the product*. This will be carried out by the quality team via quality audits (on the product, the project or the application of a process). It will include reviews of the elements produced (documentation, etc.) and control activities (monitoring of anomalies, monitoring of non-conformities, monitoring of client feedback, etc.).

1.4.3.2. *Validation*

Validation in the context of the lifecycle of a system groups together activities that ensure and build confidence in the system and in its aptitude to satisfy the anticipated uses, achieve the assigned goals and objectives.

In the CEI/IEC 61508 standard [IEC 98], validation is the activity that consists in demonstrating that the system, before or after installation, corresponds on all counts to the conditions contained in the prescription of the system. Thus, for example, validation of the software consists in confirming that the software meets the requirements specification for the safety of the software through the use of examination and the provision of evidence.

Validation therefore consists of showing that we have built the right product. Validation can be seen as an external verification.

1.5. Techniques, methods and practices

In the context of this section, we will present the different techniques and methods associated with V&V. The presentation of techniques will be limited to the bare essentials.

1.5.1. *Static verification*

Static verification is based on the absence of execution of all or part of the system.

The absence of execution enables us to carry out this type of analysis at any stage of the realization process (specification, design, coding, test, etc.). Static verification can be manual or tool driven. A few qualities expected of the code or "piece of code" (portion of code, program, file, etc.) must be:

– commented on;

– legible;

– modular;

– of mastered complexity; and

– conform to the design dossier.

1.5.1.1. *Manual static analysis*

In the context of this section, we present the two techniques of manual static analysis. These are inspection (documentary inspection, code inspection) and *software error effects analysis* (SEEA).

1.5.1.1.1. Software inspection: principles

Software inspection (see [GRA 93]) is the technique for manual static analysis, the objective of which is to discover faults as soon as possible.

DEFINITION 1.6. – *Software inspection.* This is a control technique enabling us to ensure that documentation produced during a data phase remains coherent with documentation coming from previous phases and that it respects the pre-established standards and rules.

The objective of software inspection is to look for faults (understanding, interpretation, translation, etc.), deviations – particularly with regards to quality clauses, absences or overabundances, etc. – and to supply elements to provide corrections. The aim of software inspection is not to carry out corrections.

In order to be efficient, software inspection must be prepared and carried out by a team that is separate from the realization team.

Software inspection is broken down into two types of inspection/review:

– documentary inspection/review is concerned with documents produced for a given phase. The inspection will deal with the quality, correction and relevance of the document(s); and

– inspection/review of code is concerned with elements such as "computing files": model, files that are source of a program, test scenario, etc.

1.5.1.1.2. Documentary inspection

This will enable us to verify:

– the quality instructions described in the referential of the company (QAM, procedure, standards and applicable frames of reference) and the project plans (QAP, SQAP, VVP, SAP, CMP)[1] have indeed been taken into account;

– correction of the work carried out: for this, the entries of the phase and the process to be carried out need to be known and it is necessary to have control points (a control list to be implemented);

– the conformity (relevance) of works: at the end of the documentary inspection, a formal review (meeting of people involved in the inspection) must enable us to rule on the conformity of works.

In the context of documentary inspection, anomalies can be detected and pointed out.

1.5.1.1.3. Code inspection

Code inspection will enable us to verify:

– that programming rules are respected (for example the specific frame of reference, such as MISRA-C [MIS 04], is respected);

– legibility;

---

1 Quality Assurance Plan, Software Quality Assurance Plan, Verification and Validation Plan, Safety Assurance Plan and Configuration Management Plan.

– presence and relevance of commentaries; and

– conformity of design code with the set of documents in entries.

To carry out the code review, it is necessary to have a frame of reference:

– the standard to be respected:

– trade standards;

– coding standards;

– quality procedures;

– etc.

It is also a review process that will be described by a quality procedure and is based on control lists (which question to ask, which point to examine, etc.). In particular, it is necessary for the code review to have an objective.

Here are a few examples of rules to be verified:

– *naming convention*: every object has a name that respects a syntax that is specific to its own category. For example: C_xx, V_xx, T_xx^2;

– *typing*: every object is typed (no typing by default);

– *initialization*: every declared object is initialized;

– *use*: all data produced are consumed.

Code review is a manual activity that is based on tools such as editor, word processing, etc., but it can also be based on tools for programming rule verification such as: *codewizard.*

1.5.1.1.4. Software error effects analysis

SEEA [AFN 90, GAR 94] is part of analyses that are carried out during the various stages of development. SEEA consists of examining the consequences of potential software errors.

The objectives of SEEA are to:

– identify these integrated software components with precision, and to evaluate their criticality level;

– suggest measures aiming to detect faults and to improve the robustness of the software;

---

2 xx is the name of the object.

– evaluate the amount of validation effort to be carried out on the various components of the software.

Software error effects analysis Application: Project: Language:				Built by: Date: Version analyzed:			
Module	Function	Error	Type of error	Effect on the component	Effect on the system	Recommended measure	Comments

Figure 1.8. *Example of SEEA table*

Its application is broken down into three phases:

– preliminary analysis of all the safety procedures for characterizing the development of studies for each procedure (based on safety objectives, we identify the procedures to be analyzed);

– procedure-by-procedure analysis of the consequences for safety of the envisaged software errors (analysis sheet for each procedure analyzed containing the identification of errors, safety criteria associated with each criteria and the consequences of errors);

– summary of works in view of software validation and the development of the safety dossier (list of scenarios that go against safety, the safety criteria identified and proposed means of detection).

For the first time, SEEA has been built in the context of validation of the automatic metro system called MAGGALY (*métro à grand gabarit de l'agglomération de Lyon*[3], see [MAI 93]).

These initial SEEA dealt with code, but in the context of the realization of the automatic metro, called SAET-Meteor (line 14 of the Parisian Metro, see [CHA 96]), they were built as much on the code as the specifications.

SEEA therefore enable us to analyze the impact of a failure of the inputs of a function on an output, both for the specification and the code.

Regarding the systems, sub-systems, equipment and/or materials, there is a type of study that is implemented in the context of safety functioning. This type of study

---

3 Large Scale Metro for the Lyon Agglomeration, in English. See http://www.maggaly.net/.

is called *failure modes and effects analysis* (FMEA). FMEA is a method of preventative analysis that appraises and highlights the potential risks. It is a systematic study. For more information, see [GAR 94].

SEEA is the equivalent of FMEA. The main characteristics of these studies are that they are purely "manual" and that the only tools necessary are a word processor or a spreadsheet. In general, SEEA is considered a safety study but in the context of the CENELEC EN 50128 standard [CEN 01], SEEA is seen as a verification activity.

It is worth noting that there is no tool to carry out SEEA and that each industrialist has developed his or her own methodology regarding the realization of SEEA.

1.5.1.2. *Tool-driven static analysis*

It is important to define what a static analyzer is, hence the following definition.

DEFINITION 1.7. – *Static analyzer* [ISO 85]. This is a software tool that analyses the structure and text of a program without executing it: cycles, inaccessible parts, redundancies, etc.

A static analyzer enables us to verify interfaces, identify incorrect constructions, non-initialized variables, atypical program parts and to generate a certain documentation of the software (cross references, diagram, etc.).

In what follows, we will present different types of static analysis tools, compiler, static program analysis, metric construction, abstract program interpretation, etc.

1.5.1.2.1. Compilation

A standard compiler is broken down into four phases:

– syntactic analysis;

– typing phase;

– semantic analysis; and

– generation of the executable.

Compilers are therefore tools that carry out a certain number of verification activities on the source code of an application.

DEFINITION 1.8. – *Compiler*: this is a computing tool used to translate a software design expressed in a programming language into a code that can be executed by the material.

Compilers have specific options that enable them to obtain information about the program being analyzed. This information includes:

– a cross referencing table;

– the size of the executable (code, data);

– a data location table.

Some languages, such as C, are partially "poorly defined"; hence the need to carry out complementary corrections to those of the compiler. Initially the Lint tool was created to verify latent errors linked to typing, function calls, etc. This tool has been extended to other languages (see the pcLint tool).

1.5.1.2.2. Identification of differences

Mastering of the evolutions of an application includes the analysis of differences between two versions of the software. The basic tools, such as the UNIX diff command, for example, are fairly simple.

1.5.1.2.3. Verification of coding rules

The quality control of development and properties, such as legibility and maintainability, includes the establishment a set of programming and architecture rules that must be respected for all the realization process.

The verification of these rules can be automated.

These programming rules can be induced by company constraints, the respect of a specific frame of reference (MISRA-C, for example [MIS 04]) and/or by known problems (semantics problem, legibility problem, non-determinism, poor constructions, etc.). See section 1.5.1.1.3 with regards to code inspection.

1.5.1.2.4. Measure of complexity

Mastering a software application involves mastering the complexity of the code. The complexity of the code is an indicator enabling us to validate the objectives linked to quality, to evaluate test efforts and to evaluate the maintainability and reliability of the code. The complexity of the code is one measure.

DEFINITION 1.9. – *Measure*: a measure is a formula that enables us to evaluate a quality based on different measurable parameters.

DEFINITION 1.10. – *Metric*: a metric is made up of a measure and a "theory of the measure" on the space in which we are measuring.

In our case, the theory of the measure [HAB 91] consists of defining the boundaries to be respected in the context of the project (or business) and the principles of interpretation.

A few measures (see, for example, [CAB 96]) include:

– cyclomatic number v(G): this describes the complexity of a program. It enables us to quantify the number of execution pathways of a procedure/function. This metric is measured based on the control graph, see section 1.5.1.2.5;

– number of lines of code: there a several variations (with or without commentary, with or without white line). This metric will enable us to evaluate legibility and maintainability (presence of commentary);

– Halstead metrics: this collection of metrics allows the complexity of a piece of program to be measured via the complexity of expressions (operators and operands);

– number of errors detected, number of errors corrected, number of versions, etc.

Metric	Mnemonic	LO (minimum)	HI (maximum)	Value
Instruction number	N_STMTS	1	50	70
Length of the program	PR_LGTH	3	350	85
Cyclomatic number	V(G)	1	20	11
Maximum number of levels	MAX_LVLS	1	5	3
Number of pathways without cycle	N_PATHS	1	80	29
Number of jumps	N_JUMPS	0	0	0
Frequency of commentaries	COM_R	0.2	1.0	0.17
Average size of instruction sets	AVG_S	3	7	1.21
Number of input–output points	IO_PTS	2	2	2

Table 1.1. *Example of metric measurement results using the Logiscope tool*

It is important to note that it is possible to construct direct metrics (about the code) or indirect metrics (synthesis of other metrics, analysis of the process, etc.).

As an example, Table 1.1 shows a result of metric measure on a code using the "Logiscope" tool. The table reveals the name of the metric, the minimum and maximum boundaries (chosen for the project or business) and the measure that was made.

There is currently no answer regarding the applicability of the theory of the measure in the context of object-oriented languages. Several metrics have been developed [CHI 94], but they have focused on the aspect of the complexity of the structure and it is difficult to relate them to the classic quality indicators (test effort, maintainability, etc.).

1.5.1.2.5. Structural analysis

The structural analysis of a program, P, consists of constructing an oriented graph. This graph can be used to analyze the data flow, measure the structural complexity or study execution pathways.

The directed graph provides a compact view of the control structure of the P program being analyzed:

– it is built based on the source code of the program;

– a knot = maximal bloc of consecutive instructions $i_1, \ldots i_n$:

  - i_1 is the unique point of access to the bloc,

  - instructions are always executed as $i_1, \ldots i_n$,

  - we leave the bloc after the execution of i_n;

– a unique entry knot with one or several output knots;

– arches between the knots = conditional or unconditional connections.

The control graph (see Figure 1.9) enables the structure of a program to be visualized and the singular points to be identified. It enables the structural metrics to be calculated (cyclomatic number, marked Vg, for example).

The main anomalies encountered (given in this non-exhaustive list) are:

– isolated components (never usually called into play – beware, however, of all components used by the graphic interfaces);

– level jumps;

– a call graph is structured into hierarchical levels that are not being respected;

– a jump of several levels indicates poor design of the software application;

– graph too big (poor hierarchical breakdown);

– graph too deep;

– "plate of spaghetti" (links in all directions, the impossibility of isolating a component, etc.).

```
void main()
{
    int x = 0;
    int y = 1;
    while (y < 10)
    {
        y = 2 * y;
        x = x + 1;
    }
    printf ("%d",x);
    printf ("%d",y);
}
```

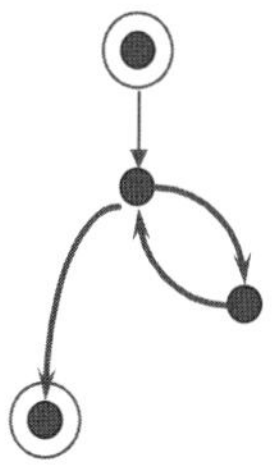

Figure 1.9. *Example of a control graph*

The software application is broken down into small components that risk no longer having precise functionalities and this can also pose problems for integration tests.

The control graph can be annotated in order to study the data flow, as Figure 1.10 shows.

The anomalies detectable using data flows are mainly:

– use of a variable with no prior allocation;

– allocation of a variable with no previous use; and

– redefinition of a variable without having used it before.

The control graph is a summary of a program that can be analyzed from various angles in order to understand the complexity, the testability (sequence of branches and pathways) and can even be used to identify anomalies.

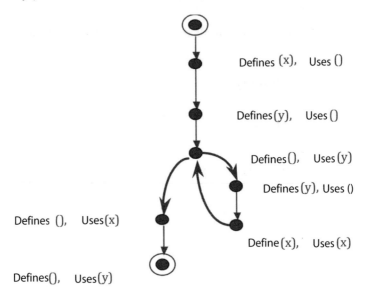

Figure 1.10. *Data flow analysis*

1.5.1.2.6. Symbolic execution

Based on a software application, *P*, the symbolic execution builds symbolic expressions linking data in input, *E*, to data in output, *S*.

These expressions generally include conditions that ensure a certain path is followed during the execution.

	X0	Y0
Begin	X0-Y0	Y0
x: = x-y;	X0-Y0	Y0+X0-Y0
y: = y+x;		X0
x: = y-x;	X0-Y0+X0	X0
End	Y0	

Figure 1.11. *Example of a symbolic execution*

Symbolic execution consists of carrying out the execution of a software application but changing the type of data. Indeed, we have gone from a software application that handles numbers to a handling of algebraic expressions (see Figure 1.11).

The complete symbolic execution of a software application is impossible, as a limit – the number of turns of the cycles – is often dependent on the execution.

1.5.1.2.7. Abstract program interpretation

Abstract interpretation [COU 00] is a technique for automatic static analysis. Abstract interpretation consists of replacing a precise element of a program by a less detailed abstraction in order to try to calculate the properties of the program.

Abstraction leads to a loss of sure information, which leads to the inability to devise conclusions for all the programs.

Abstract program interpretation enables us to detect runtime errors, such as division by 0, overflow, etc., and also detects the use of shared variables and dead codes.

The main advantage of these tools is that the test is done with no preparation, based on sources of the project. If we carry out a comparison with the costs of unitary arguments, it represents a sizeable argument.

There are two main uses of the abstract interpretation:

– *acceptance of the final product*: the project manager can use an abstract interpretation to accept the code provided by the supplier; and

– *debugging of the product* during development:

- during development, the developers use an abstract interpretation to detect the design anomalies (unitary tests),

- the verification team can use it to detect shadow zones to be examined as a priority.

1.5.1.2.8. Modeling

The realization of a model, M, is a means by which to understand and/or apprehend a problem/situation. In general, the specification phase, which enables us to appropriate the specifications sheet, includes the creation of a model, M.

The static view (see Figure 1.12) has two viewpoints:

– hierarchical point of view, which allows the visualization of the decomposition tree;

– composition point of view, which enables communications between models of the same level to be visualized.

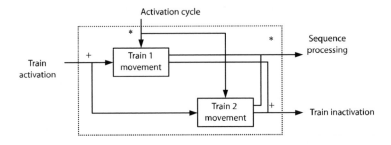

Figure 1.12. *Example of static introducing different types of communication*

This favors the black box vision of modules.

Figure 1.13 presents an example of a dynamic model in the form of state/transition diagrams. It is worth noting that this example could be completed with conditions for transitions and/or actions.

Modeling is often based on a graphic representation of the system that is described in the form of a tree structure of distinct and autonomous entities that communicate among themselves and with the system environment.

The first modeling was based on functional analyses of the system (see works around SADT[4] [LIS 90]).

A model closely resemble the system being studied or can be more generally representative, whereupon we speak of abstraction. The closer the modeling is to the system, the closer the results obtained will be to those observed in the final system.

Another characteristic of models comes from whether or not the support language has a semantic. The presence of a semantic enables us to implement reasoning techniques that guarantee the correction of the results obtained. Two complementary modelings are frequently used with this specification:

---

4 The acronym SADT stands for *structured analysis and design technique*. This method was perfected by Softech in the United States. The SADT method involves analysis by successive levels of approach, descriptive of an ensemble, whatever it may be.

– a static modeling describing the entities that make up the system and the states with which they can be associated;

– a dynamic modeling describing the authorized changes in state.

The model, *M,* describes the behavior of the system:

– states/transitions system;

– logical equations;

– etc.

The model, *M,* has access to data that are:

– controllable (known, fixed, etc.); and

– probabilistic.

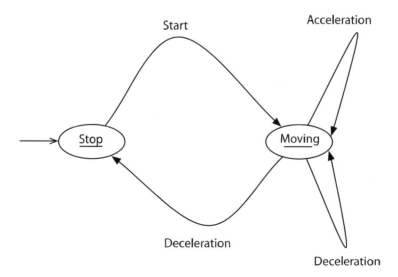

Figure 1.13. *Example of a dynamic model*

In summary and globally, modeling consists of translating a physical situation into a symbolical model and then into a more or less abstract language of iconic type (graphic symbols, tables, curves, diagrams, etc.) or logic-mathematical type (function, relation, etc.). For example, the unified modeling language (UML)[5] notation [OMG 06a, OMG 06b] is one way to create a model (see, for example, Figure 1.14).

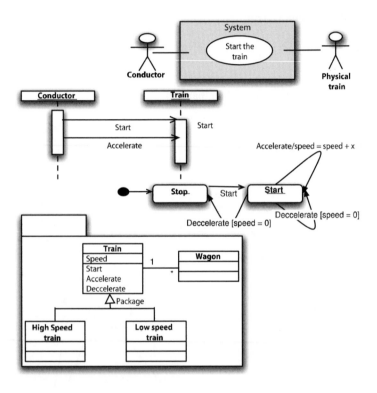

Figure 1.14. *Example of a UML model*

1.5.1.2.9. Simulation

Based on a model of the product to be analyzed, it is possible to carry out behavior analyses via an interactive (or automatic) simulation and/or exhaustive simulation (*model checking*).

DEFINITION 1.11 – *Simulation*: the simulation of a model, *M*, corresponds to the carrying out of a controlled execution of the model.

─────────────

5 To find out more, visit the OMG site: www.omg.org.

The aim of the simulation is to:

– understand the functioning of a complex system;

– highlight properties of:

  - safety,

  - performance,

  - etc;

– carry out experiments that are:

  - difficult (for example, a nuclear explosion),

  - costly (for example, biological experimentation),

  - impossible (for example, modeling of a system that is being interpreted),

  - etc;

– validate the specifications;

– validate the behavior.

Simulation can be carried out continuously until it is asked to stop according to the diagram. Simulation requires:

– the choice of inputs;

– the execution of a calculation step; and

– output recuperation.

For the simulation, inputs to the model are variables that come from an environment. There are two cases: either there is an environment, or there is not.

In the absence of modeling of the environment (see Figure 1.15), it will be necessary to select inputs by hand (randomly, in the worst case scenario). Two problems then arise:

– coherence between the different inputs; and

– a link between the outputs and the state of the model.

Figure 1.15. *Model without an environment (open model)*

The implementation of an environment (see Figure 1.16) involves an additional development and validation efforts in order to demonstrate the validity of this environment.

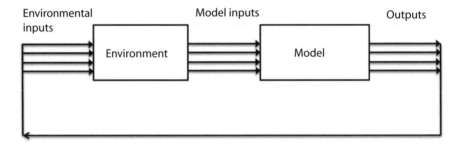

Figure 1.16. *Model with an environment (closed loop)*

With the simulation, there are three possibilities:

– "step-by-step" simulation: the model is executed step-by-step (interactive); the user chooses which transitions to execute among those that are "executable":

- there is always an initial state,

- a transition is said to be "executable" if the start state is activated, the event associated with the transition is produced and if the condition associated with the transition is true;

– "automatic" simulation: a process chooses the transitions to be executed from among those that are "executable". There is a possibility that the environment can be taken into account via modeling. The choice of transitions is still the most difficult task: "computing hazard";

– "exhaustive" (model checking): the graph is a construction of all the possible executions and it is then possible to analyze the graph using:

- property verification,

- sub-tree search,

- selection of test case,

- etc.

Exhaustive simulation [BAI 08] enables the properties of a model to be automatically verified. The implementation of an exhaustive simulation (see Figure 1.17) requires there to be a semantic and is based on the use of temporal logic to express the properties.

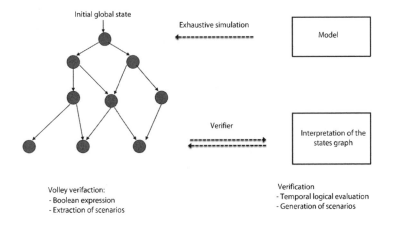

Figure 1.17. *Exhaustive simulation and operation*

The properties that can be verified can be classed into families:

– *the safety properties*: a property that is true in all states and says that some things never occur. Example: there is no train collision;

– *liveliness properties*: a property that can be true in some states and introduces the possibility that some things will occur (in particular good things). Example: if we call the elevator, it will arrive in the near future.

The main difficulty with the implementation of exhaustive simulation is in mastering the memory size of the graph of the system states, the analysis of which is ongoing. We are frequently confronted with the problem of combinatory explosion: the number of states of the system is too great for analysis. There are then several solutions. We can:

– implement optimization algorithms of the size of the graph in memory: for example BDDs (*binary decision diagrams*);

– implement an abstraction of the model;

– implement a strategy for the analysis of the system based on trajectories (partial analysis);

– implement other state management strategies, for example we can replace the state memorization by memorization of the properties of the these states;

– etc.

1.5.1.2.10. Model for verification

Based on a program, P, its specification, SP, and a set, A, of the safety properties on P expressed in the form of the expression of the variables of P, it is possible to construct a model, M, that has an input, E, and the Boolean outputs S and S'.

The formal verification of a program, P, then consists of simulating the model (interactively or exhaustively) with inputs in order to verify that we always have the correct ouput (see Figure 1.18).

In order to facilitate the verification phase, it is preferable to close the model by introducing an environment that will enable us to generate inputs and will react to outputs. The dynamic behavior of such a model in its environment is represented by Figure 1.16.

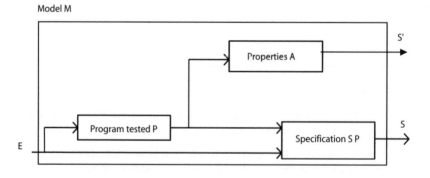

Figure 1.18. *Example of the principle of verification*

An example of safety properties applicable for the SAET-Meteor system [BOU 06] includes:

– P1: only trains that are equipped, located and are automatically driven can have a target;

– P2: the internal state of the PAS (trackside equipment) representing the occupation of the track must be coherent with the rest of the trains (equipped or not) present in the zone managed by the PAS.

In the context of [BOU 99], we have shown the realization of a model based on the principles of Figure 1.18, which enables us to verify a textual verification and enables us to select validation tests.

1.5.1.2.11. Model for proof

In order to demonstrate that a property, *P*, is true in relation to the description of a system, *S*, it is necessary to have a model, *M*, described in a language, *L*, that has a semantic. The mathematical proof of the property, *P*, is a finite sequence of inferences in the logic of the language, *L*.

Above all it is necessary to note that formal proof is indeed a static technique in so far as it is does not require the execution of the model, *M*.

There are two types of corrections that can be studied via the proof:

– *partial correctness*: the program produces the correct result if its execution finishes;

– *total correctness*: partial correctness + end of program.

The proof techniques are based on the Hoare triples [HOA 69]. Intuitively the triple {P} S {Q} (P and Q are predicates that characterize the state of the variables of the system and S is a piece of program) means: "if P is true before executing S, and if S terminates, then Q is true after".

Applying the rules, it is then possible for Hoare triples [HOA 69] to be used to implement a reasoning (set of inferences) that enables the correction of the program to be demonstrated. The rules of handling triples are expressed via a "sequent".

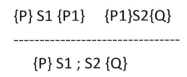

Figure 1.19. *A sequent of the sequence*

For example, the sequent in Figure 1.19 shows that to execute S1 and S2 in sequence starting from P and to arrive at Q, there must be a state, P1, that is a state of arrival for S1, and a state of departure for S2.

The implementation of a proof is therefore based on an inference process that enables a tree of proof to be obtained. As an example, we show the tree of proof (see Figure 1.20) associated with a piece of program containing a loop "as long as".

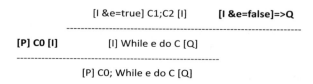

[I &e=true] C1;C2 [I]   **[I &e=false]=>Q**

[P] C0 [I]   [I] While e do C [Q]

[P] C0; While e do C [Q]

Figure 1.20. *Tree of proof*

Tools to help demonstration have been developed. There are three categories:

– interactive proof tools: these help the management of the demonstration;

– tools of automatic proof: these are capable of carrying out the proof of a theorem based on a mathematical rule;

– tools for verification of the proof: these, based on the a tree of proof, are able to verify the correction of the demonstration that has been carried out.

1.5.1.2.12. Formal methods

Formal methods [MON 00] are based on the use of discreet mathematics to prove that programs verify properties. In the context of [OFT 97], we have examples of the use of different formal methods in industry.

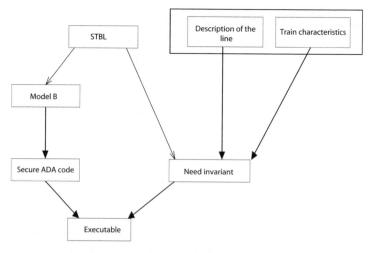

Figure 1.21. *Formal development process of a configured application*

The formal methods group together languages of which the semantic is defined mathematically and transformation and verification techniques are based on mathematical proof.

Among these methods, we find: Petri nets, the B method [ABR 96], SCADE®6 [DOR 08], VDM (Vienna Development Model) [JON 90], Z [SPI 89], etc.

As an example of implementation, we will present the SAET-Meteor system. Line 14 of the Parisian metro [CHA 96] is managed by SAET[7] which is a complex distributed real-time system whose the main function is to ensure the transport of passengers, all the while guaranteeing a very high level of safety.

The separation between data and code (see Figure 1.21) enables the elimination of compatibility errors between pieces of equipment, and – especially important – enables a generic description of pieces of equipment to be obtained. From the description of the software needs of a piece of equipment, it is possible to construct a B model and to define a set of data, called *invariants*, which are derived from topological invariants. Invariants are associated with particular types of equipment.

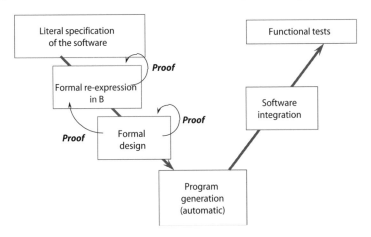

Figure 1.22. *Development process of a formal application*

Figure 1.22 presents an example of the development process for a formal application. This process is the one that was implemented in the context of use of the

B method [ABRI 96] during the development [BEH 96, BOU 06, chap. 3]) of the SAET-Meteor.

Translation of the B model [ABR 96] into a safe subset of Ada language [ANS 83] is carried out automatically by the tool. The safety aspect is obtained via a subset of the Ada code and the use of the safe coded processor (SCP) [BOU 09, chap. 2], which secures the safety of the execution.

The presence of the formal proof of conformity of the code in relation to the specifications has enabled a significant reduction in the test phases of the V-cycle. This is represented in Figure 1.22.

The implementation of the B method in SAET-Meteor [BOU 06, chap. 3] enabled the demonstration that was possible to replace the test activities (unit tests and integration tests) with proof activities.

However without starting a debate on the use of formal methods in the context of safety-critical software, in [BEH 96] it is said that the unitary tests and integration tests are redundant with complete proof and the secured generation of code. [WAE 95] recommends preserving all test phases, while waiting for feedback on the methodology and validation of B tools. This discussion is still valid if the development is carried out without a SCP [BOU 09, chap. 2].

Indeed it is necessary to remark that realizing and validating a B model does not guarantee that the code generator, tools for production of the executable (compiler, linker, etc.), installation tools, configuration management tools, etc., will not transform the binary file execution and therefore render the proof void.

In context of Figure 1.21, we have introduced the notion of generic software configured by data. This practice is very topical in the context of rail and/or automotive applications. In the context of [BOU 03, BOU 07], we have shown that it is possible to implement formal techniques for the V&V of conformity of data associated with a rail application.

Properties linked to data can be safety or other types of properties. They are introduced within the verification tool via a formal language based on set theory. The collective language enables us to express properties with classic mathematical operators ($\forall$, $\exists$, $\in$, $\subseteq$, $\Rightarrow$, $\Leftrightarrow$, $\wedge$, $\neg$, $\vee$, etc.).

A constraint is verified by exploration of the space of possibilities (topological data), which is equivalent to a proof by case. The constraint verification tool applied in the context of the SAET-Meteor application is based on a similar algorithm to *model checking*.

This verification tool [DEL 99] enables us to formally verify data; there are now more than a hundred safety rules that can be verified. Here, for example, are a few safety properties regarding the data:

– P3: all of the track circuits form a partition of the track (track connectivity);

– P4: a switch is associated with – at most – two itineraries.

1.5.2. *Dynamic verification*

Dynamic verification is based on the partial or total execution of the system.

DEFINITION 1.12. – *Dynamic analysis* [ISO 85]: a dynamic analyzer is a software tool analyzing the behavior of a program by monitoring its execution. This tool enables us to record the paths covered, execution times, resources consumed, etc.

1.5.2.1. *Analysis of execution*

There are several types of execution analysis:

– efficiency of resource use (execution time, memory management, management of tasks, management of processes, etc.);

– memory management (allocation/de-allocation) in order to master leaks and poor uses;

– covering of tests;

– etc.

1.5.2.2. *Test*

The test [MYE 79, XAN 99] is a dynamic verification technique that consists of making the system (or one of its components) function by providing it with input values.

DEFINITION 1.13. – *Testing a software application* [MYE 79]: testing involves executing the program with the intention of finding anomalies or faults.

The test and the implementation of a program are two separate activities that are closely linked:

– the test enables us to reveal the existence of faults in a program and to verify that the development properly corrected them and did not generate any new faults;

– development begins when a fault is identified. It enables us to locate the fault in the program, and to design and carry out the correction.

The development cycle is separated into two phases, and the test occurs in several phases. As Figure 1.23 shows, there are unitary tests, integration tests and functional tests.

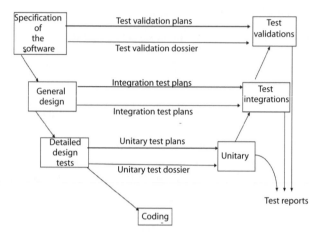

Figure 1.23. *The different test campaigns*

Activities (see Figure 1.24) that are linked to tests can be broken down into:

– the selection of test games;

– submission;

– scoring (the need to have an oracle); and

– assessment.

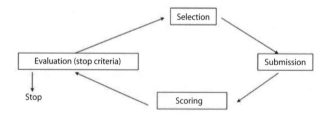

Figure 1.24. *Activities linked to tests*

Hence a few questions arise:

– How can we choose the program inputs?

– How can we decide whether the result is good or bad (the issue of the oracle)?

– When should we test?

– Which tools should we use?

– When should we stop the tests (the issue of the measure of the cover of tests)?

– etc.

Sections 1.5.5.2.1 to 1.5.5.2.5 introduce the general concepts in order to present the test as the V&V techniques of a software application.

1.5.2.2.1. Selection of case tests

The selection of case tests is an essential manual activity which in certain cases can be done using tools.

According to the stage of the test, the frame of reference can be very different:

– UT: we have the sources. An analysis of the sources therefore enables us to select the best tests to be carried out. Here we talk of a *white box* test;

– IT: we have a description of the software architecture and a description of the interactions between the material and the software;

– FT: we only have specifications. The tests are said to be *black box*.

With the IT and FT phases, there are two types of activities:

– manual selections of test cases: in the absence of model, the tester must construct his or her test catalog from his or her knowledge;

– selection by exploration: it is possible to carry out a model of specifications and exploration of this model enables us to select the case test. We then use the tools described in section 1.5.1.2.10.

1.5.2.2.2. Execution of test cases

UT and IT software are generally created and executed on the development computer (host machine). It consists of the realization of specific programs written in the application language. For these test families, it is important to be able to re-run the same test, both to demonstrate the correction and to manage evolutions (induced by the correction of anomalies). There are test environments that, based on a description of the test case (inputs to be provided and anticipated output), are capable of carrying out all executions, archiving results, analyzing results and producing a file with the trial reports.

For FT, they can be carried out on a "host" machine or on a "target machine". They require the implementation of specific environments that are generally dedicated to the project. These environments must enable us to more or less realistically simulate the environment.

1.5.2.2.3. Test scoring

Test scoring is an essential phase that aims to verify that the results obtained conform to those expected. The scoring of results can be carried out manually or automatically.

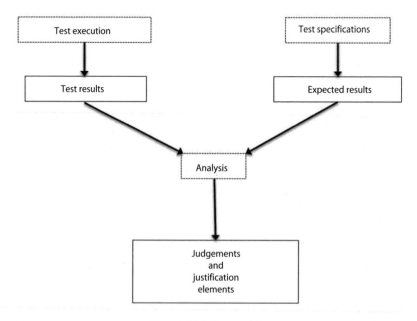

Figure 1.25. *Scoring phase*

1.5.2.2.4. Measure of the cover

One of the important questions a tester must ask him- or herself when judging a project is "how can I decide when to stop the tests?" There are several possible answers to this. It can be when:

– a sufficient confidence level has been reached (purely subjective);

– an instruction covering the objective has been reached;

– a structural cover has been reached;

– an objective input and output cover objective has been reached;

– a cover has been reached;

– the number of estimated residual errors is acceptable;

– etc.;

– as a last limitation, the budget has been spent.

The notion of cover level involves the possibility of having information on the execution path associated with each test. This information can be obtained via two mechanisms:

– a code instrumentation: here there is a modification of the source code. This modification can have an impact on the behavior of the application (at least from a temporal point of view). This type of instrumentation is carried out when working on the "host" equipment;

– a physical instrumentation in the processor (probe), in the bus, etc. This type of instrumentation is carried out when we are working on the "target" equipment.

1.5.2.2.5. Test and verification

After having presented the activities linked to tests, it is important to highlight that the selection activities of test cases are verification activities in their own right that must be conducted as early as possible.

Indeed, as soon as the software requirement specification (SRS) is realised, it must be used as input data for the selection of validation test cases (see Figure 1.23).

1.5.3. *Validation*

Validation is normally carried out on the final product. Validation is based on functional tests that are carried out on the final (target) equipment. The issue of tests has been presented in the context of section 1.5.2.2.

1.6. New issues with verification and validation

This chapter has given us the opportunity to very briefly present all of the applicable techniques (see section 1.5) in the context of V&V activities, that is to say reviews (code reviews, document review, etc.), the static analysis of coding, etc.), the dynamic analysis of code (unitary tests, integration tests, validation tests, etc.), etc.

As stated in the introduction (see section 1.1) the standards that are applicable to the different domains (aeronautical [ARI 92], automotive [ISO 09], rail [CEN 01a], nuclear [IEC 06], generic [IEC 98], etc.) recommend the implementation of quality assurance (section 1.4.2) based on the implementation of a development cycle, such as the V-cycle (see section 1.4.1, and more specifically Figure 1.3).

It is worth noting that these different standards define the notion of the "safety level to be attained" (design assurance level (DAL) in aeronautics, safety integrity level (SIL) for the generic standard, software SIL (SSIL) for rail and automotive SIL (ASIL) for automotive). The safety level is generally linked to an effort to be implemented; this effort can be linked to an objective to be attained (aeronautical field) or to the means to be implemented (automotive, rail and generic fields).

	SSIL0	SSIL1	SSIL2	SSIL3	SSIL4
Formal methods including, for example, CCS, CSP, HOL, LOTOS, OBJ, temporal logic, VDM, Z and B	-	R	R	HR	HR
Semi-formal methods	R	R	R	HR	HR
Structured methods including, for example, JSD, MASCOT, SADT, SDL, SSADM and Yourdon	R	HR	HR	HR	HR

Table 1.2. *CENELEC EN 50128, specification of the software requirements (Table A.2 [CEN 01a]; R refers to recommended, HR refers to highly recommended*

As an example, Table 1.2 is applicable to the realization phase of a *specification of software requirements*. It is taken from the EN 50128 standard [CEN 01a]. It is worth noting that this always gives a description of the problem in a natural language and all the mathematical notations necessary to describe the application. It is worth noting that similar tables appear for the architecture and design phase in rail applications. In the context of automotive [ISO 09], rail [CEN 01a] and generic [IEC 98] standards, formal methods are recommended (see Table 1.2) as a means to capture the needs and to produce mastered code. Indeed, formal methods such as B [ABR 96] or SCADE[®8] method [DOR 08] enable us to determine a need, formalize it in the design of a model, demonstrate that it respects properties and produce a code that is in the image of the model.

If the tools implemented (simulator, approver, code generator, etc.) are shown to respect the application's desired safety objectives, this type of approach enables us to replace the V&V activities with other activities (for example unitary tests can be replaced with a qualification/certification of the code generator [BOU 06]).

---

8 SCADE[®] is distributed by Esterel-Technologies, see www.esterel-technologies.com.

Standards therefore take into account the use of formal techniques when they are associated with modeling (see sections 1.5.1.2.10, 1.5.1.2.11 and 1.5.1.2.12), which are in turn associated with design documents (specification, architecture and design).

The coding phase is currently based on the use of a programming language such as Ada [ANS 83], C [ISO 99] and/or C++. Originally, these languages were not associated with formal verification techniques.

As we will see in the following chapters, it can be quite difficult to carry out V&V activities, such as review and tests on the final code (like Ada, C or C++). It is, however, worth implementing formal techniques, such as abstract interpretation [COU 00] and/or proof (such as Hoare proof [HOA 69]), which will enable the properties respected by the code to be identified and/or the demonstration that the code verifies certain properties.

1.7. Conclusion

The development of a certifiable software application is constrained by the requirements of standards associated with each domain (aeronautical [ARI 92], automotive [ISO 09], rail [CEN 01a], nuclear [IEC 06] and generic [IEC 98]). These standards recommend the implementation of a development process such as V-cycle, which is based on V&V activities surrounding testing (UT, IT, FT).

The implementation of test activities suffers from several problems, which include:

– the cost and complexity of test activities;

– the late detection of faults;

– difficulty in carrying out all the tests;

– etc.

This is why it is necessary to implement other practices that must enable us to detect the faults of the software application as early on in the process as possible in the broadest possible manner. One of the possible orientations consists of implementing formal methods (for example B [ABR 96], SCADE [DOR 08], VDM [JON 90], Z [SPI 89], etc., methods), which on the basis of a model and a set of properties enable us to demonstrate that the software produced verifies the said properties.

On the basis of classic development languages (such as C) it can be worth exploring the behaviors of the program and demonstrating that they verify a certain number of properties. Such demonstration is only possible via the addition of annotations describing local conditions (pre-condition, post-condition, invariant) and a propagation and/or proof mechanism.

In the following chapter, we will present examples of the implementation of techniques for the static analysis of code based on abstract interpretation [COU 00] and program proof [HOA 69]. It is worth noting that one of the difficulties in the implementation of these techniques is the absence of their recognition in current standards. Indeed, certain standards (see Table 1.2, taken from the CENELEC EN 50128 standard [CEN 01a], for example) recommend the implementation of formal methods but they do not mention the notion of abstract interpretation (or derived methods).

1.8. Bibliography

[ABR 96] ABRIAL J.R., *The B Book – Assigning Programs to Meanings*, Cambridge University Press, Cambridge, 1996.

[AFN 90] NF F 71-013, Installation fixes et matériel roulant ferroviaires, informatique, sûreté de fonctionnement des logiciels – méthodes appropriées aux analyses de sécurité des logiciels, AFNOR, December 1990.

[ANS 83] ANSI, Standarde ANSI/MIL-STD-1815A-1983, Langage de programmation Ada, ANSI, 1983.

[ARI 92] ARINC, Software Considerations in Airborne Systems and Equipment Certification, *DO 178B, n° ED12, edition B*, l'EUROCAE 1992.

[BAI 08] BAIER C., KATOEN J.-P., *Principles of Model Checking*, MIT press, Cambridge, MA, 2008.

[BEH 96] BEHM P., "Formal development of the safety critical software of METEOR", *First B Conference*, Nantes, November 24-26, 1996.

[BOU 99] BOULANGER J.-L., DELEBARRE V., NATKIN S., "METEOR: Validation de spécification par modèle formel", *Revue RTS*, vol. 63, pp. 47-62, 1999.

[BOU 03] BOULANGER J.-L., "Validation des données liées à la sécurité", *Qualita 2003, Quality and dependability* (RAMS), Nancy, March 19-21, 2003.

[BOU 06] BOULANGER J.-L., Expression et validation des propriétés de sécurité logique et physique pour les systèmes informatiques critiques, thesis, University of Technology of Compiègne, 2006.

[BOU 07] BOULANGER J.-L., "Etat de l'art de la validation des données dans le domaine ferroviaire", *Revue REE*, vol 3, pp.25-31, 2007.

[BOU 09] BOULANGER J.-L. (ed.), *Sécurisation des Architectures Informatiques – Exemples Concrets*, Hermès Lavoisier, Paris, 2009.

[CAB 96] CABE J.-MC., WATSON A.H., Structured Testing – A methodology Using the Cyclomatic Complexitry Metric, *NIST Report 500-235*, NIST, 1996.

[CEN 01a] CENELEC, NF EN 50128, Applications Ferroviaires. Système de signalisation, de télécommunication et de traitement – logiciel pour système de commande et de protection ferroviaire, July 2001.

[CHA 96] CHAUMETTE A-M., LE FEVRE L., "Système d'Automatisation de l'exploitation des trains de la ligne METEOR", *REE*, vol. 8, pp.1-79, September 1996.

[CHI 94] CHIDAMBER S.R., KEMERER C.F., "A metric suite for object oriented design", *IEEE Transactions*, Vol. 20, No 6, pp. 476-493, June1994.

[COU 00] COUSOT P., "Interprétation abstraite", *TSI*, vol. 19, no. 1-2-3, pp. 155-164, www.di.ens.fr/ ~cousot/COUSOTpapers/TSI00.shtml, 2000.

[DEL 99] DELEBARRE V., GALLARDO M., JUPPEAUX E., NATKIN S., "Validation des constantes de sécurité du pilote automatique de METEOR", *ICSSEA'99*, CNAM, Paris, France, December 8-10, 1999.

[DOR 08] DORMOY F.-X., "Scade 6 a model based solution for safety critical software development", *Embedded Real-Time Systems Conference*, Toulouse, France, January 29-31, February 01, 2008.

[GAR 94] GARIN H., *AMDEC-AMDE-AEEL L'Essentiel de la Méthode*, AFNOR, Paris, 1994.

[GRA 93] GILB G., *Software Inspection*, Addison Wesley, London, 1993.

[HAB 91] HABRIAS H., *La Mesure du Logiciel*, (2nd edition), Teknea, Paris, 1991.

[HOA 69] HOARE C.A.R., "An axiomatic basis for computer programming", *Communications of the ACM*, vol. 12, no. 10, pp. 576-580-583, 1969.

[IEC 98] IEC, *IEC 61508:* Sécurité Fonctionnelle des Systèmes Électriques Électroniques Programmables Relatifs à la Sécurité, Standarde Internationale, IEC, 1998.

[IEC 06] IEC, *IEC 60880:* Centrales Nucléaires de Puissance – Instrumentation et Contrôles-commande Importants pour la Sécurité. Aspects Logiciels des Systèmes Programmés Réalisant des Fonctions de Catégories A, Standards Internationale, IEC, 2006.

[ISO 85] ISO, *ISO Z61-102,* Traitement de l'Information – Vocabulaire de la Qualité du Logiciel, ISO, July 1985.

[ISO 99] ISO, ISO C Standard 1999, Technical Report, ISO, 1999 (available at: www.open-std.org/jtc1/sc22/ wg14/ www/docs/n1124.pdf).

[ISO 00] ISO, *ISO 9000:2000,* Systèmes de Management de la Qualité – Principes Essentiels et Vocabulaire, ISO, 2000.

[ISO 04] ISO, *ISO 90003* Ingénierie du Logiciel – Lignes Directrices pour l'Application de l'ISO 9001:2000 aux Logiciels Informatiques, ISO, 2004

[ISO 08] ISO, *ISO 9001:2008,* Systèmes de Management de la Qualité – Exigence, ISO, December 2008.

[ISO 09] ISO, *ISO/CD-26262*, Road Vehicles – Functional Safety, ISO, 2009 (unpublished).

[JON 90] JONES C.B., *Systematic Software Development using VDM*, (2nd edition), Prentice Hall, Engelwood Cliffs, 1990.

[LIS 90] LISSANDRE M., *Maîtriser SADT*, Armand Colin, Paris, 1990.

[MAI 93] MAIRE A., "Présentation du système MAGGALY", *Symposium international sur l'Innovation Technologique dans les Transports Guidés*, ITIG'93, Lille, September 1993.

[MIS 04] MISRA, MISTRA-C:2004, Guidelines for the Use of the C Language in Critical Systems, MISTRA, 2004.

[MON 00] MONIN J.F., *Comprendre les Méthodes Formelles*, Hermès, Paris, 2000.

[MYE 79] MYERS G.J., *The Art of Software Testing*, J. Wiley & Sons, London, 1979.

[NAU 69] NAUR P., RANDELL B., (eds.), *Software Engineering: A Report on a Conference Sponsored by NATO Science Committee*, NATO, 1969.

[OFT 97] OFTA, "Application des techniques formelles au logiciel", *Arago 20*, 1997.

[OMG 06a] OMG, OMG Document ptc/06-01-02, Unified Modeling Language: Superstructure, Version 2.1, OMG, January 2006.

[OMG 06b] OMG, OMG Formal Document/05-07-05, Unified Modeling Language: Infrastructure, Version 2.0, OMG, March 2006.

[RTA 92] RTCA, DO-178B/ED-12B, Software Considerations in Airborne Systems and Equipment Certification, RTCA, 1992.

[SOM 07] SOMMERVILLE I., *Software Engineering 8*, Addison Wesley, London, 2007.

[SPI 89] SPIVEY J.M., *The Z Notation – a Reference Manual*, Prentice Hall, New York, 1989.

[VIL 88] VILLEMEUR A., *Sûreté de Fonctionnement des Systèmes Industriels*, Eyrolles, Paris, 1988.

[WAE 95] WAESELYNCK H., BOULANGER J.-L., "The role of testing in the b formal development process", *ISSRE'95*, Toulouse, October 25-27 1995.

[XAN 99] XANTHAKIS S., REGNIER P., KARAPOULIOS C., *Le Test des Logiciels*, Hermès, Paris, 1999.

Chapter 2

Airbus: Formal Verification in Avionics

2.1. Industrial context

Avionic systems are involved in the main functions of the plane, such as its piloting (flight commands, automatic pilot, propulsion, breaking), making information available to the pilots regarding the situation of the plane in its environment and the state of its systems, signaling of alarms, electric generation, air conditioning, etc.

2.1.1. *Avionic systems*

Avionic systems are composed of mechanical, hydraulic and electronic devices. Among the mechanical organs are the mobile surfaces of the plane (flight control surfaces), motors, breaks, etc. Devices such as flight-control surfaces are activated by power organs, such as hydraulic jacks controlled by servo-commands that modulate hydraulic power according to electric currents produced by avionic calculators, and true onboard computers that constitute the intelligent part of systems. A great many sensors enable calculators to take into account the exterior environment the plane is in as well as the state of its internal devices.

Calculators that make up the systems of the plane are increasingly communicative: among themselves via avionic networks and, for some, with the ground via classic VHF radio (very high frequency) or satellite liaisons.

Chapter written by Jean SOUYRIS, David DELMAS and Stéphane DUPRAT.

Finally, we must note the major impact of safety, reliability and availability constraints on the development of systems.

Figure 2.1. *The A380 Airbus*

2.1.2. *A few examples*

Fly-by-wire functions (see [TRA 05] and/or Chapter 6 in [BOU 09]) that – since the A380 – are grouped together with the autopilot (AP), which is the most critical system on the plane. The first of these two functions (flight controls) ensures that the flight control surfaces are controlled so that the plane responds to the orders of the pilot or AP, and that the plane does not leave its flight domain (protection). The second function, the AP, is a control loop aiming to make the plane follow a trajectory that conforms to the flight plan.

The *flight warning system* enables the crew to be informed of any alarm signaled by the plane's systems and give the procedure to follow in order to deal with it. This signaling occurs via luminous buttons, sounds and on-screen display. It is also worth noting the vocal announcement function, giving the altitude of the plane when in the approach phase.

Similarly to alarm systems, the maintenance system centralizes all information relative to failures signaled by the systems of the plane. This information is not received by the crew but by the personnel of air companies responsible for the maintenance of their planes.

2.1.3. *Regulatory framework*

For a plane to be used in air space, it needs to be certified by the appropriate air safety authority. In Europe, this is the European Aviation Safety Agency.

Beyond the very first certification, which is a mandatory prerequisite for the start of a new aircraft type, any evolution, however small, must be subject to a partial "recertification".

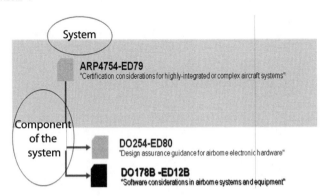

Figure 2.2. *Links between the three norms*

For the development of systems, electronics and software for avionic calculators, the Authority and/or companies use the following documents:

– the ARP 4754/ ED-79 [SAE 10];

– the DO-254 / ED-80 [RTC 06];

– the DO-178B / ED-12B [RTC 92].

These documents fix the objectives for all aspects of a development project and sometimes, also impose techniques for reaching them. Thus, the fixed normative frame also concerns the different development phases (specification, design and realization) and verifications associated with project management, configuration management, (mastering of successive versions, modifications and evolutions), and quality monitoring.

2.1.4. *Avionic functions*

As the central organs of avionic systems, calculators respond to specifications written by the system designers. The requirements they contain are attributed either to electronics or to the calculator software.

In general, the requirements relative to the function of the calculator in the software are allocated to the software. The hardware must provide the processing power necessary for the software to fulfill its function as well as all the peripherals enabling the calculator to be connected to other electronic or electric organs in the system. These safety functioning, reliability and availability requirements also apply to the hardware.

Figure 2.3. *Onboard calculator*

The specification of the software is often given in a graphic way according to an approach that we can call "model based".

The most widespread language is SCADE®. A specification in SCADE® is very detailed, enabling the production of corresponding code to be done with the help of an *automatic code generator* (ACG), a kind of compiler that, for example, produces C code based on SCADE® models [DOR 08].

This approach is sometimes qualified as "semi-formal" in so far as the specification language is formalized, but – to date – the passage to code does not occur via a sequence of transformations that are formally proved.

Before the A380, excluding a fairly innovative calculator, there was at most one function of a system in a calculator; the electronics of the latter being specific to the function in question. With the A380, the concept of *integrated modular avionics* (IMA) appeared.

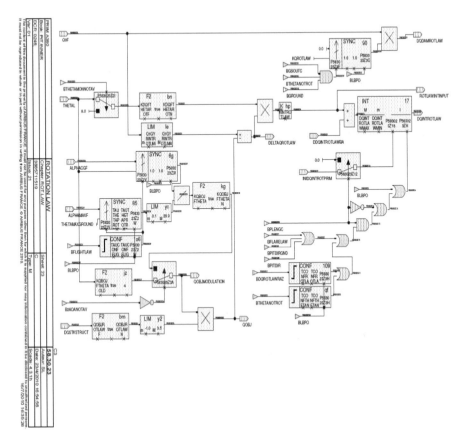

Figure 2.4. *Example of the SCADE® model*

This new form of avionics is comprised of identical hardware modules that, equipped with an avionics operating system meeting the ARINC 653 [ARI 03] norm, harbors more than one function. It is worth noting that the various functions running in an integrated modular avionics (IMA) module can belong to different systems.

A very important element for the development process of an avionic function, both for hardware and software, is its *development assurance level* (DAL). This is assigned to the avionics function by the safety analysis that includes the function. These assurance levels range from A (the highest) to E (the lowest). The attribution criteria of various levels of an avionic function are summarized in Table 2.1.

Consequence of failure	Safety objective	Assurance level
Catastrophic	$< 10^{-9}$	A
Dangerous	$<10^{-7}$	B
Major	$<10^{-5}$	C
Minor	None	D
No impact on safety	None	E

Table 2.1. *Definition of assurance levels*

2.1.5. *Development of avionics levels*

2.1.5.1. *Regulatory and development frame*

What follows is a succinct presentation of the model for the development of avionics software that is strongly recommended by docuement DO-178B [RTC 92].

Four processes are identified:

– the *software specification* process produces high-level requirements (HLRs) based on the specifications of the system that are assigned to the software;

– the *software design* process produces low-level requirements (LLRs) as well as the software architecture based on HLRs;

– the *software coding* process produces the source code based on the high-level architecture and requirements;

– the *integration* process loads the object code onto the calculator material and carries out the software/material integration.

Each of the activities mentioned above is a stage in the development of the software product. Figure 2.5 presents these different stages.

For its software developments made from textual specifications, Airbus calls "low-level requirements (LLR)" – requirements related to design entities implemented as modules and functions of the programming language.

The manner in which these entities cooperate to implement LLRs is defined at an earlier time, during the architecture phase of the software.

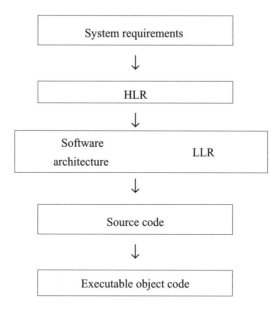

Figure 2.5. *The DO-178B development process [RTC 92]*

The products of all development activities must be *verified*. Detailed objectives are defined for each stage of the development. Systematically, some objectives apply to products of a development activity whereas others concern the conformity of these products with the inputs of the activity.

For example, Figure 2.6 presents objectives relative to *LLRs*.

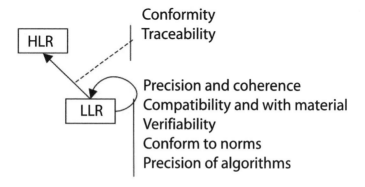

Figure 2.6. *Verification process associated with LLRs*

On one hand, LLRs must be precise and coherent, compatible with the target machine (the avionic calculator), verifiable, conform to the specification norms, and specify precise algorithms. On the other hand, LLRs must conform to HLRs. They must correctly implement them. The traceability between these two types of requirements must be ensured.

The verification means identified by document DO-178B are reviews, analyses and testing:

– reviews procurement and qualitative evaluation of the correction;

– analyses provide a reproducible means of evaluating the correction. Review and analyses are used for verification objectives relative to LLRs and HLRs, to the software architecture and the source code;

– testing is employed for the verification of conformity of the code to LLRs and HLRs. It is always based on requirements (functional test) and must include nominal and robustness cases. A structural coverage analysis was carried out in order to ensure that the software had been sufficiently tested (there are different structural coverage criteria depending on the criticality level of the software).

2.1.5.2. *Development of avionic software*

The process elaborated by Airbus for the development of its avionic software is rigorously copied from that strongly recommended by document DO-178B (see section 2.1.3.1). Formal verification methods are not discussed in any detail in this norm dating from 1992.

It is nonetheless in this context that Airbus implements the formal tool-driven techniques described in this chapter. Their adequacy with regards to the requirements of DO-178B and more generally the introduction of these techniques to the development process was the subject of [SOU 09].

The new version of the norm, the DO-178C, [RTC] suggests a *formal method* supplement. Such supplements are now seen as an alternative to the test to meet verification objectives.

2.2. Two methods for formal verification

Two formal methods for the verification of programs or models are presented in this section. These are *static analysis by abstract interpretation* [COU 77, COU 92, COU 00] and *program proof by calculation of the weakest pre-condition* [DIJ 75]. It is not a matter of an overview of all the formal techniques, but a presentation of the principles of those put into practice via tools in the industrial experience related to this chapter, that is to say those identified by Airbus as being the most promising in the long term [SOU 04b].

These two theoretical approaches resolve the problem posed by verifying that a program satisfies a certain specification in different manners. The objective is to obtain verification software tools that are as automatic as possible so that they can be used industrially.

Before examining these two methods, the general principle of program proof must be recalled. This is the subject of the following section.

2.2.1. *General principle of program proof*

A specification is met by a program if and only if there is an invariant that:

– P1: is true for the initial states of the program;

– P2: remains true after the execution of any instruction of the program;

– P3: implies the specification.

This principle expresses equivalence (if and only if) it can be broken down into two subprinciples in the form of an implication):

– If a specification is met by a program then there is an invariant which satisfies the properties P1, P2 and P3.

– If there is an invariant which satisfies P1, P2 and P3 then the specification is satisfied by the program.

The first implication establishes *completeness* and the second *safety*.

When it is a matter of automatic verification, completeness cannot be attained. Indeed, the undecidability principle means that it is impossible to design a software tool that automatically calculates the invariant which, satisfying P1, P2 and P3, enables us to prove that an arbitrary program meets its specification.

However, the second implication – safety – can be guaranteed by an automatic verification tool.

The formalization of this principle is based on that of a program as a system of transitions. A program is thus defined by a set of states among which we can distinguish the initial states, the final states and a transition relation joining the passage of one state to another. The state of a program has two components: a memory state (variables, registers, etc.); and a "program point" (or control point), i.e. a place in the text of the program that we can "tag" by a label (or sticker) before an instruction.

A finite execution of the program is then a sequence of states, from an initial state to a final state, if it finishes. In the opposite case, we have an infinite execution.

Thus, both the specification and the invariant can be seen as execution sets and property P3 of the principle proof can be interpreted in the following manner: the set of executions of the program "captured" by the invariant is included in the ensemble of the specified executions.

2.2.2. *Static analysis by abstract interpretation*

Generally, and very informally, a static analyzer by *abstract interpretation* [COU 77, COU 92, COU 00] takes the program and a few directives (or annotations) as the input in order to calculate an abstract semantic of the program in the form of an abstract invariant. If the analyzer is used to prove a specification, the analysis ends by the test including the invariant in the specification. The invariant being a sure abstraction of the semantic of the program analyzed, if it is included in the specification the latter is satisfied.

This inclusion test is an application of the general principle of proof presented in the previous section.

In the event of non-inclusion, the responsible locations of code in the program are signaled to the user. Non-inclusion provides alarms that are either true – i.e. each is revealed by at least one real execution of the program being analyzed – or false – in the case where their conditions of appearance are due to imprecision introduced by the abstraction. The user has to decide whether an alarm is true or false, often with the help of an analyzer in an interactive session.

2.2.2.1. *Calculation of the abstract invariant by a static analyzer*

Once the text of the program has been converted into an internal form that can be used by the analysis (e.g. an abstract syntax tree), its instructions are interpreted by no longer considering the concrete values of variables, but by considering the abstract values.

The abstract values represent a superset of values that can be taken on by the variables of the program. Thus, it is not the real state of the program that the analyzer is changing but its abstract state. The analysis begins with the abstract values of the input variables of the program and propagates them instruction-by-instruction until it finishes. In the absence of loops, this propagation of abstract values enables us to calculate the abstract state in one go after each instruction, and therefore also at the end of the program.

If the abstraction is safe, then each abstract invariant represents a superset of the concrete states after each instruction. In the presence of the loop – with an exception when a local directive is specified by the user – a static analyzer cannot generally successively interpret all the iterations, if only because the loop can be infinite in reality or in abstraction. The repeated interpretation of loop instructions leads to the abstract invariant getting bigger and then stabilizing, a fixed point having been reached.

It is the abstract invariant corresponding to this fixed point that is propagated in the rest of the program. The fact that the analyzer cannot engage in all the iterations of a loop is translated, in the calculation of a fixed point, by a passage to the limit (termed widening) to try and quickly exceed the fixed point followed by a narrowing to try and reduce over approximation.

Here is an illustration of this calculation of an abstract invariant, taking the very basic example of abstraction by intervals.

The program portion is written in C, with x being an integer variable:

L0:	x = 1
L1:	while (x<10000) {
L2:	x = x + 2
L3:	}
L4:	

The labels Li, for $i \in [0,4]$ are labels of different points of the program. In L0, the variable x is in an unknown state. The abstract invariant of this piece of program is made of five local abstract invariants, with one per program point. The memory state of the program being reduced to the content of the sole variable x, let Xi represent these local abstract invariants, $i \in [0,4]$. Xi refers to the abstraction in the form of an interval of the set of possible values for variable x at the program point Li.

The abstract invariant is obtained from the following semantic equations:

$$X0 = ?$$
$$X1 = [1,1]$$
$$X2 = (X1 \cup^{\#} X3) \cap^{\#}]{-\infty},10000[$$
$$X3 = X2 +^{\#} [2,2]$$
$$X4 = (X1 \cup^{\#} X3) \cap^{\#} [10000, +\infty[$$

Table 2.2 gives the evolution of the abstract state until its stabilization, where we then have the abstract invariant of this piece of code.

Abstract	Init	1	2	Widening	Guard
X0	?	?	?	?	?
X1	∅	[1,1]	[1,1]	[1,1]	[1,1]
X2	∅	[1,1]	[1,3]	[1, +∞]	[1, 9,999]
X3	∅	[3,3]	[3,5]	[3, +∞]	[3, 10,001]
X4	∅	∅	∅	∅	[10,000, 10,001]

Table 2.2. *Abstract execution*

2.2.2.1.1. Commentary regarding Table 2.2

Before the start of the analysis, only X0 is non-empty. The question mark means that x can take on all of the values anticipated by its type. If x is an integer number signed on 32 bits then X0 = [-2,147,483,648, 2,147,483,647].

Column 1 gives the result of the first step of the loop analysis and column 2 the result of the second step. Once there, the analyzer notes that the right bound of the intervals is increasing: he therefore carries out a passage to the limit (widening), hence the [1, +∞] and [3, +∞] of the "Widening" column. Once at this point in the analysis, abstract states X2 and X3 can no longer grow and an overapproximation of the accessible states is reached. Then, a last analysis step takes into account the guard "x < 10000" to reduce the "+∞" to 9999 or 10001, according to the program points, to arrive at the result: [10,000, 10,001] in X4 (last column).

The abstract domain contains the set of possible abstract values that have an order. In this case it includes intervals $\subseteq^{\#}$, collective operators $\cap^{\#}$ and $\cup^{\#}$, as well as a set of operators enabling us to interpret the expressions, either Boolean or arithmetic, in abstract form and the control structures of the programming language.

A static analyzer, by abstract interpretation, can therefore be assimilated to a mathematical function $F^{\#}$ that transforms the abstract state before an instruction into the next abstract state.

Still using the same example: $F^{\#}$ ("x = x +2", X2 = [1,3]) gives the abstract state X3 = [3,5]. The evaluation of the loop condition $F^{\#}$ ("x < 10000", X3 $\cup^{\#}$ X1 = [1,5]) gives TRUE and X2 = [1,5]. The operation carried out here is an intersection of intervals: X2 = [1,5] $\cap^{\#}$]-∞, 10000[= [1,5].

When intervals are stabilized, the evaluation of the loop condition gives:

TRUE case: $X2 = (X3 \cup^{\#} X1) \cap^{\#}]\text{-}\infty,10000[$

$\qquad\qquad = [1,10001] \quad \cap^{\#}]\text{-}\infty,10000[$

$\qquad\qquad = [1, 9999];$

FALSE case: $X4 = (X3 \cup^{\#} X1) \cap^{\#} [10000,\text{-}\infty[$

$\qquad\qquad = [1,10001] \cap^{\#} [10000,\text{-}\infty[$

$\qquad\qquad = [10000, 10001]$

The columns in Table 2.2 correspond to the successive iterates, with widening, of the calculation of the fixed point: $X = F^{\#}(X)$, X being a vector of X_i components for $i \in [0,4]$, starting from $X_i = \varnothing$ for all $i > 0$.

2.2.2.1.2. Abstract domains

The example given above cannot account for the vast application field of abstract interpretation, even when only considering static analysis. There are several reasons for this, that we will not go into here, but we refer the reader to publications already referenced on the subject. We can nonetheless open the door to this immense field by specifying that the abstract domain of intervals is not the only one, that some have already been developed and that nothing *in theory* limits the number of domains.

These domains, current and future, are split into two fundamental categories, depending on whether or not they are relational.

We could not introduce this notion of relation in the example because, for reasons of simplicity, it is limited to a single variable. Of course a real program has numerous variables and it is essential to establish relations between them that a static analyzer must be able to "discover" in order to prove certain properties.

EXAMPLE 2.1. – Before the instruction we have two integer variables, x and y, and a set of possible memory states $\{(x=1, y=0), (x=2, y=0),(x=3, y=0)\}$.

The instruction given is "y = 2 * x;".

After the instruction, we get: $\{(x=1, y=2), (x=2, y=4), (x=3, y=6)\}$. This new memory state shows the relation that has been established between x and y. An analysis using the abstract domain of intervals gives an abstract state of (X=[1,3], Y=[0,0]) before the instruction and an abstract state of (X=[1,3], Y=[2,6]) after the instruction.

Thus, in the abstract relation "y is worth two times x" is lost, since from the abstract state resulting from the instruction the set of couples (value of x, value of y) that must, for safety, be reconstituted is:

{(1,2), (1,3), (1,4), (1,5), (1,6), (2,2), (2,3), (2,4),.... (3,2), (3,3), (3,4), (3,5), (3,6)}.

2.2.2.1.3. Non-relational domains

The above example shows that the domain of intervals is non-relational. Indeed, the mathematical relation (a set of couples in the example) deduced from the abstract analysis is much less precise than that stemming from the concrete analysis. The positive offset of this lack of precision is the weak complexity of the analysis (reduced calculation time with regards to relational domains).

2.2.2.1.4. Relational domains

It is theoretically possible to discover all of the relations between the variables of a program but in practice this leads to impossible analyses from the point of view of calculation and consumption of memory, if we wish to analyze industrial programs.

Nonetheless, relational domains are very useful if they are dedicated to the analysis of such-and-such family of programs and if they are activated according to *ad hoc* heuristics (see section 2.3.2.3 for a good overview of the existing abstract relational domains).

2.2.2.2. Safety (soundness) of the abstract invariant

For the inclusion test of the abstract invariant of the specification to be safe (i.e. sound), it is necessary to have the guarantee that it represents a superset of all possible executions of the program. The formalization of this safety (also called soundness) is the central notion of the theory of abstract interpretation. Such formalization is instigated by the use of the mathematical notion of "Galois correspondence" adapted by Patrick and Radhia Cousot:

$$< p, \subseteq > \underset{\alpha}{\overset{\gamma}{\rightleftarrows}} < Q, \subseteq^{\#} >$$

In this formula, P is all of the parts of a set S of concrete objects (traces, states, etc.), $\subseteq$ is the order given on this set and Q is a set of abstract values with the order $\subseteq^{\#}$. This formula, from left to right, enables us to go from concrete to abstract and, from right to left, from abstract to concrete values. To do this, two functions are defined: α for the abstraction and γ for concretization, with the following properties:

– α and γ are increasing;

– $\forall\, x \in P,\, x \subseteq \gamma\,(\alpha\,(x))$;

– $\forall\, y \in Q,\, \alpha(\gamma(y)) \subseteq\# y$.

Let us once more take the example of code written in C and dealt with by abstraction using the intervals described in the previous section. Let us call x_i, with i in [0,4] the concrete values of x per program point.

Table 2.3 shows the evolution of all the concrete values of the program during its execution.

	Init	1	2	End of program
x_0	?	?	?	?
x_1	$\varnothing$	{1}	{1}	{1}
x_2	$\varnothing$	{1}	{1,3}	{1, 3, 5, 7,...,9,999}
x_3	$\varnothing$	(3)	{3,5}	{3, 5, 7, 9...,10,001}
x_4	$\varnothing$	$\varnothing$	$\varnothing$	{10,001}

Table 2.3. *Concrete execution*

2.2.2.2.1. Commentary regarding Table 2.3

Let us first of all note that there are no more intervals as we have moved onto the concrete side. We find the sets for all the values of x, depending on which point of the execution we are at, in this table. The value of x at the end of the program is unique: 10,001; and the sets only contain odd numbers.

Applying the concretization function to what the analyzer calculated gives us Table 2.4.

	Init	1	2	End of the program
x_0	?	?	?	?
x_1	$\varnothing$	$\gamma([1,1]) = \{1\}$	$\gamma([1,1]) = \{1\}$	$\gamma([1,3]) = \{1,2,3\}$
x_2	$\varnothing$	$\gamma([1,1]) = \{1\}$	$\gamma([1,3]) = \{1,2,3\}$	$\gamma(1, 9,999])$ $=\{1, 2, 3, 4, 5, 6,..., 9,999\}$
x_3	$\varnothing$	$\gamma([3,3]) = \{3\}$	$\gamma([3,5]) = \{3,4,5\}$	$\gamma(1, 10,001])$ $=\{3, 4, 5, 6, 7, 8...,10001\}$
x_4	$\varnothing$	$\varnothing$	$\varnothing$	$\gamma(10,000,10,001])$ $=\{10,000, 10,001\}$

Table 2.4. *Concrete expression of the abstract execution*

2.2.2.2.2. Commentary on Table 2.4

The comparison of Tables 2.3 and 2.4 reveals the over approximation due to the analysis. Two differences are worth noting. First, whereas in the real execution (Table 2.3) all the values x takes are odd (except in x_0), the analysis also considers pairs (Table 2.4). The second difference concerns the final value: it is unique and is worth 10001, following the execution of the real program; whereas the analysis envisages two possibilities: 10000 and 10001.

2.2.2.2.3. Safety of $F^{\#}$

As we have seen, the analyzer implements a mathematical function, $F^{\#}$, which makes the abstract state of the program evolve from instruction to instruction. This function abstracts function F, which plays the same role on the concrete side.

The safe construction of $F^{\#}$ in relation to F must satisfy:

$$F^{\#} = \alpha \circ F \circ \gamma$$

or, if not then,

$$\alpha \circ F \circ \gamma \subseteq^{\#} F^{\#}.$$

As already mentioned, the abstract invariant is obtained by the calculation of the least fixed point (lfp).

The safety of the calculation is then expressed as:

$$\alpha \, (\text{lfp } F) \subseteq^{\#} \text{lfp } F^{\#}.$$

When it is a matter of widening, it is on an upper bound, $\text{Inv}^{\#}$, from the lfp that the calculation stabilizes. We therefore have:

$$\alpha \, (\text{lfp } F) \subseteq^{\#} \text{lfp } F^{\#} \subseteq^{\#} \text{Inv}^{\#}.$$

2.2.2.2.4. Verification

The abstract invariant $\text{Inv}^{\#}$ serves to verify a certain specification, *Spec*. Broadly speaking, *Spec* is a set of executions. From a theoretical point of view, verification is achieved by the following inclusion test:

$$\gamma \, (\text{Inv}^{\#}) \subseteq Spec.$$

Let us once again take our example and let us give ourselves the following specification: "none of the integer expressions calculated must overflow". Verifying this specification with the calculated abstract invariant is the same as verifying (see Table 2.4 for the set of concrete values):

– L0: γ ([-2, 147,483,638, 2,147,483,647]) $\subseteq$

$\{i \mid i \in$ [-2,147,483,638, 2,147,483,647]$\}$: TRUE;

– L1: γ ([1,1]) $\subseteq \{i \mid i \in$ [-2,147,483,638, 2,147,483,647]$\}$: TRUE;

– L2: γ (1,9999]) $\subseteq \{i \mid i \in$ [-2,147,483,638, 2,147,483,647]$\}$: TRUE;

– L3: γ (1,10001]) $\subseteq \{i \mid i \in$ [-2,147,483,638, 2,147,483,647]$\}$: TRUE;

– L4: γ (10000,10001]) $\subseteq \{i \mid i \in$ [-2,147,483,638, 2,147,483,647]$\}$: TRUE.

If the specification is: "in L4 x must be worth 10001" then the inclusion test gives:

γ (10000,10001]) = $\{10,000, 10,001\} \subseteq \{10001\}$: FALSE.

However the execution of the program does indeed give x = 10001 in L4. The verification failure is therefore due to the abstraction: it is a false alarm.

Let us note that this way of verifying the specification is not applicable in practice (in a static analyzer) since it would be necessary to implement the concrete expression function. Therefore the verification stage is done abstractly, by a process that involves the inclusion test presented above, but the implementation of which does not require the γ function.

2.2.2.2.5. $F^{\#}$ is a result of the composition of several abstractions

Passing safely from the concrete semantic of a program to its abstract semantic "by intervals", for example, proceeds by successive abstractions, each passage from one semantic to another, that is more abstract and vice versa, gives rise to a Galois correspondence. The composition of these correspondences enables us to apply the safety $F^{\#}$ formula cited above.

2.2.3. *Program proof by calculation of the weakest precondition*

The fundamentals of the proof of logical properties on an imperative language program were put forward by Hoare [HOA 69] in 1969. Based on the precise semantic definition of a computing program in imperative language, Hoare proposed proving certain expected properties by mathematical deductive reasoning, generally at the end of the program.

He introduces a notation called the *Hoare triple*, which associates a program, Q, start hypotheses, P, and expected output properties, R:

P {Q} R

The logical sense of this triple corresponds to: if P is true, then after program Q, R will be true if Q ends.

This foundational approach brings into play the most important notions of program proof, which are still valid today.

On one hand, the notion of formalization of an expected behavior: a functionality that is informally described is then presented in the form of logical assertion in a mathematical language, which makes it a lot more precise.

On the other hand, the global nature of the assertion is valid for all executions of the program that satisfies starting hypotheses that are also formalized in a mathematical language. This second characteristic is a marked difference from the test that enables us to verify a functionality in a very precise and rigorous way, but only on an input test pack.

The Hoare test process is a purely intellectual process with the objective of resulting in the final Hoare triple relative to a program that we call (P MyProg} R).

To arrive at this final result, Hoare gave the definition of Hoare triples for each type of instruction, as well as axioms, enabling him to establish P {Q} R relations on a block of instructions, branches and loops.

Through a deductive process, the different rules are applied until the whole program is processed.

The basic rule is that of assignment:

$P[x{\leftarrow}e]$ { $x := e$ } P   (assign)

where x is a variable that is assigned the value of expression e. $P[x{\leftarrow}e]$ corresponds to the property *P* where all the occurrences of x are replaced by e.

Example: $(x+1{\geq}0)$ x: $= x+1$ $(x{\geq}0)$

Name	Rule	Condition
Composition	If P {Q1} R1 and R1 {Q2} R: then P {Q1;Q2} R	
Condition	If B ∧ P {Q1} R and ¬B ∧ P {Q2} R: then P {if B then Q1 else Q2}R	
Loop	If (B ∧ P) {Q} P: then P {while B do Q} (¬B ∧ P)	With P: invariant of the loop

Table 2.5. *Other rules enabling us to process the composition of instructions, branches and iterations*

The proof activity by application of the Hoare rules is an intellectual process and is not tool driven. It is up to the author of the proof to define the correct properties between each instruction of the program and to establish its demonstration by applying the different theorems. This activity requires fairly specialized mathematical skills and is not adapted to process thousands of lines of code in an acceptable time.

An initial automation of the process of program proof was brought by the calculation of the *WP* (*weakest precondition*) from Dijkstra [DIJ 75]. The principle consists of automatically calculating the most general property holding before a statement S such as the property P holds after execution of S. We then have:

$$WP(S,P) \{S\} P$$

WP is then defined according to the same model of Hoare logic:

– calculation of the *WP* of the affectation:

$$WP(x:=e, P) \equiv P[x \leftarrow e]$$

Examples:

$$WP(x:= y + 5, x>0) \equiv y > -5$$

$$WP(x:= 5, x = 5) \equiv \text{true}$$

$$WP(x:= 3, x = 4) \equiv \text{false}$$

$$WP(x:= 3, y = 3) \equiv y=3$$

– calculation of the *WP* of the composition of two instructions:

$$WP(S1;S2, P) \equiv WP(S1, WP(S2, P))$$

The calculation of the *WP* of two instructions is the same as calculating the *WP* of the first instruction based on the result of the calculation of the *WP* of the second instruction.

– calculation of the *WP* of a branch:

$$WP(\text{if } (c) \text{ then } S1 \text{ else } S2, P) \equiv c \wedge WP(S1, P) \vee \neg c \wedge WP(S2, P)$$

– calculation of the *WP* of the loop: the case of *WP* in the event of a loop requires the definition of a loop invariant that cannot be automatically calculated. The loop invariant describes the relations between the variables in valid packs for all the iterations of the loop. They are defined by the user. For the Caveat tool (see section 2.3.1), the calculation of *WP* for a loop is defined as follows:

$$WP(S0; \text{ while } (c) \text{ Sb, } P) \equiv$$

In the event where the loop is executed:

$$WP(S0, B \wedge \text{Inv} \Rightarrow WP(Sb, \neg B \Rightarrow P))$$

In the event where the loop is not executed:

$$WP(S0, \neg B \Rightarrow P)$$

With S0: sequence of instructions before the loop.

The processing of a program consists of calculating the *WP* by going back up the control flow from the end of the function (where the P property must be valid) until the beginning of the start function. It is therefore a backward analysis technique.

At the end of the calculation of *WP*, the hypotheses given at the start of the program are introduced. The proof of the property is the same as demonstrating that:

$$H \Rightarrow WP(\text{MyProg, P})$$

The predicate returning of a calculation of *WP* can rapidly become fairly complex, depending on the instructions in the source code, the property P to be proved, and the possible loop invariants. The proof tools must implement automatic theorem provers if we want to be able to automate the process.

The proof tools for code C Caveat (see section 2.3.1), Frama-C/Jessie and Frama-C/WP[1] are built from this model. Frama-C/Jessie is particular in that it does not calculate *WP* directly on the C code, but on its transformation to a pivot language (the "why" language). Frama-C WP is designed to embed different memory models and *WP* computations.

One of the greatest advantages of deductive proof techniques is that it is able to specify and prove very specific functional properties defined by the user. The problems encountered in the implementation relate to the non-automated nature of the process.

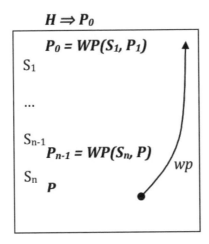

Figure 2.7. *Retro-propagation of the WP*

The addition of invariants necessary for the calculation of *WP* is a blockage point that was identified at the same time as the theory. It can be avoided in some cases by automatic generation of invariants by inductive methods.

Another break to the fluidity of an ideal process is the work of automatic theorem provers that work at the end of *WP* calculations with predicates that are very complex to prove. They are not always capable of automatically demonstrating all the true properties that come from *WP*. In the case of failure of the automatic procedures, it is possible to end the process manually with a proof assistant such as Coq.

---

1 For more information on Frama-C *plug-ins*, see frama-c.com/plugins.html.

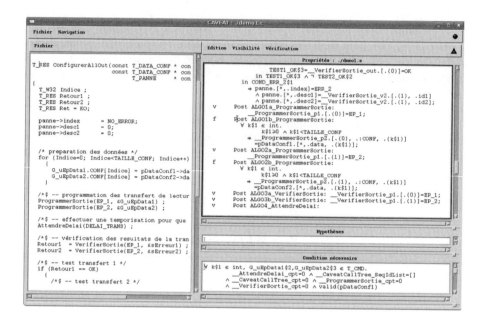

Figure 2.8. *The Caveat tool*

2.3. Four formal verification tools

2.3.1. *Caveat*

The Caveat tool[2] [RAN 99], see Figure 2.8, used on one of the pieces of software in the A380 (see Figure 2.1), is based on the calculation of the *WP* (Pg, P). Once this precondition has been calculated, it is necessary to try to prove it so as to be able to ensure, in the event of success, that the post-condition P of the program is verified. Thus, in addition to the calculation of *WP*, Caveat incorporates three other tools:

– an algebraic simplificator;

– an automatic theorem prover (or demonstrator);

– an interactive predicate transformer (IPT).

2.3.1.1. *Simplifier*

The calculation of *WP* handles predicates in their syntax form (see section 2.2.3) so that during the retro-propagation formulas grow very rapidly. The objective of the simplifier is to limit this inflation in order to facilitate the proof at the end of

---

2 To find out more about Caveat, see www-list.cea.fr/labos/fr/LSL/caveat/ index.html.

retro-propagation as much as possible (that is to say, the proof of *WP*(PR, P)). The simplifier is also called by the demonstrator.

2.3.1.2. *Demonstrator*

Once the calculation of *WP* has finished, the *WP*(PR, P) of the program is submitted to the demonstrator, which is tasked with trying to prove that the predicate result is true. This demonstrator is based on the theory of sequents.

A sequent is a sequence of hypotheses followed by a sequence of conclusions. The two sequences are separated by the symbol "−". For example:

H,P |− Q

Inference rules enable us to deduce a consequent sequent from an antecedent sequent:

$$\frac{antecedent}{consequence}(name)$$

Axioms enable us to express a sequent which is valid in all cases. Here are a few examples of rules and axioms:

$$\frac{H,P|-Q}{H|-P\Rightarrow Q}(\Rightarrow) \quad \frac{H|-Q \quad H|-Q}{H|-P\wedge Q}(\wedge) \quad \frac{}{H,P|-P}(ax)$$

2.3.1.3. *Proof process*

Once the user has submitted the code of the program, PR, and a post-condition, P, Caveat begins by calculating the *WP*(PR, P). Then, without user intervention, it submits this *WP*(PR, P) to the demonstrator, which either returns "true", meaning that the proof is complete, or returns a predicate.

If we are not proceeding by abstraction, this predicate returned by the demonstrator is the manifestation of the indecidability principle: This must then be handled by the user within Caveat's Interactive Predicate Transformer (IPT).

The reason the user can succeed where the demonstrator has failed is due to the ability of the human operator to spot the terms to be "brought together" within a logical expression (a predicate) in order to complete a stage in the proof and thus, more or less quickly, be able to conclude either by finishing the proof or by understanding why it is not possible.

2.3.1.4. *Interactive transformer of predicates*

This interactive part of Caveat enables the user to apply a transformation chosen from a set of menus to the predicate returned by the demonstrator. This transformation is applied to the predicate by the IPT if and only if it is mathematically correct. If this is the case, the predicate before transformation is replaced by the one after transformation, the latter being equivalent to the former. If after successive transformations, that is to say by application of a "proof tactic", the predicate obtained is "true", then due to the successive equivalences guaranteed by the IPT the predicate returned by the demonstrator is replaced by "true" and Caveat then marks this post-condition to be proved by a "V" meaning "Verified".

Heuristics

During the proof campaign, if the user is led to end a certain number of proofs by implementing the same tactic, thanks to the *control language* of the Caveat tool, he or she can program the said tactic (we then speak of heuristics) and automatically invoke it.

2.3.2. *Proof of the absence of run-time errors: Astrée*

Astrée is a static analyzer by abstract interpretation that is capable of proving the absence of *run-time errors* in programs written in C. First developed by the computer science laboratory at the *Ecole normale supérieure*, today it is marketed by AbsInt Angewandte Informatik GmbH[3].

2.3.2.1. *Implicit specification*

A run-time error is:

– any use of the C language defined in section J2 of the international norm [ISO 99] as being undefined behavior, that is to say an operation that produces a result that is incorrect or undefined (such as a division by zero or an indexation of the table outside the markers);

– any use of the C language that is contrary to aspects of section J3 of the norm [ISO 99] specific to implantation of the program on a given machine (such as the size of integer numbers and arithmetical overflows);

– all aspects of the C language linked to current conventions of the users of C (like the fact that we do not want arithmetic on signed integer numbers to be modular, even it is implanted this way in the machine on which the program is running);

---

3 See www.absint.com.

– any violation of an assertion provided by the user.

2.3.2.2. *Characteristics*

The Astrée analyzer is:

– *Sound*: some commercial tools, called *bug-finders*, implement incomplete search heuristics for the most common *run-time errors* but are unable to guarantee the absence of a run-time error on a program that does not have any. Astrée, on the other hand, cannot omit signaling a run-time error in a program that has one. Indeed, its analysis exhaustively takes into account all possible run-time errors for all possible executions of the program being analyzed.

– *Automatic*: the tools based on deductive methods, such as the Caveat tool, require an important interaction with the user, who must annotate the program being analyzed with numerous inductive invariants adapted to the properties to be proven, and interactively finish the difficult proofs. The Astrée static analysis, in comparison, is completely automatically carried out and is based on very few (if any) user annotations.

– *Efficient:* Astrée is able to prove the absence of run-time errors in synchronous industrial control–command programs containing several hundreds of thousands of lines in just a few hours.

– *Specialized*: unlike generalist analyzers, Astrée is specialized in the analysis of synchronous control–command programs. It implements abstract domains that take into account the underlying control theory, which is necessary to automatically prove sophisticated properties.

– *Parametric*: the options and directives (local and global) provided by Astrée enable the user to have a very subtle control of the compromise between the cost and precision of the analysis.

– *Modular*: Astrée is made up of modules called abstract domains, the choice and configuration of which enable us to freely construct new analyzers that are specialized in a particular domain. This modularity is favored by the implementation in the Objective Caml language [LER 11].

– *Extensible*: Astrée can easily be extended by the development of new abstract domains that are adapted to a use domain;

– *Precise*: like any sound and automatic analyzer, Astrée can produce false alarms. Generic analyzers have many: 10–20% of alarms triggered per C language operation are false. Such rates are unacceptable for industrial programs, which have hundreds of thousands of lines of code. Astrée, in contrast, is able to obtain the "zero alarm" objective, at least for programs in the domain in which it is specialized. Experience shows us that Astrée is also precise for other program families.

2.3.2.3. *Abstract domains*

Astrée implements abstract domains chosen to enable the precise and efficient analysis of synchronous control–command programs. The following sections describe a few of the main domains.

2.3.2.3.1. Intervals domain

The intervals domain [COU 77] enables us to capture invariants of the type $a \leq v \leq b$, where v is a numeric variable (integer or floating point), and a and b are numerical constraints discovered automatically by the analysis. This domain does not capture any of the possible relations between the two variables v and w of the program being analyzed. It is a basic domain that is not very expressive but the good thing is that it is not very costly either. It can be implemented in any value analysis tools by abstract interpretation.

2.3.2.3.2. Octagon domains

Octagon domains [MIN 01, MIN 04] enable us to capture invariant relations of the type $x \pm y \leq c$, where x and y are integer or floating-point numerical variables, and c is a constant automatically discovered by the analysis.

The octagon domain is a weakly-relational domain [MIN 04b, chap. 4] in the sense that it enables us to represent part of the relations between two variables, x and y.

2.3.2.3.3. Domain of the decision trees

The domain of the decision trees [BLA 03, section 6.2.4] (or domain of Boolean relations) enables us to establish invariant relations between Boolean variable values and numerical values.

As an example, this domain is used to prove the absence of division by zero in the example in Figure 2.9.

```
1 typedef enum {FALSE = 0, TRUE = 1} BOOLEAN;
2 BOOLEAN B;
3 void main () {
4     unsigned int X, Y;
5     while (TRUE) {
6         B = (X == 0);
7         if (!B) Y = 1 / X;
8     }
9 }
```

Figure 2.9. *Example of C code*

2.3.2.3.4. Domain of the arithmetic–geometric deviations and clocks

The arithmetic–geometrical deviation domain [FER 05] deals with arithmetic–geometric progressions with a common difference that is slightly bigger than 1 (slowly divergent progressions). When a variable, v, is updated in the body of a loop, B, if the successive values of v correspond to the terms of such a progression, and the number of maximum turns of B is known, this domain enables us to bound all the values accessible by v in a sound and precise way.

A particular instance of this domain is the domain of clocks. It enables us, for all synchronous programs, to take into account the existence of a synchronous clock exterior to the program that is incremented with each execution of the body of the reactive loop. In this way, the analyzer can compute sound supersets for the intervals of values of variables diverging slowly with every clock tick, from the period of the clock and the maximum mission duration.

2.3.2.3.5. Linearization domain for floating-point expressions

The linearization domain for floating-point expressions enables us to approximate a floating-point expression in a linear form, the coefficients of which are intervals (to take rounding errors into account). The propagation of these linear forms in the program, and the algebraic simplifications when several occurrences of a same variable appear in the same form, enable floating-point expressions to be simplified while taking into account rounding errors[4].

This domain also works for integer expressions.

2.3.2.3.6. Filter domains

These specific domains [FER 05] enable us to calculate invariants of digital filters that are currently implemented in control–command programs. Astrée implements a domain for the high-pass filters and a domain for the second-order filters, as well as a simplified domain for the second order.

2.3.2.3.7. High-pass filters

These filters receive an input, $(E_n)_{n \in \mathbb{N}}$, and calculate a response, $(S_n)_{n \in \mathbb{N}}$, such as:

$$S_0 = cst$$

$$S_{k+1} = \alpha.S_k + \beta.(E_{k+1} - E_k)$$

with $E_k \in [-m,m]$ for any $k \in \mathbb{N}$.

---

4 To find out more see [GHO 09, chap. 5] and [GOU 06, chap. 6].

2.3.2.3.8. Second-class filters

These filters calculate a response such as:

$$S_0 = cst_0$$

$$S_1 = cst_1$$

$$S_{k+2} = \alpha.S_{k+1} + \beta.S_k + \gamma.E_{k+2} + \delta.E_{k+1} + \epsilon.E_k$$

with $\beta \in \ ]0,1[$, $\alpha^2 + 4.\beta < 0$ and $(cst_0, cst_1, E_k) \in [-m,m]^3$ for any $k \in \mathbb{N}$.

Even if these filters only carry out linear computations, the relations that they establish between the values of the variables in play are nonlinear. The specialized domains of Astrée are therefore essential for a precise analysis of the values computed by these filters.

2.3.2.3.9. Partitioning domain

When the behavior of the program analyzed strongly depends on the precise values of certain expressions, such as test conditions or array indexes, the direct use of abstract numerical domains can produce results that are too imprecise to prove the absence of run-time errors. In cases like these, it is advisable to proceed by case analyses, that is to say by conducting several local analyses of a same part of a program so as to join results later in the program where the problematic expressions no longer play an important role. This case analysis is called partitioning [BLA 03, MAU 05].

The grouped analysis of different concrete execution traces is split at the partition point (according to partitioning criteria, e.g. the possible values of a variable) into several analyses that are then later joined together at a merging point. For example, without partitioning Astrée cannot prove the absence of division by zero in the example in Figure 2.10.

```
1  typedef enum {FALSE = 0, TRUE = 1} BOOLEAN;
2  volatile BOOLEAN B;
3  void main () {
4       unsigned int X, Y;
5       if (B)    {X = 0; Y = 1;}
6       else      {X = 1; Y = 0;};
7       X = 1 / (X + Y);
8  }
```

Figure 2.10. *Example of code where Astrée cannot prove the absence of division by 0*

Indeed, the other abstract domains show the invariants $X \in \{0,1\}$ and $Y \in \{0,1\}$ before the division, but none automatically captures the (implicit) relation $X + Y = 1$.

```
 1  typedef enum {FALSE = 0, TRUE = 1} BOOLEAN;
 2  volatile BOOLEAN B;
 3  void main () {
 4      unsigned int X, Y;
 5      __ASTRÉE_partition_control
 6      if (B)    {X = 0; Y = 1;}
 7      else      {X = 1; Y = 0;};
 8      X = 1 / (X + Y);
 9      __ASTRÉE_partition_merge(());
10  }
```

Figure 2.11. *Example of code with a partition request*

However, if the user asks Astrée to carry out a well-chosen partitioning (see Figure 2.11) then Astrée conducts two separate analyses of the division:

– one for the case where the test "if (B) turns out to be true" and therefore X=1/(0 + 1);

– one for the case where the test "if (B) turns out to be false", and therefore X=1/(1 + 0).

This partitioning enables us to prove the absence of division by zero, as well as the invariant $X = 1$ after the division.

2.3.3. *Stability and numerical precision: Fluctuat*

All control programs are based on control theory, which describes the physical data that are manipulated, together with control algorithms, in the realm of (ideal) real numbers.

In practice, the effective implantation of such algorithms in onboard computers is carried out by means of floating-point arithmetic, based on a finite representation of real numbers. Floating-point arithmetic is an approximation of real arithmetic, in so far as each operation can have a rounding error – which is generally very small. Even if this approximation is fairly precise for most applications, there are pathological cases where accumulations of rounding errors produce results that are grossly false, even if the subjacent numerical schemes are stable with the real mathematical numbers.

Even if the control algorithms on board a plane are correctly constructed for real numbers, it is necessary to verify that the imprecisions introduced by the floating-point implantation are still negligible in the face of uncertainties on the sensors and actuators of the system.

2.3.3.1. *The IEEE-754 norm*

The IEEE-754 norm [IEE 85] describes the format of floating-point numbers as well as the basic arithmetical operations that any processor that conforms to this norm must implement.

It defines two floating-point formats:

– the simple precision format represents the exponent, exp, on 8 bits, the mantissa, m, on 23 bits and sign, s, on 1 bit;

– the double precision format represents the exponent on 11 bits, the mantissa on 52 bits and the sign on 1 bit.

It distinguishes several categories of floating-point numbers, presented here for double precision:

– normalized floating-point numbers have a non-null and non-maximal exponent and 53 bits of significant mantissa (the bit of the strong weight, which is implicit, is worth 1):

$$f = (-1)^s \times (1.0 + m / 2^{52}) \times 2^{exp - 2^{(11-1)} + 1};$$

– the denormalized floating-point numbers have a null exponent and a non-null mantissa with $\lfloor \log_2(m) \rfloor$ significant bits (the bit of strong weight, implicit, is worth 0):

$$f = (-1)^s \times (0.0 + m / 2^{52}) \times 2^{0 - 2^{(11-1)} + 2};$$

– +0 (resp. −0) has a null exponent and mantissa, and a positive sign (resp. negative);

– $\pm \infty$ have maximal exponents and null mantissas;

– the NaN (*Not a Number*) have maximal exponents and non-null mantissas.

The norm also defines four rounding modes:

– round $o_\sim$ to the nearest floating-point number;

– round $o_{-\infty}$ to $-\infty$;

– round $o_{+\infty}$ to $+\infty$;

– round o_0 to zero.

The basic arithmetical operations $+$, $-$, $\times$ and $\div$ are rounded exactly, in the sense that their evaluation always produces a floating-point number equal to the rounding of the real result with the chosen rounding mode.

More formally, if we note $\uparrow_o$: $|R \rightarrow F$ the function with floating-point values that returns the rounding of a given real with the rounding mode $o \in \{o_-, o_{-\infty}, o_{+\infty}, o_0\}$ and $\diamond \in \{+,-,\times,\div\}$ an elementary operation, then for all floats $(f_1,f_2) \in F^2$:

$$f1 \diamond_{F,o} f_2 = \uparrow_o (f_1 \diamond_{|R} f_2)$$

Despite this useful property of floating-point arithmetic defined by IEEE-754 [IEE 85], finite precision induces subtle pitfalls from which big relative errors, even abnormal functional behaviors, can result. Among the principal sources of error, we can cite:

– *representation errors*: for example, the rational number 1/10 cannot be represented exactly by a floating-point number in base 2;

– *absorption*: high loss of precision during the addition of two numbers of very different orders of magnitude;

– *cancellation*: strong loss of relative precision during the calculation of the difference between two very close numbers;

– *unstable tests*: tests inducing a discontinuity of data flow, with different control flows for real and floating-point arithmetic.

– *accumulation of rounding errors*: which can cause a catastrophic amplification of errors, and a drift of computations.

In addition to this, an optimizing compiler can transform the code in a way that invalidates the analysis of numerical precision carried out on the source code. Several solutions exist to deal with this problem:

– Study the compilation *patterns* and write source code in such a way that it behaves like the executable. This solution is often used for critical embedded software, where the optimizing compilation is not currently used. Indeed, the applicable norms [RTC 92] require traceability between the source code and the compiled code.

– Use a certified compiler [LER 06].

– Use a separate validator to verify the conformity of the compiled code with the source code [RIV 04].

– Verify the numerical precision on the compiled code – a specific version of Fluctuat directly analyses the assembler for a digital signal processor [MAR 04].

2.3.3.2. *The Fluctuat static analyzer*

2.3.3.2.1. General presentation

The non-specific version of Fluctuat [DEL 09] is a static analyzer using abstract interpretation developed by the French nuclear research center (*Commissariat à l'énergie atomique et aux énergies alternatives*, CEA), and dedicated to the numerical precision analysis of programs in C.

To do this, it computes value intervals that variables of the program can take at each control point, for all possible executions, with two different semantics:

– semantics corresponding to executions of the program on an ideal machine that handles real mathematical numbers;

– semantics corresponding to the implementation of floating-point numbers and modular integers with finite precision, by means of IEEE-754.

Fluctuat then computes an upper bound for the difference between values taken by variables for these two semantics, and breaks it down according to the contributions of the different control points. This enables the user to determine the main sources of numerical imprecision in his or her program.

The graphic interface of the tool (see Figure 2.12) enables us to visualize the graph of rounding errors introduced by each line of code for each variable at the end of the program.

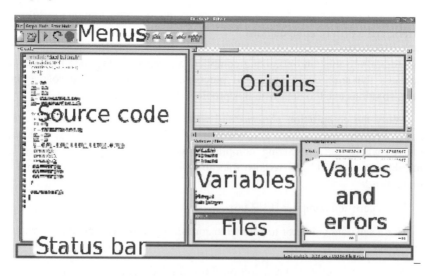

Figure 2.12. *The graphic interface of Fluctuat*

2.3.3.2.2. Abstract domains based on affine arithmetic

To compute value and error intervals for each variable, Fluctuat uses weakly relational abstract numerical domains based on affine forms [GHO 09, GOU 06, GOU 08].

Domain for real numbers

Affine arithmetic is an extension of interval arithmetic and improves its precision by taking into account the linear correlations between variables. The real value of variable x is represented by an affine form $x^{\#}$:

$$x^{\#} = x_0 + x_1 \varepsilon_1 + \ldots + x_n \varepsilon_n$$

where:

– the noise symbols $\varepsilon_i \in [-1,1]$ are independent symbolic variables with undetermined values;

– the coefficients $x_i \in |R$, called partial deviations in the centre $x_0 \in |R$ of the linear form, express uncertainties regarding the values of variables.

The sharing of noise symbols between several affine forms enables us to represent implicit dependencies between the associated variables.

In practice, these affine forms are themselves represented with floating-point coefficients. The implementation is made sound by overapproaching the rounding errors on these coefficients and by agglomerating these errors into additional noise symbols.

The joint concretization of these affine forms is a center-symmetric polytope, which is a zonotope. Zonotope-based abstract domains provide a good trade-off between computational cost and accuracy.

Domain for floats and errors

This abstract domain extends the above linear forms to represent the floating-point values of variables, as well errors on variables (differences between floating-point values and real values):

$$f^x = \left(\alpha_0^x + \sum_i \alpha_i^x \varepsilon_i \right) + \left(e_0^x + \sum_i e_l^x \eta_l + \sum_i m_i^x \varepsilon_i \right)$$

where:

$-f^x$ is the floating-point abstract value of variable x;

$-\alpha_0^x + \bigoplus_i \alpha_i^x \varepsilon_i$ is the affine form representing the real value of x, with a noise symbol per control point i of the program;

$-e_0^x$ is the center of the error;

– the noise symbols η_l express dependencies between errors, so that $e_i^x \eta_l$ represents the rounding error committed at the control point l;

– each $m_i^x \varepsilon_i$ term describes the propagation of the uncertainty on the value of the error term at control point i, which enables us to express the dependencies between errors and values.

A new noise symbol is created for each rounding error introduced by computations of the program analyzed. Thus at the end of the program, each variable Fluctuat is able to associate each error term of its affine form to the control point where it has been introduced. This is the information presented on the graph of rounding errors.

2.3.4. *Calculation of the worst case execution time: aiT (AbsInt GmbH)*

AbsInt's aiT is a family of tools for the calculation of the *Worst Case Execution Time* (WCET) for different microprocessors on board planes, automobiles, etc. These tools have an executable program and an annotations file (directives given to the tool) as input. Among these annotations, we find the description of memories (external) and buses of the target board in the form of a list of address zones with associated access time. Finally, the user must also provide the program point (generally the beginning of the task) from which the calculation of WCET must occur. The task here requires a portion of code that must be executed sequentially (no *threads*, parallelism or waiting for external events). The way in which aiT calculates the WCET of a task is broken down into several phases.

First of all there is the construction of the *control flow graph* (CFG). This initial internal analysis identifies the instructions and reconstructs the CFG based on the executable (or binary) program provided in entry. Annotations written by the user can help aiT identify the targets of computed jumps or calls.

Then, the *value analysis* calculates the value intervals for registers and addresses brought into play in the calculation of accesses to memory. The phase of *loop-bound analysis* calculates the upper bounds of the number of iterations of the loops (for the simpler ones) for the task being analyzed. Such bounds are necessary to obtain a WCET.

Cache analysis classifies the access to memory as "Hits", "Miss" or "indeterminate". This classification is very useful to the following analysis, particularly in the case of *Hit* or *Miss* classification; thus reducing the number of indeterminate situations, which can be costly in analysis time and consumption of memory by aiT.

Pipeline analysis is a safe symbolic execution of the program (represented by its CFG) analyzed on a model of the target processor. Thus *pipeline analysis*, benefiting from the results of previous analyses, predicts the temporal behavior of the task analyzed and calculates the WCET of all the basic blocks, the latter being assembler instruction sequences finished by a jump (or routine call).

Based on this, the *analysis of paths* calculates the longest path of the task being analyzed.

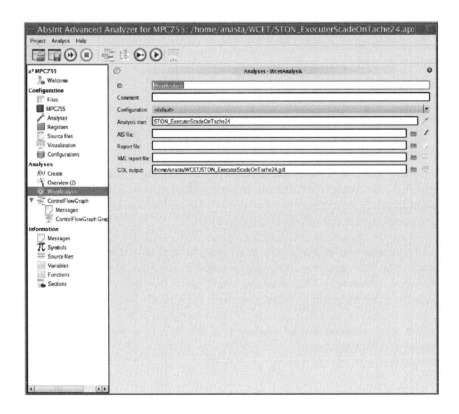

Figure 2.13. *aiT for PowerPC MPC755*

The *value analysis* is a static analysis by abstract interpretation including abstract domains that are non-relational (intervals) or weakly relational (*difference bound matrices*). The results of the value analysis are used to determine the bounds of loop iterations, to predict the addresses calculated by the task being analyzed as well as to exclude impossible paths for later analyses. Such paths appear when the value analysis is able to determine that the logical values always evaluate true or always false. The knowledge of the addresses of access to data in memory is very useful to the cache analysis.

Cache analysis therefore uses results from the value analysis to predict the behavior of the *data cache*. Those of cache analysis are used in the pipeline analysis to predict *pipeline stalls* in the event of *cache misses*. The combined results of cache and pipeline analyses are then used to calculate the WCET of the task being analyzed. The separation of the WCET calculation into successive phases renders the use of techniques adapted to each one possible. Analyses of value, cache and pipeline are static analyses with abstract interpretation. Path analysis is carried out by the calculation of an upper bound in *integer linear programming*.

2.4. Examples of industrial use

2.4.1. *Unitary proof (verification of low level requirements)*

2.4.1.1. *Introduction*

Unitary proof constitutes the first use of formal proof techniques by Airbus applied to the context of critical avionic software. The first motivations are mastering of the verification process and its costs in the face of a constant increase in the complexity of the software being developed.

The implementation of unitary proof was decided by the total replacement of unitary tests that were previously implemented in the type of software subset that was being processed. This decision could only be made after research and development by Airbus in partnership with the CEA [RAN 99].

This work enabled the development of the tool to a level of maturity that satisfied a certain number of criteria defined as prerequisites to the decision. These criteria were:

– ease of use;

– the adaptation of the process to software development engineers who are not specialists in formal methods;

– a rapid return on investment;

– reduced impact on the global development cycle.

The implementation of unitary proof gave rise to the development of a very automatic workshop based on the Caveat tool and coupled with the avionics software development workshop [DUP 06, SOU 04].

We will see how the unitary proof process is made up of two activities: formal specification and proof.

The activity of formal specification consists of the expression of the LLRs in a formal language. This formalism allows a functional description that is unambiguous and complete. This activity is without intervention of the tool.

Proof has the objective of verifying that the source code is correct with regards to its formal specifications. This activity is essentially automatic, the user having a role to play in order to end up with the proof of 100% of the defined properties.

This part of the activity of the prover is crucial for the evaluation of the method, since the more automatic the proof is, the more efficient it is with regards to testing in terms of engineers' workload.

The whole challenge of the unitary proof method is to define the conditions enabling an optimal progression of all phases, particularly in the proof phase.

2.4.1.2. *Methodology of unitary proof*

2.4.1.2.1. Reminder of the methodology of unitary tests

As a foreword to unitary proof, it is necessary to give a few reminders about the classic development cycle (as it was before the use of unitary proof).

The technique of unitary tests is the most frequently used technique to verify LLRs on the most critical software (Development Assurance Level A).

In the classic process, the HLRs are taken into account by defined design elements. The design presents itself in the form of a structural decomposition in machines.

We will distinguish an abstract machine that can be broken down into submachines and terminal machines.

These terminal machines contain elements corresponding to types, data that are constant or not, exported or private, and services that are later implemented by C functions.

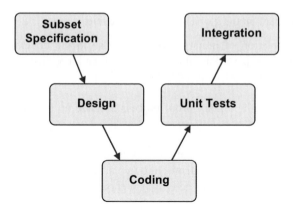

Figure 2.14. *Development cycle before unitary proof*

The notion of LLRs corresponds to the complete and unambiguous definition of a service. This precise description of the services describes, among others, which are the variables in read–write access and which are the services of the other machines that are used. This is what we call flow description.

It also describes the relationship between inputs and outputs by using an algorithmic vision.

This description is complete and unambiguous and allows the definition of unitary verification test plans.

The definition of unitary tests must follow a strict methodology so as to be certain to completely cover all functionality. For example, when several inputs are in play it is necessary to verify the impacts of each input on the subsequent outputs.

The consequence of respecting this methodology is a very weighty test plan definition activity with a large number of tests in output.

2.4.1.2.2. Integration of unitary proof in the development cycle

Moving from unit tests to unit proof has had a minimal impact on the development process.

Thus, the cycle is globally the same (see Figure 2.15), as are the verification objectives, but the means and activities are modified.

The design activity is modified to integrate the formalization of functional requirements.

The unitary verification activity does not require tests and consists of the verification of flows and the unitary proof of properties defined in the design stage.

The process of unitary proof intervenes from the design until the unitary verification.

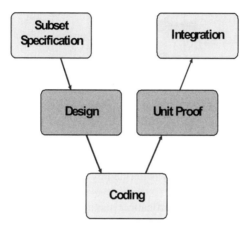

Figure 2.15. *Development cycle with unitary proof*

During the design phase, the designer produces a formal specification of the functional requirements expected. This formalization is described by a set of properties relating to functions or constants.

These properties are described in the Caveat language (a first-order predicate language).

The way in which properties are written is defined by the formal specification method, which is described in the following section. The definition of this method is an essential component of the industrialization of this process of unitary proof.

The *coding phase* is not impacted by unitary proof, although the source code must respect certain constraints imposed by the proof tool (Caveat) that are, for example, no function pointers, no forward jumps in the code and others.

The *verification phase* consists of the proof of formal specification on the code. It is examined in detail in section 2.4.1.2.5.

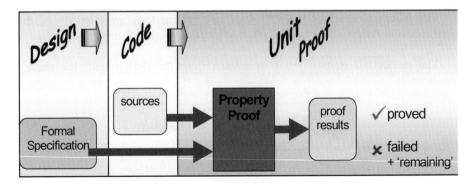

Figure 2.16. *Process of unitary proof*

2.4.1.2.3. Specification phase

The way of specifying formally is defined by a dedicated method.

The application of this specification method gives a standardized solution enabling the production of a complete, legible and maintainable specification.

The unitary approach of proof

Unitary proof is to the formal verification of a program what the unitary test is to test techniques, that is to say a unitary verification.

Here it is applied in its strictest definition. Each function is verified in a context that is isolated from its called functions.

The objectives of unitary verification deal with the relations between inputs and outputs. Inputs are the parameters of the function, the global variables read and the returned values of the called functions. The values returned by the output parameters of the called functions.

In this example, considering function f:

– the inputs are parameter p1;

– the global variable is Glob;

– the return of function f2 is during its first and second call;

– the return of function f3 is during its second call;

– the outputs are the return of function f1 and the value of Glob.

```
int Glob;
int f1(int p1)
{
        int local;
        local =f2();

        if (p1<10)
                local += f2();
        else
                local += f3(&Glob);

        return local ;
}
```

Figure 2.17. *Example illustrating the method of unitary proof*

We can freely and without formal language describe the expected properties in terms of relations between inputs and outputs. For example:

– if p1 is strictly less than 10, function f1 returns the sum of values returned by each call to function f2 (and not twice the return value of function f2, as nothing tells us that f2() is a pure function);

– if p1 is strictly less than 10, the value of global variable Glob is unchanged;

– if p1 is greater or equal to 10, global variable Glob is assigned the value given during the first call of f3 to its First rank output parameter;

– if p1 is greater or equal to 10, function f3 is called once with the address of global variable Glob passed by reference into First rank parameter;

– if p1 is greater or equal to 10, the function calls of f1 are in the order of a call to f2, followed by a call to f3.

And so on. We can give assertions in a natural language scrupulously describing all of the expectations of our function f1.

Unitary proof provides the means by which to apply this principle with a formalized language and in a way that is verifiable by the tool.

The chosen solution is mainly based on the notion of simulated functions that replace true functions that are called by the function to be proved.

We have understood in the previous example that we are not basing our analysis on the real behavior of functions f2 and f3.

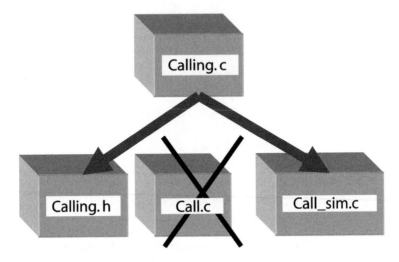

Figure 2.18. *Example illustrating the method of unitary proof*

These simulations, in the proving environment, produce instrumentation output operands enabling us to carry out the verifications sought by the unitary proof.

The organization of properties

As a necessity, we have previously presented the definition of a standard format of formal description. This standardization involves the identification of several property categories enabling us to process several aspects of a function.

We have, for example:

– the robustness properties on the incoming parameters of a function;

– the properties on the variation domain of output operands;

– the properties on the values of output operands and others on the call conditions of the functions called;

– the order they are called in.

This classification into categories offers an initial split of properties. To this initial split into several categories is added the notion of execution conditions (comparable to the notion of *behavior* in JML[5] and in ACSL[6]). The execution conditions are defined by conditions on inputs, according to which the behavior of the function can be different.

In the previous example, we have two execution conditions corresponding to p1 < 10 and to p1 ≥ 10.

Dividing up functionality by categories and conditions of execution offers a very fine reading grid for the expected functionality. This enables very reliable control by rereading the written properties.

2.4.1.2.4. Example

We will deal with the example of the Test Output function. The functionality is informally described.

The algorithm is defined in three stages:

– two outputs corresponding to EP_1 and EP_2 are called upon one after the other with data defined by a table;

– a wait time is respected;

– the two outputs are verified.

IF both tests are correct, the function returns OK. In the opposite case, it returns KO and follows a specific breakdown following the KO test.

Stage 1: execution conditions

The first stage consists of defining the "execution conditions" of the function. We have identified three, corresponding to:

– both tests go well;

– the first test is KO;

– the first test is OK, but the second is KO.

---

5 The *Java Modeling Language* (JML) is a specification language for Java. It is based on the paradigm of programming by contract.
6 To find out more, see frama-c.com/acsl.html

```
T_RES ConfigurerAllOut(
   const T_DATA_CONF * const  pDataConf1,
   const T_DATA_CONF * const  pDataConf2,
   T_PANNE       * const  panne)
{
   T_W32 Indice ;
   T_RES Retour1 ;
   T_RES Retour2 ;
   T_RES Ret = KO;

   panne->index      = NO_ERROR;
   panne->desc1      = 0;
   panne->desc2      = 0;

   /* preparation des données */
   for (Indice=0; Indice<TAILLE_CONF; Indice++)
      {
         G_uEpData1.CONF[Indice] = pDataConf1->data[Indice] ;
         G_uEpData2.CONF[Indice] = pDataConf2->data[Indice] ;
      }

   /*$ -- programming of reading transfers */
   ProgramOutput(EP_1, &G_uEpData1) ;
   ProgramOutput(EP_2, &G_uEpData2) ;

   /*$ -- carry out a temporization so that the process is carried
out */
   WaitDelay(DELAI_TRANS) ;

   /*$ -- verification of the transaction results */
   Retour1  = VerifyOutput(EP_1, &sErreur1) ;
   Retour2  = VerifyOutput(EP_2, &sErreur2) ;


  /*$ -- test transfer 1 */
  if (Retour1 == OK)
     {
        /*$ -- test transfer 2 */
        if (Retour2 == OK)
        {
          Ret = OK;
        }
        else
        {
        /*$ -- Transfer failure 2 */
        /*$ -- maj of the breakdown describer */
        panne->index      = ERR_2;
        panne->desc1      = sErreur2.id1;
        panne->desc2      = sErreur2.id2;
        }
     }
  else
     {
        /*$ -- Transfer failure 1 */
        /*$ -- maj of the breakdown describer */
        panne->index      = ERR_1;
        panne->desc1      = sErreur1.id1;
        panne->desc2      = sErreur1.id2;
     }
   return Ret ;
}
```

Figure 2.19. *C code of the example*

The formalization of these three execution conditions occurs according to Figure 2.20.

```
-- 1- Definitions des conditions d'execution du service
--------------------------------------------------------
LET TEST1_OK = (__VerifierSortie_out.[.(0)]=OK);
LET TEST2_OK = (__VerifierSortie_out.[.(1)]=OK);

-- Definition des conditions d'assert
-- sans objet

-- Definition des conditions de panne

-- le test 1 est ko
LET COND_ERR_1 = ¬TEST1_OK;

-- le test 1 est ok le test 2 est KO
LET COND_ERR_2 = TEST1_OK ∧ ¬TEST2_OK ;

-- Definition des conditions fonctionnelles

-- les deux tests se sont bien passés
LET COND_FCT_OK = TEST1_OK ∧ TEST2_OK ;
```

Figure 2.20. *Execution conditions*

The term "VerifySortie_out.[.(0)]" enables us to designate the return value of the first call to the function "VerifySortie." and the term "VerifySortie_out.[.(1)]", that of the second call.

Stage 2: Verifications for the execution conditions

The second stage consists of verifying certain expected properties of execution conditions themselves.

Execution conditions form a partition of the input space, i.e. they are mutually disjoint and their union contains all possible combinations of the values of the inputs. This is very useful when the different cases are numerous and complex.

The property COND0 enables us to verify that all three execution conditions deal with all the cases.

The three other properties enable us to verify that there is no crossover between each of the defined execution conditions.

```
-- 2- Verification des conditions d'execution
------------------------------------------------
-- Completude des conditions du service
Always COND0: COND_FCT_OK ∨ COND_ERR_1 ∨ COND_ERR_2;

-- Disjonction des conditions

-- Disjonction entre les conditions fonctionnelles et les conditions d'erreur
Always COND_DIS1: ¬(COND_FCT_OK ∧ COND_ERR_1);
Always COND_DIS2: ¬(COND_FCT_OK ∧ COND_ERR_2);
Always COND_DIS3: ¬(COND_ERR_1 ∧ COND_ERR_2);
```

Figure 2.21. *Properties of execution conditions*

Stage 3: expression of output variation domains

This category of properties enables us to express the different values possible for outputs when applicable (in the case of an index or enumerate). In the example shown, we express the fact that the output equals OK or KO, as well as the possible values of the index field of the failure parameter (*panne*).

```
-- 4- Verification des operandes de sortie (Post VAR)
------------------------------------------------------

-- domaine de variation du retour de la fonction
Post VAR1_RET : ConfigurerAllOut ∈ {OK, KO};

-- domaine de variation des erreurs
Post VAR2_PANNE : panne.[*, .index] ∈ {NO_ERROR, ERR_1, ERR_2};
```

Figure 2.22. *Specification of output variation domains*

Stage 4: expression of output values

By basing our analysis on the partitioning of execution conditions, we define the values expected from each of the outputs in all cases.

The output value is represented in the properties by the name of the function "ConfigurerAllOut".

In each of the three execution conditions, we define the values of the function return and output parameter.

```
-- 5- Verification des resultats du service (Post RES)
---------------------------------------------------------

-- valeur de retour de ConfigurerAllOut
Post RES1a_ConfigurerAllOut :
  COND_FCT_OK ⇒ ConfigurerAllOut=OK;

Post RES1b_ConfigurerAllOut :
  COND_ERR_1 ∨ COND_ERR_2 ⇒ ConfigurerAllOut=KO;

-- valeur de panne
-- verification des appels a DeclarerPanne
Post ALGO2a_DeclarerPanne: COND_FCT_OK ⇒
    panne.[*, .index] = NO_ERROR
  ∧ panne.[*, .desc1] = 0
  ∧ panne.[*, .desc2] = 0;

Post ALGO2b_DeclarerPanne: COND_ERR_1 ⇒
    panne.[*, .index] = ERR_1
  ∧ panne.[*, .desc1] = __VerifierSortie_v2.[.(0), .id1]
  ∧ panne.[*, .desc2] = __VerifierSortie_v2.[.(0), .id2];

Post ALGO2c_DeclarerPanne: COND_ERR_2 ⇒
    panne.[*, .index] = ERR_2
  ∧ panne.[*, .desc1] = __VerifierSortie_v2.[.(1), .id1]
  ∧ panne.[*, .desc2] = __VerifierSortie_v2.[.(1), .id2];
```

Figure 2.23. *Specification of outputs*

Stage 5: expression of the algorithmic properties

This category of properties concerns all the contexts of function calls. It is a matter of specifying the values of input parameters of the called functions.

The terms used with the prefix "__" enable these values to be identified.

For example, the term "__AttendreDelai_p1.[.(0)]" designates the value of the first argument passed during the first call to the function "AttendreDelai".

We thus express the value of parameters passed during the calls to "ProgramSortie", "VerifySortie" and "AttendreDelai".

```
-- 6- Verification de l'algorithme du service (Post ALGO)
----------------------------------------------------------
▮- verification des appels a ProgrammerSortie

-- verif du premier parametre lors du premier appel
Post ALGO1a_ProgrammerSortie :
  __ProgrammerSortie_p1.[.(0)] = EP_1;

-- verif du second parametre lors du premier appel
Post ALGO1b_ProgrammerSortie :
  ∀k∈int. k≥0 ∧ k<TAILLE_CONF ⇒
    __ProgrammerSortie_p2.[.(0),.:CONF,.(k)] = pDataConf1.[*,.data, .(k)];

-- verif du premier parametre lors du second appel
Post ALGO2a_ProgrammerSortie :
  __ProgrammerSortie_p1.[.(1)] = EP_2;

-- verif du second parametre lors du second appel
Post ALGO2b_ProgrammerSortie :
  ∀k∈int. k≥0 ∧ k<TAILLE_CONF ⇒
    __ProgrammerSortie_p2.[.(1),.:CONF,.(k)] = pDataConf2.[*,.data, .(k)];


-- verification des appels a VerifierSortie
Post ALGO3a_VerifierSortie :
  __VerifierSortie_p1.[.(0)] = EP_1;

Post ALGO3b_VerifierSortie :
  __VerifierSortie_p1.[.(1)] = EP_2;


-- verification des appels a ASTP_AttendreDelai
Post ALGO4_AttendreDelai :
  __AttendreDelai_p1.[.(0)] = DELAI_TRANS;
```

Figure 2.24. *Specification of the algorithmic properties*

Stage 6: expression of sequential properties

This stage enables us to describe precisely which functions are called and in which order.

To do this, we express the different functions in their call order, in the form of a sequence. In our example, the call sequence is immutable and a single property suffices.

```
Post SEQ1_OK :
  __CaveatCallTree_SeqIdList = [ID_PROGRAMMERSORTIE,
              ID_PROGRAMMERSORTIE,
              ID_ATTENDREDELAI,
              ID_VERIFIERSORTIE,
              ID_VERIFIERSORTIE];
```

Figure 2.25. *Specification of sequential properties*

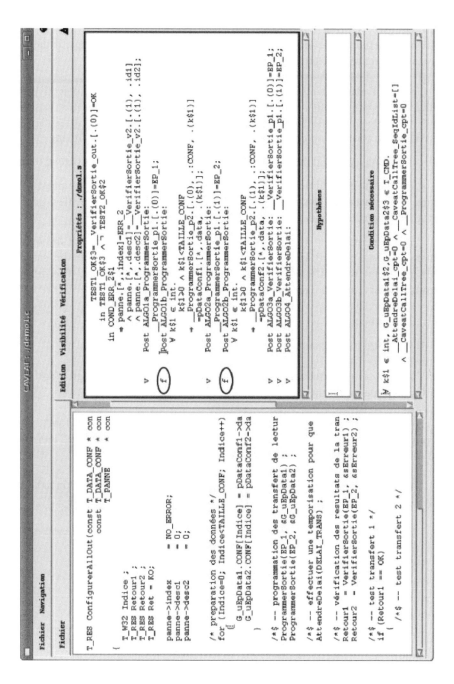

Figure 2.26. *No proven properties (lack of invariants)*

2.4.1.2.5. The proof phase

The objective of the proof phase is to detect all of the coding bugs, if there are any, or, if there are not, prove 100% of the specified properties.

The proof phase involves the Caveat formal proof tool and the objective is to prove the properties with a maximum amount of automation.

When the proof of a property fails, the cause can be one of the following:

– the source code and the properties are incoherent. This is case for bugs; or

– the tool needs additional information, which is the case with the presence of loops in the code. In this case the user must add additional properties, such as invariants and/or loop ends, before restarting the proof; or

– it is a matter of a weakness of the automatic theorem prover of the tool. In other words, the property is true but the tool was not able to show it. In this case, the user intervenes with different means in order to generate the proof. The different means of intervention are presented in section 2.4.1.2.6 below.

2.4.1.2.6. Example

If we return to our example, which properties are proven?

The answer to this question is that all except two – ALGO1b_ProgramSortie and ALGO2b_ProgramSortie – are proven (see Figure 2.25).

By linking these two properties, we see that they correspond to a functionality involving the loop *for* in the source code and we know that the proof tool needs additional information in this particular case.

This information consists of invariant and termination properties that the tool cannot always synthesize. The properties to be added are given in Figure 2.27.

```
Inv 1 I1_VAR1 : Indice≥0 ∧ Indice<TAILLE_CONF;

Inv 1 I1_SET1 : ∀k∈int. k≥0 ∧ k<Indice ⇒
     G_uEpData1.[.:CONF,.(k)] = pDataConf1.[*,.data, .(k)];

Inv 1 I1_SET2 : ∀k∈int. k≥0 ∧ k<Indice ⇒
     G_uEpData2.[.:CONF,.(k)] = pDataConf2.[*,.data, .(k)];
```

Figure 2.27. *Loop invariants*

Once added, we notice that on one hand the invariants have been automatically proven; and on the other hand the properties ALGO1b_ProgramSortie and ALGO2b_ProgramSortie are still unproven. What is the reason for this?

If all the additional information required for the proof has been given to the tool, it must either be a bug or a weakness in the automatic demonstrator.

It is always advisable to carefully re-read the part of the code involving an unproven property before diving into the interactive demonstration activity. This loop case with properties in the form of quantifiers, is however, a classic case where it is necessary to guide the tool in its demonstration process.

To convince us and achieve what we want, we have the proof remainder and the IPT (see section 2.3.1.4).

The proof remainder is a logical predicate that remains on failure of the proof of the property. It is interpreted as "the property is proven on condition that the remainder is true".

Thus, either the remainder is true but could not be proven by the tool, or it is untrue and the property is false. In our case, the remainder is given in Figure 2.28.

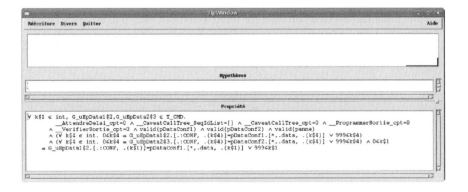

Figure 2.28. *Window of interactive proof containing the remainder*

This predicate is in true logic and can be demonstrated interactively in a single pinpointing operation, which enables the property to be moved to the *proved* state. The remainder after the pinpointing operation is given in Figure 2.29.

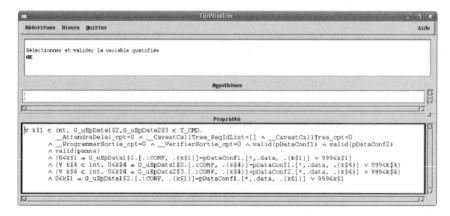

Figure 2.29. *Remainder after pinpointing*

Then, it is reduced to *true* by the automatic demonstrator.

The same goes for the second unproven property, which enables us to successfully arrive at the proof of this example.

In practice, several alternatives are available to the user to delay the requirement to engage in the IPT. Thus, heuristics enable the automatic execution of certain processing that has become common for the IPT and can be *called upon* by the user.

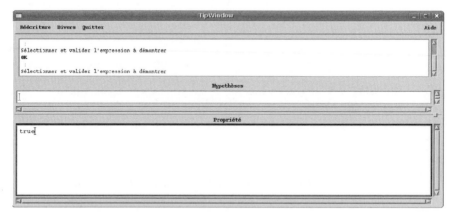

Figure 2.30. *Remainder after activation of the automatic demonstrator*

Recently, the Caveat tool opened up to the *why* platform so as to activate more powerful theorem provers. Indeed, this multi-prover platform offers a proof power that is much greater than the initial Caveat one. The problem encountered in the example is then proven automatically, on the condition of having laid down the right invariants.

2.4.1.3. *Report*

This example enables us to illustrate how it is possible to specify a C function in a unitary and standardized way as well as go to the end of the proof process. This method has been applied to a software subset of more than 30,000 lines of code. The number of properties written is greater than 5,000. The initial objectives of workload optimization have been met. This software subset has indeed been replicated with the unitary proof method on three aircraft programs.

Regarding maintenance, the hindsight that we now have enables us to judge the maintenance qualities of this type of verification solution very positively. Indeed, the functional evolutions are taken into account by an update of the properties, which is easier to carry out than the update of a battery of tests.

2.4.2. *The calculation of worst case execution time*

2.4.2.1. *Presentation of the software analyzed*

2.4.2.1.1. From SCADE® to C

The functional part of the software now presented is a synchronous control–command application specified in SCADE®. It represents 90% of the complete calculator code, the remainder being made up of the initialization of the computer, of the sequencer of functional tasks, of auto-tests and input/output drivers.

The code of this functional part is automatically produced from the SCADE® specification with the help of an automatic code generator. The automatic code generator for each SCADE® model (a graphic sheet) produces a C file made up of invocations of macro-operations taken from a library of software components. Each of these macro-operations implements one of the types of graphic symbols of which any SCADE® sheet is made. A C code file of the same name corresponds to one of these sheets.

2.4.2.1.2. Dynamic architecture

On a dynamic level, this software includes four periodic tasks that are executed on a single processor, the sequencing of which is fixed once and for all. This means that the sequencer of the application is completely determinist and there is no pre-emption. This serialization by design is as follows: let us call these four periodic tasks C1, C2, C3 and C4. The periodic activation of the tasks is ensured by a clock (electronic device) with a 5 ms period. The activation periods of the tasks are P1 = 10 ms for C1, P2 = 20 ms for C2, P3 = 40 ms for C3 and P4 = 120 ms for C4. Each SCADE® sheet of the application, and therefore each routine of the program generated, is affected to one of the four tasks. Also taking into account the priority rules (this sheet must be executed before that one) the construction of the application from a temporal point of view is done by distributing the sheets (once automatically coded) over 24 code clusters, each of them being activated 5 ms (basic clock) after the previous one (except for the very first). Once the 24th has been executed, the first is executed once again, and so on.

Here is how the periods of our four periodic tasks are respected by this mechanism. The periodic tasks Ci, i in [1,4], are divided into subtasks Ci_Ji, with: J1 in [1,2]; J2 in [1,4]; J3 in [1,8]; and J4 in [1,24]. Thus to completely carry out the task Ci, it is necessary to execute the Ci_Ji in order, with one every 5 ms (period of the clock). For i = 1, we have a complete execution C1 (C1_1 then C1_2) every 2 x 5 ms = 10 ms, which is the period of C1. For C2, 4 x 5 ms = 20, etc.

By "unfolding" the principle, we have:

– A t0 (origin of time):	T1: C1_1, C2_ 1, C3_ 1, C4_1;
– A t0+5 ms:	T2: C1_2, C2_ 2, C3_ 2, C4_2;
– A t0+10 ms:	T2: C1_1, C2_ 3, C3_ 3, C4_3;
– A t0+15 ms:	T2: C1_2, C2_ 4, C3_ 4, C4_4;
– A t0+20 ms:	T2: C1_1, C2_ 1, C3_ 5, C4_5;
– A t0+25 ms:	T2: C1_2, C2_ 2, C3_ 6, C4_6;
– A t0+30 ms:	T2: C1_1, C2_ 3, C3_ 7, C4_7;
– A t0+35 ms:	T2: C1_2, C2_ 4, C3_ 8, C4_8;
– A t0+40 ms:	T2: C1_1, C2_ 1, C3_ 1, C4_9;
– A t0+45 ms:	T2: C1_2, C2_ 2, C3_ 2, C4_10;
– A t0+50 ms:	T2: C1_1, C2_ 3, C3_ 3, C4_11;
– A t0+55 ms:	T2: C1_2, C2_ 4, C3_ 4, C4_12;
– A t0+60 ms:	T2: C1_1, C2_ 1, C3_ 5, C4_13;

....

– A t0+115 ms:	T2: C1_2, C2_ 4, C3_ 8, C4_24;
– A t0+120 ms:	T2: C1_1, C2_ 1, C3_ 1, C4_1;
– A t0+125 ms:	T2: C1_2, C2_ 2, C3_ 2, C4_2;

....

....

and so on throughout the mission.

This very determinist sequence enables us to reduce the temporal verification during the production of the software to this: the WCET of each of these 24 processes must be inferior to 5 ms, the period of the clock which cadences them.

The calculation of these WCETs is done with the aiT analyzer that has already been presented.

2.4.2.2. *Calculation of the WCET by static analysis*

2.4.2.2.1. Why static analysis?

The reason for choosing static analysis for the calculation of the WCET [SOU 05] for the control–command software, rather than the method previously used, stems essentially from that of the (modern) processor, the complexity of which has made the old method obsolete. For this control–command software, we have gone from the AMD 486 processor to the PowerPC MPC755. If we add this to a certain number of specifications and technological constraints, a same type of software executed by an AMD 486 without use of the cache is now executed by a super-scalar process, instruction cache and static branch prediction being active.

The memory has also become more complex as dynamic RAM with a one-page "cache" has been implanted on the CPU board. These new characteristics have the effect of making the execution time of an instruction from the program dependent on "what happened before", and for a length of history that can be considerable.

The method of calculating the WCET previously used for this type of control–command software has therefore become obsolete from the moment the processor has been retained. It has become too over-approaching and its soundness too difficult to demonstrate. This way of operating initially consisted of measuring the WCET. The WCET of each cluster Ti, i in [1,24], was obtained by summation of the WCET of the SCADE components (those measured during their test), which make up Ti.

This very simple and sound method was made possible for three main reasons:

– any instance of a SCADE® component in a Ti is executed once and only once during the execution of Ti;

– with a sequential processor, without using the cache, it was possible to measure each component's basic WCET in the worst initial conditions for safety reasons;

– during the summation of the WCET of components to obtain that of a Ti processing, the implicit accumulation of the time cost induced by the execution of each component in the worst initial conditions during the tests was acceptable, in terms of overestimation.

The situation is different with a processor such as the PowerPC MPC 755, moreover with the use of its instruction cache. Putting each basic component in the worst conditions to measure its WCET requires us to identify such conditions with precision, which is far from being easy with features such as branch prediction, the parallelism of the execution (superscalar execution), and the cache. These initial conditions – the worst from the point of view of execution times – are worse than an empty cache and empty pipeline. However, if the WCET of each basic component was measured in these conditions, the summation to obtain the WCET of a Ti would lead us to consider that during the real execution of Ti the cache and the pipeline are empty before any instance of a component. A gross overestimation of the Ti WCET would then ensue, a reason that, in itself, makes this method obsolete.

By the use of a static analysis tool by abstract interpretation, which proceeds by over-approximation on all possible executions of each Ti, the safety of the WCET calculation is ensured as a matter of principle. The problem of overestimation remains. Contrary to the method based on time measurement basic components are not considered in isolation in an initial phase, but *in situ* during the static analysis of each Ti. This enables the analyzer to take into account the effects of mechanisms that accelerate the processor. Indeed, cache analysis being extremely efficient on the type of software analyzed here, the WCET of a basic component *in situ* (i.e. taken in the complete software) is considerably lower than the old approach if its code is already in the cache. Thus, the calculation of the WCET of the Ti in this software is much more precise (less overestimated) than the traditional approach.

2.4.2.2.2. Calculation of the WCET of a Ti

Development of the analysis: annotations

The first analysis by aiT of a software product requires a development that we do not find in later versions. This phase consists of the creation of annotations enabling aiT to calculate the WCET as precisely as possible, i.e. the least amount of overapproach possible.

Here are the most frequently used annotation categories for the analysis of this software:

– assignment of the content of a register before an instruction;

– asignment of the content of variables in memory;

– maximum number of iterations of a loop;

– waiting time due to a *hardware* mechanism that is not modeled in aiT;

– locally forced control flow as a branch condition that is always true or always false for non analysis of certain parts of the program.

Automatic generation of annotations

The annotations contained in the file presented in the context of Figure 2.31 are automatically produced by an *ad hoc* tool integrated into the chain of automatic code generation. To understand the requirement of this automatic generation, it is necessary to remember that the code produced from SCADE® sheets is an assembly of macro operations.

The latter come from the library of basic components graphically used in SCADE® sheets. During the preparation phase of the analysis by aiT, imprecision sources of the calculated WCET were identified in the code of various macro operations. If the components of the SCADE® library were coded in the form of C functions (or assembly routines) and therefore called via the standard "call – return" mechanism in the code of the SCADE® sheets, an annotation relative to an address within a SCADE® component would be unique.

The implementation of a SCADE® component in the form of macro-operation, however, means that its code is inserted in any point at which it is used. The consequence is that there are as many addresses to which an annotation is applied as there are code insertions in the corresponding macro operation. This is the calculation of addresses that is automatically carried out for each annotation that can be applied to a SCADE® component, based on files produced by the automatic generator of SCADE® sheets code.

Analysis of an annotation

In the annotation file (Figure 2.31) we find, for example, an annotation for the macro operation COS (cosine). It tells aiT that the address "Nm_111610" + 0x10c, the register r31 of the processor, contains a value comprised between 0 and 360. In order to understand this annotation, it is important to know that COS is calculated via a table with 361 inputs and that at the address specified in the annotation, r31 contains the value of the index used to access a value of the table.

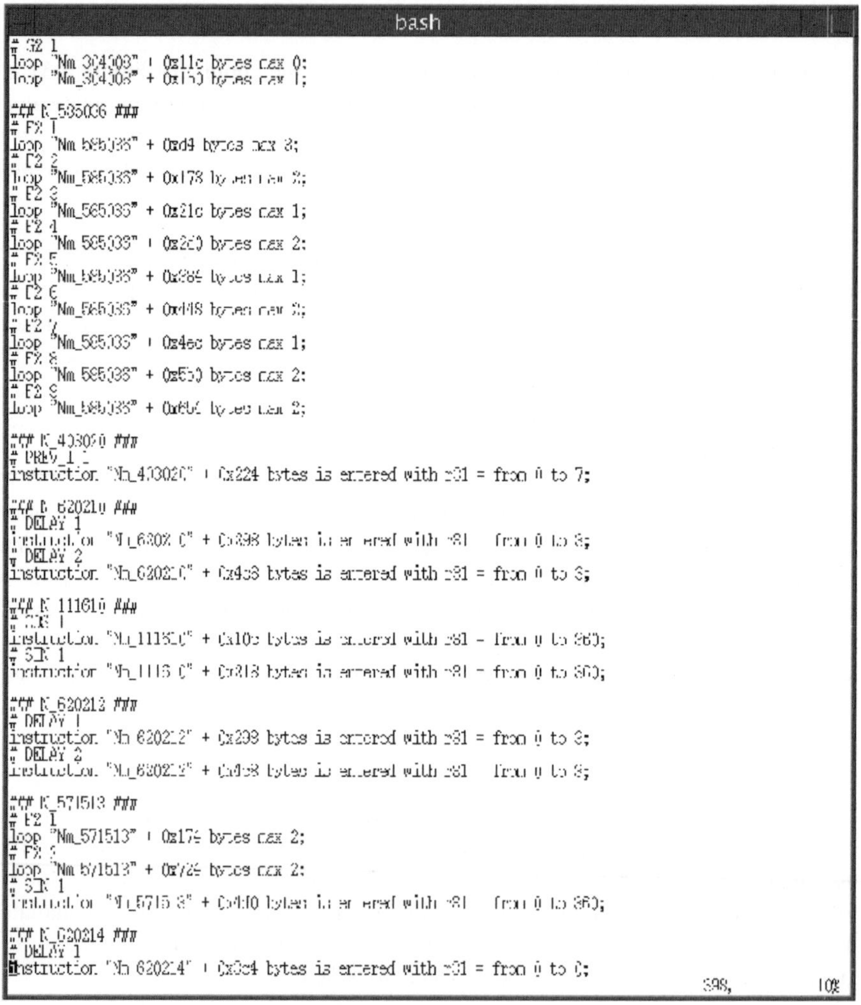

Figure 2.31. *Annotation file*

This index is an integer number calculated from a floating-point value. However aiT does not analyze the floating-point numbers in a precise enough way to calculate the intervals of possible values of the index (r31): [0,360]. It is even worse than this, since it considers any possible value in the range of 32 bits. During the cache and pipeline analyses, access to the table in memory will be analyzed. aiT will consider that it can be done far beyond the real limits of the table, particularly in zones that have much higher response times than those of the memory that contains this table. From here a WCET is calculated that is considerably overestimated.

WCET calculation

Once all the sources of imprecision have been processed, the WCET that is calculated by aiT is as accurate as possible, with the minimum amount of overestimation.

Total WCET of a Ti: addition of additional times

The WCET calculated by aiT must be increased by the accumulation of asynchronous access times on the processor's bus. In fact, as such times do not result directly from Ti processing instructions, it is impossible for aiT to take them into account. The time accumulations come from statistic analyses of events, the occurrences of which create "interferences" on the bus in the form of accesses that compete with those desired by the program.

2.4.2.3. Report

The use of static analysis by abstract interpretation (aiT analyzer) to calculate the WCET for the processing of Airbus' synchronous software has, so far, always produced more precise results than the previous method based on measures. Among the hardware targets these analyzed programs are produced for, there are PowerPC MPC 755 (e.g. this chapter), TMS320C33, Intel 386 and AMD 486. For the latter three, it is the precision as well as automacity of the calculation that have prevailed with the choice of this technique. As for software made to be executed by PowerPC MPC755, it is more than that, since no safe method would have enabled us to demonstrate that the WCET of each process was inferior to the time allocated.

Some of the software now analyzed by aiT was in maintenance when the decision was taken to replace the old technique with the new one. This scenario is very interesting since it enables us, during the transition phase, to show that the processor is not as heavily loaded, the new method being more precise than the old one. This "liberation" of CPU power then improves the evolutivity of the software that is in maintenance.

2.4.3. *Proof of the absence of run-time errors*

Proof of the absence of run-time errors is conducted with the help of the Astrée abstract interpretation based the Astrée static analyzer. This tool enables the analysis of embedded programs with several hundreds of thousands of C lines in an automatic and precise manner, particularly control–command applications whose code has been automatically produced based on SCADE® [DOR 08] or Simulink graphic specifications.

Analysis activity with Astrée is an iterative process:

– preparation of the program;

– configuration of the analysis;

– execution of the analysis;

– while the analysis returns alarms:

  - the study of alarms;

  - configuration adjustment and/or correction of the code;

  - re-execution of the analysis.

2.4.3.1. *Preparation of the program*

Astrée exclusively analyses pre-processed C code. To analyze a given program, it is therefore advisable to:

– *delete, transcode* in C language or with the help of Astrée directives model:

  - any occurrence of assembly code;

  - any built-in function of the used compiler; and

  - any standard library function used.

For example, the code below enables us to provide the analyzer with hypotheses regarding outputs of the *sine* function:

```
1 double sin(double x) {
2     double y;
3         __ASTRÉE_known_fact((y>=-1.0));
4         __ASTRÉE_known_fact((y<=1.0));
5     return y;
6 }
```

– pre-process the whole program using the option dedicated to the compiler used, gcc -E, for example.

2.4.3.2. *Configuration of the analysis*

Once the pre-processed C source files are available, it is necessary to configure the analysis project.

First of all, we must describe the inputs of the program and their variation intervals. This is done with the help of directives such as __Astrée_volatile_input

((V, [min, max])), which tell the analyzer that each reading of variable V produces a (potentially different) value in the interval [min, max].

The name of the C function acting as the entry point of the program (and therefore to the analysis) must then be provided. In some cases, it is necessary to specify the execution model of the program. In particular, for a synchronous program it is advisable to:

– define the fraction of the program executed at each iteration of the reactive loop with the directive __Astrée_wait_for_clock(());

– bound the number N of iterations of this loop (i.e. the duration of the mission) with the help of a directive __Astrée_max_clock((N)); particularly for the domain of arithmetic–geometric deviations presented previously.

For an initial analysis, the other parameters (choice and configuration of abstract domains in particular) are generally left to their "default" values.

2.4.3.3. *Execution of the analysis*

With this minimal configuration, the very first analysis of a program by Astrée generally produces false alarms:

– in a limited number for all control command programs, for which the analyzer has been specialized;

– more numerous for programs that do not belong to this family.

The rest of the analysis process involves distinguishing:

– *true alarms*: these are bugs that it is advisable to correct in the program;

– *false alarms*: due to imprecision of the analysis by abstract interpretation, which will need to disappear in a later analysis after a more subtle tuning of the analyzer's parameters.

The targeted objective is to obtain an analysis that returns zero alarm.

2.4.3.4. *Study of alarms*

2.4.3.4.1. Why zero alarm?

Astrée is not a simple *bug finder*, that is to say a tool that implements incomplete heuristics for detecting potential run-time errors. Unlike such tools, Astrée is able to prove the absence of run-time errors in software that does not have any.

As the goal is to guarantee the absence of errors, we cannot be satisfied with an analysis that signals "a certain number of alarms", without the assurance that they are all false. Indeed, when Astrée returns an alarm to a given control point, it continues the analysis downstream of this control point by assuming that the alarm is false, i.e. by restricting the analysis to executions that do not produce the feared run-time error – if there are any. Such a simplification is essential, in so far as the behavior of the program analyzed cannot be defined downstream of certain run-time errors. For example, accessing an array out of bounds could destroy the code to be executed.

Thus, one alarm can hide another. For example, in Figure 2.32 Astrée returns an alarm in line 11. It is a real bug, as an array out of bounds occurs if x = 4. Astrée does not signal any other alarm, although an execution of this program with x = 4 will typically overwrite the stack at line 11 for certain compilers and certain architectures. The result of this is that z is set to zero, so that line 12 produces a division by zero.

This is why the "zero alarm" objective is necessary. The user must be able to make any alarm disappear, or failing this prove "by hand" that any residual alarm is necessarily false in the real execution environment of the program being analyzed.

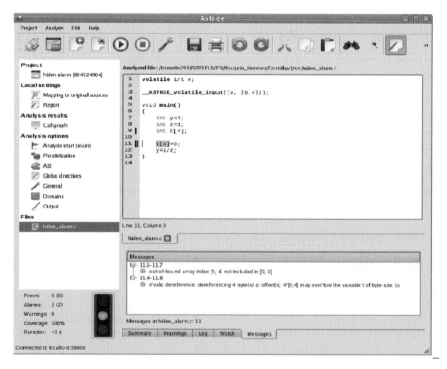

Figure 2.32. *One alarm may hide another*

2.4.3.4.2. Investigating an alarm

An alarm message refers to a control point in the pre-processed C code[7]. For example, in Figure 2.32 Astrée returns that in line 11, between columns 6 and 7, the value of array index x can be outside the bounds of table t. Between columns 4 and 8, Astrée specifies that, in this case, the expression t[x] constitutes an invalid dereference.

When Astrée is not able to prove an operation is free from run-time errors, it produces an alarm message containing a precondition: the operation produces a run-time error if this precondition is satisfied. Most preconditions are expressed in terms of intervals of values. For example, in Figure 2.32 Astrée returns that x varies in interval [0,4], whereas access to elements in table t is only legal for the index that takes their values in the interval [0,3].

To investigate an alarm, it is therefore necessary to begin by knowing the variation intervals of variables intervening in the execution of the operation that is incriminated. This information is available in the local invariants that Astrée can export for each instruction, instruction block, function or loop head, according to the configuration of the analysis. In this case, the information is available in the graphical user interface (GUI) of the tool.

It is costly to export detailed information from the very big synchronous programs. *At the very least*, we use the invariant of the reactive loop in the program calculated by Astrée that contains variation intervals of the global variables of the program. This information can be completed by a limited number of local invariants chosen by the user.

With this information, the investigation of an alarm consists of a backward analysis of the data flow upstream of the alarm, in order to find the origin: either a bug or insufficient precision of the automatic analysis. This activity can be difficult for large programs. The task is easier for control–command programs for which a SCADE® or Simulink graphic specification is available [DEL 07, SOU 07].

Indeed, the user can then start from the alarm and browse the data flow backwards by labeling each arrow that represents a variable with the variation interval computed by Astrée for this variable. The origin of the problem is generally found when a sudden and unexpected inflation of variation intervals is encountered.

At this moment of the analysis process, we know whether the alarm originated in some local program part with local effect, or in a specialized operator. This

---

7. The Astrée graphic interface enables us to simultaneously visualise *the source* before and after *pre-processing*, which will facilitate understanding.

information is useful, as an efficient approach initially concentrates on the alarms in operators that are frequently used by the program, especially if several alarms with different call contexts point to the same operators. Indeed, alarms such as these generally affect the analysis of calling functions, causing other alarms in these functions, and so on. Making them disappear generally enables us to erase all related alarms in the calling functions at the same time.

For control–command applications with a very linear call graph, it is also recommended that the alarms that appeared furthest upstream in the data flow are analyzed first of all. By making them disappear, we erase other related alarms that appeared downstream of the data flow at the same time.

2.4.3.5. *Parameter tuning*

Once the origin of the alarm has been found, it remains to be decided whether it is a bug or a false alarm. When the case is not trivial, an efficient method consists of extracting a "reduced example", that is to say a "slice" of the complete program in which the problem occurs.

To do this, we:

– write a small program containing the code at stake;

– create a new analysis project for this program, where the variation intervals of the inputs are taken from the Astrée invariant over the complete program; and

– execute the analysis on this reduced example.

For big programs, in which the Astrée analysis time is non-negligible, this approach enables instantaneous local analyses to be executed. In addition, this process is usually conservative in terms of alarms produced.

If the analysis turns out to be more precise on the reduced example than on the complete program, it is because:

– this reduced example is not a true slice of the complete program (it is advisable to verify this); or

– the non-monotonous character of Astrée's widening strategies improves the precision by "zooming" in on the imprecisely analyzed code – which is very rare. In this case, the results of the local analysis can be re-injected in the form of hypotheses for the global analysis.

In the vast majority of cases, the results are the same on the reduced example and on the complete program. It is then easy to experiment on this analysis of a mini-project by:

– inserting directives into the source, to locally refine the precision of the analysis. For example, partitioning directives can enable us to erase imprecision introduced by the analysis of loops. It is also possible to require the unrolling of certain complex loops. The local triggering of certain abstract domains, such as octagons, can allow us to use certain important implicit relations between variables that automatic configuration would not have picked up on;

– refining the global options of the analysis. In particular, a good compromise between cost and precision of the analysis needs to be found in the unrolling of loops and the expansion or folding of the large arrays in the memory of the analyzer handled by the program analyzed;

– trying various variations around the code of the reduced example itself, to better understand the origin of the problem.

When a satisfactory solution has been found, it is re-injected into the configuration of the analysis of the complete program. In almost all cases, this causes a decrease in the number of alarms.

2.4.3.6. *Conclusion*

Once the analysis process has run its course, we generally reach a situation where there are zero alarms, or failing this a handful of residual alarms that we can get rid of by providing Astrée with a few additional hypotheses regarding the environment of the program to be independently verified. In both cases, the absence of run-time errors in the program analyzed is guaranteed.

This objective has been reached for numerous programs developed at Airbus, including the synchronous control–command applications of more than 500,000 lines of C code, carrying out massive floating-point computations, and including numerous numerical filters. For these large programs, the volume of the source code affected by the analysis process (transcoding of the assembler, insertion of directives to improve the precision of the analysis, etc.) does not exceed around 100 lines.

2.5. Bibliography

[ARI 03] ARINC 653, Avionics Application Software Standard Interface, Aeronautical Radio Incorporated.

[BLA 03] BLANCHET B., COUSOT P., COUSOT R., FERET J., MAUBORGNE L., MINÉ A., MONNIAUX D., RIVAL X., "A static analyzer for large safety – critical software", in *Proc. of the ACM SIGPLAN Conference on Programming Language Design and Implementation (PLDI'03)*, pp. 196–207, San Diego, United States, June 2003.

[COU 77] COUSOT P., COUSOT R., "Abstract interpretation: a unified lattice model for static analysis of programs by construction or approximation of fixpoints", in *Proceedings of the 4th Symposium on Principles of Programming Languages*, pp. 238–252, ACM Press, Los Angeles, United States, 1977.

[COU 92] COUSOT P., COUSOT R., "Abstract interpretation frameworks", *Journal of Logic and Computation*, vol. 2, no. 4, pp. 511-547, 1992.

[COU 00] COUSOT P., "Interprétation abstraite", *Technique et Science Informatique*, vol. 19, no. 1-2-3, pp. 155-164, 2000.

[DEL 07] DELMAS D., SOUYRIS J., "Astrée: From research to industry", *Computer Science, SAS*, vol. 4634, pp. 437-451, 2007.

[DEL 09] DELMAS D., GOUBAULT E., PUTOT S., SOUYRIS J., TEKKAL K., VÉDRINE F., "Towards an industrial use of fluctuat on safety-critical avionics software", *Lecture Notes in Computer Science, FMICS*, vol. 5825, pp. 53-69, 2009.

[DIJ 75] DIJKSTRA E.W., "Guarded commands, nondeterminacy and formal derivation of programs", *ACM*, vol.18, no. 8, pp.453-457, 1975.

[DOR 08] DORMOY F.-X., "Scade 6 a model based solution for safety critical software development", *Embedded Real-Time Systems Conference*, Toulouse, France, January 29 – February 01, 2008.

[DUP 06] DUPRAT S., SOUYRIS J., FAVRE-FÉLIX D., "Formal verification workbench for avionics software", *European Congress ERTS 2006 (European Real Time Software)*, SIA R-2006-01-2A2, Toulouse, France, January 25 –27, 2006.

[FER 04] FERET J., "Static analysis of digital filters", in *European Symposium on Programming (ESOP'04)*, no. 2986, LNCS, Springer-Verlag, Heidelberg, 2004.

[FER 05] FERET J., "The arithmetic-geometric progression abstract domain", in *Verification, Model Checking and Abstract Interpretation (VMCAI'05)*, no. 3385, Lecture Notes Computer Science, pp. 42–58. Springer-Verlag, Heidelberg, 2005.

[GHO 09] GHORBAL K., GOUBAULT E., PUTOT S., "The zonotope abstract domain taylor1+", *Computed Aided Verification conference, CAV'09*, Lecture Notes in Computer Science, vol. 5643, pp. 627–633, Grenoble, France, 2009.

[GOU 06] GOUBAULT E., PUTOT S., "Static analysis of numerical algorithms", *SAS'06*, vol. 4134, pp. 18–34, Lecture Notes in Computer Science, Seoul, Korea, 2006.

[GOU 08] GOUBAULT E., PUTOT S., "Perturbed affine arithmetic for invariant computation in numerical program analysis", *CoRR*, abs/0807.2961, 2008.

[HOA 69] HOARE C.A.R., "An axiomatic basis for computer programming", *ACM*, vol. 12, no. 10, pp. 576-580, 1969.

[IEE 85] IEEE, IEEE 754: Standard For Floating-point Arithmetic. Floating-Point Copyright 1985 by the Institute of Electrical and Electronics Engineers, Inc, New York, USA, 1985

[ISO 99] ISO, ISO C Standard 1999, Technical Report, ISO, 1999 (available at: www.open-std.org/jtc1/sc22/wg14/www /docs/n1124.pdf).

[LER 06] LEROY X., "Formal certification of a compiler back-end, or: programming a compiler with a proof assistant", *33rd ACM Symposium on Principles of Programming Languages*, pp. 42-54. ACM Press, 2006.

[LER 11] LEROY X., DOLIGEZ D., GARRIGUE J., RÉMY D., VOUILLON J., The Objective Caml system, www. caml.inria.fr/pub/docs/manual-ocaml/index.html.

[MAR 04] MARTEL M., "Validation of assembler programs for dsps: a static analyzer", *PASTE '04: Proceedings of the 5th ACM SIGPLAN-SIGSOFT Workshop on Program Analysis for Software Tools and Engineering*, pp. 8-13, ACM Press, 2004.

[MAU 05] MAUBORGNE L., RIVAL X., "Trace partitioning in abstract interpretation based static analyzers", in *European Symposium on Programming (ESOP'05), Lecture Notes in Computer Science*, vol. 3444, pp. 5-20, Springer-Verlag, Heidelberg, 2005.

[MIN 01] MINÉ A., "A new numerical abstract domain based on difference-bound matrices", *2nd Symposium on Programs as Data Objects (PADO II), Lecture Notes in Computer Science*, vol. 2053, p. 155–172, Springer, Aarhus, Denmark, May 2001. (Work in Progress, available at: www.di.ens.fr/~mine/publi/article-mine-padoII.pdf.)

[MIN 04a] MINÉ A., "Relational abstract domains for the detection of floating-point run-time errors", *European Symposium on Programming (ESOP'04), Lecture Notes in Computer Science*, vol. 2986, pp. 3–17, Springer, Barcelona, Spain, 2004.

[MIN 04b] MINÉ A., Weakly relational numerical abstract domains, PhD thesis, Ecole Polytechnique, Palaiseau, France, December 2004 (available at: www.di.ens.fr/~mine/these/these-color.pdf).

[RAN 99] RANDIMBIVOLOLONA F., SOUYRIS J., BAUDIN P., PACALET A., RAGUIDEAU J., SCHOEN D., "Applying formal proof techniques to avionics software: A pragmatic approach", *World Congress on Formal Methods*, pp. 1798-1815, Springer, 1999.

[RIV 04] RIVAL X., "Symbolic transfer functions-based approaches to certified compilation", in LEROY X., (ed.), *31st Symposium on Principles of Programming Languages*, pp. 1-13, ACM Press, January 2004.

[RTC 92] RTCA, DO-178B/ED-12B, Software Considerations in Airborne Systems and Equipment Certification. RTCA, 1992.

[RTC 06] RTCA, DO254/ED80, Design Assurance Guidance for Airborne Electronic Hardware, RTCA, 2006.

[RTC] RTC, DO-178C, RTCA, forthcoming.

[SAE 10] SAE, *ARP4754/ED79*, Certification Considerations for Highly-integrated or Complex Aircraft Systems, SAE, 2010.

[SOU 04a] SOUYRIS J., FAVRE-FELIX D., "Proof of properties in avionics", *Proceedings of the IFIP Congress, Topical Sessions,* pp. 527-536, Kluwer Academic Publishers, 2004.

[SOU 04b] SOUYRIS J., RANDIMBIVOLOLONA F., "Towards product-based assurance", *European ERTS (European Real Time Software) Congress*, R-2004-01-1A1 SIA, 2004.

[SOU 05] SOUYRIS J., LE PAVEC E., HIMBERT G., JÉGU V., BORIOS G., HECKMANN R., "Computing the worst case execution time of an avionics program by abstract interpretation", *Proceedings of the 5th International Workshop on Worst-Case Execution Time (WCET) Analysis*, pp. 21-24, Palma de Mallorca, Spain, 5th July, 2005.

[SOU 07] SOUYRIS J., DELMAS D., "Experimental assessment of Astrée on safety-critical avionics software", *SAFECOMP, Lecture Notes in Computer Science*, vol. 4680, pp. 479–490, 2007.

[SOU 09] SOUYRIS J., Wiels V., DELMAS D., DELSENY H., *Formal Verification of Avionics Software Products*, pp. 532-546, Springer, 2009.

[TRA 05] TRAVERSE P., LACAZE I., SOUYRIS J., *A Process Toward Total Dependability – Airbus Fly-by-Wire Paradigm*, EDCC, January 2005.

Chapter 3

Polyspace

3.1. Overview[1]

The development of embedded systems encompasses a large range of practices and development methods. For critical projects destined for extremely robust applications, the production of very high quality software is essential. Development and test teams need to carry out code reviews and test the target operating system.

But is this really enough? What would happen if a critical problem went unnoticed during the development phases in the operational use of the code?

Methods based on mathematical techniques can partly enable us to alleviate doubt.

The application of formal methods based on code verification using *abstract interpretation* can provide development teams with a precise report on the piece of code that will work well, and those that have or risk having errors. This chapter presents the practical application of these techniques for software verification.

In the context of the application of this quality improvement technique, this chapter explores the techniques that can be used with Polyspace®, one of the MathWorks® products.

Chapter written by Patrick MUNIER.

1 This chapter describing the Polyspace® product and its main uses in industry comes from an internal MathWorks report from January 2011.

3.2. Introduction to software quality and verification procedures

Most software development teams aim to maximize both quality and productivity. During software development, however, there are always three interdependent variables: cost, quality and time.

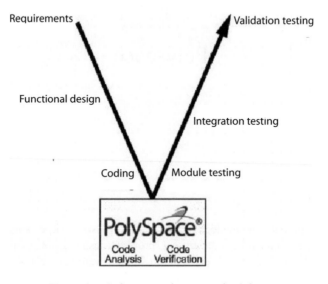

Figure 3.1. *Software verification and validation*

Generally, the criticality of the final use determines which of these variables is to be favored. With classical testing processes, development teams usually try and reach their quality objective by testing all the modules of an application until each meets the required quality level. Unfortunately, this procedure is often stopped before the quality objectives are reached as the allocated time and/or budget has expired.

Furthermore, code verification and testing that is only carried out at the end of the development process is not enough to attain maximum quality and productivity. It must be integrated into the whole verification process, while respecting time and budgetary constraints.

The verification and validation process (often referred to as V&V) of complex embedded systems consists of determining whether the requirements of the software are correctly and completely implemented, and whether they are traceable to the system requirements.

The main objective of a V&V process is to analyze and test the software during development and the test phase to ensure that the software does indeed perform its intended functions correctly, to make sure that it does not perform any unintended operations, and to provide information about its quality and reliability.

Software V&V also enables us to determine whether the software meets its technical specifications, as well as its needs in terms of security, robustness and reliability. V&V analyses, reviews, demonstrates or tests everything that is produced by software developments. This process is often described in the form of a V diagram, as presented in Figure 3.1.

The specific classes of software defaults that, strictly speaking, can be introduced into the design and coding phases of the V&V procedure are coding and design errors, as well as execution or *run-time* errors (software errors that are often considered latent).

Coding errors refers to improper implementation of code as compared to the requirements or specification. For example, the specifications require the existence of three fault conditions, but the code only implements two of them. Design errors occur when the code does not behave as it should for a specific operating environment. For example, a variable that is a 16-bit type for which the program produces a result greater than the highest value that can be represented on 16 bits.

Run-time errors are due to a faulty code, for example, a mathematical operation leading to division by zero. Run-time errors are insidious, as these faults can exist in the code, but without carrying out very specific tests under certain conditions it is possible that these faults will not occur in the system. The code therefore seems to be working normally, but this can result in unexpected failures of the system. Software including such errors cannot be considered robust.

Here are a few types of run-time errors (in a non-exhaustive list):

– *non-initialized variable*: if a variable is not initialized before being read, it can contain an unknown value when it is read;

– *access outside the bounds of an array*: this represents reading or writing of data outside the bounds of the allocated memory;

– *dereference of a null pointer*: this occurs when attempting to reference memory with a pointer that is NULL. Any dereference of this pointer leads to a crash;

– *incorrect arithmetic calculation*: these errors are caused by arithmetic errors such as *overflows*, divisions by zero, or for example by taking the square root of a negative value;

– *concurrent access to shared variable*: this error is caused by two (or more) variables declared in different tasks that want to access the same memory location;

– *illegal type conversions*: these can lead to data corruption;

– *dead code*: even though dead code (code that cannot be executed) does not strictly speaking represent a run-time error, it may be important to explain its presence. We can note that standards such as DO-178B [RTC 92] forbid the presence of non-justified dead code;

– *non-justified infinite loops*: these errors are caused by incorrect guard conditions on program loop operations (for example *for*, *while*, etc.) and may result in system hangs or halts.

The following sections present various techniques that can be used to minimize or eliminate these errors in software, and how these techniques can be integrated into a V&V process to create high quality embedded software.

3.3. Static analysis

Static analysis, or static verification, is a generic term that can be applied to any tool that derives the dynamic properties of a program but without executing it. Most static analysis or verification tools only verify the complexity of the software and look for constructions that can potentially be dangerous.

As described in [BES 10], these tools can usually find errors in the code, but will miss errors that are strongly dependent on data flow (such as run-time errors or design errors).

Due to the fact that they do not exhaustively analyze all possible behaviors, these tools are not considered sound (they miss errors) and thus produce "false negatives" (undetected real errors). Decreasing the risk of false negatives will increase the probability of false positives, that is to say the production of alarms that are not linked to real problems in the code.

The use of classic static analysis tools can contribute to the automation of part of the verification procedure, but this advantage must be carefully weighed against the ability of tools to generate false negatives and thus not detect errors.

3.4. Dynamic tests

Dynamic tests verify software execution flow. Wagner describes this methodology and explains the applications of these tests according to the dimension of types (both functional and structural) and granularity, such as unitary tests, integration tests and functional tests [WAG 06].

Dynamic tests lead to the creation of test cases or test vectors as well as the execution of the software with these tests. A comparison between the results and the standard or expected behavior is carried out. Wagner [WAG 06] also includes a summary of varied compiled statistics with regards to the efficiency of dynamic tests. His analysis shows that the efficiency of dynamic tests is around 47%. In other words, less than half of potential errors, on average, are detected by dynamic tests.

3.5. Abstract interpretation

Abstract interpretation is a formal mathematical method based on techniques that enable us to abstract the semantic of a program. It can be an efficient method for certain types of software verification. The benefits of abstract interpretation can be illustrated in a trivial way by the multiplication of the three big whole numbers in the following equation:

-4,586 x 34,985 x 2,389 = ?

Even though the calculation of the solution to the problem takes time if it is done by hand, it is possible to apply the rules of the multiplication sign to determine that the result is negative. The determination of the sign of this calculation is an example of the application of abstract interpretation. The technique enables us to verify a set of properties of a final result, such as the sign, with certainty without having to do the whole calculation.

By applying these rules it is also possible to know that the result of this calculation will never be positive. This property of the program at this point can be useful if, for example, the result of this calculation must be used as a parameter of the function calculating the square root of a number. Similarly, abstract interpretation can be applied to the semantic of software to prove certain properties of the software. Abstract interpretation enables us to relate the techniques for conventional static analysis with dynamic tests by verifying certain dynamic properties of the source code without having to run the program.

Abstract interpretation takes into account all the possible behaviors of a program, that is to say all the combinations of values, and can thus determine whether the program contains certain categories of run-time errors. The results that come from abstract interpretation are considered as sound as their mathematic proof.

3.6. Code verification

Code verification or code verifiers based on abstract interpretation can be used as static analysis tools to detect and mathematically prove the absence of certain run-time errors in the source code, such as overflows, divisions by zero and out-of-bounds array access.

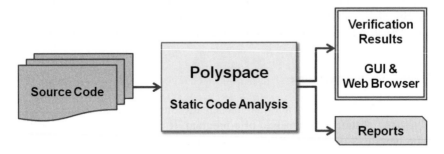

Figure 3.2. *Polyspace inputs and outputs*

Verification does not require us to run the program, instrument the code or write test cases. In [COU 96], Patrick Cousot described the success of the abstract interpretation in the analysis of programs. In [DEU 96], Alain Deutsch described the application of this technique to a commercial solution.

To describe the use of the code verification based on abstract interpretation, we will use Polyspace® [MAT 10], from MathWorks® in this chapter. Polyspace® is a code verifier that detects and proves the absence of certain run-time errors, such as overflows, divisions by zero and out-of-bound array access.

As presented in Figure 3.2, Polyspace® accepts input from source code C, C++ or Ada.

Polyspace® starts by examining the source code to determine where run-time errors could potentially occur. Polyspace® then uses a color code to indicate the status of each element in the code (see Figure 3.3).

Polyspace® results in green mean that the code does not contain certain run-time errors (see Table 3.1). In the event a certain or possible run-time error has been detected, the code is colored red or orange.

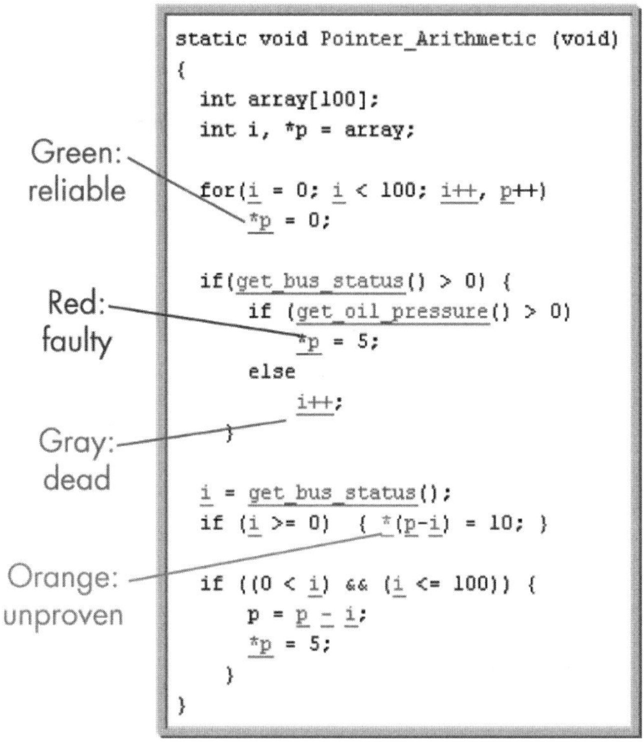

```
static void Pointer_Arithmetic (void)
{
    int array[100];
    int i, *p = array;

    for(i = 0; i < 100; i++, p++)
        *p = 0;

    if(get_bus_status() > 0) {
        if (get_oil_pressure() > 0)
            *p = 5;
        else
            i++;
    }

    i = get_bus_status();
    if (i >= 0)  { *(p-i) = 10; }

    if ((0 < i) && (i <= 100)) {
        p = p - i;
        *p = 5;
    }
}
```

Green: reliable

Red: faulty

Gray: dead

Orange: unproven

Figure 3.3. *Example of an analysis result provided by the Polyspace® tool (for a color version of this figure see www.iste.co.uk/boulanger/static.zip)*

Color	Explanation
Green	Indicates that the code is reliable – no run-time error can occur
Red	A run-time error exists in this point of the program
Gray	Dead or unreachable code
Orange	A run-time error is possible in this program

Table 3.1. *Color code used by Polyspace®*

Software developers and testers can use this information to fix run-time errors. Polyspace® also calculates the bounds of the variables of code and displays in the graphical interface, as Figure 3.4 shows.

```
rtb_Merge = (int16_T)(controller_B.limit_ratio + in_pressure);
```

variable 'in_pressure' (int 16): [-15000 .. 15000]
conversion from int 16 to int 32
   right: [-15000 .. 15000]
   result: [-15000 .. 15000]

Figure 3.4. *The bounds of the variables displayed in the graphical interface(for a color version of this figure see www.iste.co.uk/boulanger/static.zip)*

Polyspace® results can also be displayed in the form of a summary in a dashboard accessible via a Web interface (see Figure 3.5). This functionality is called Polyspace Metrics.

Polyspace® can also be used to verify standard coding rules (MISRA-C [MIS 04], MISRA-C++ [MIS 08] and JSF++ [JSF 05]), and produce complexity measures of the code (cyclomatic number of functions, density of commentaries, etc.).

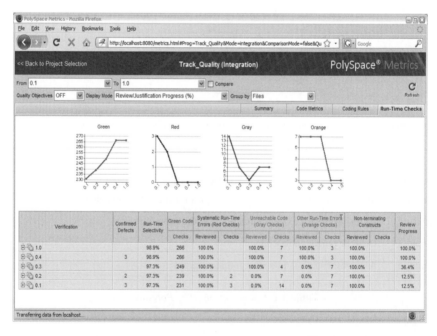

Figure 3.5. *Display of a summary of Polyspace® results in the interface Web Polyspace Metrics (for a color version of this figure, see www.iste.co.uk/boulanger/static.zip)*

The graphic interface of Polyspace® also includes project management options (see Figure 3.6). This graphic interface enables the user to specify the target environment and compilation settings, as well as other Polyspace® configuration parameters.

The tool can also be directly launched on the user's files or via the intermediary of a plug integrated into the Eclipse and Visual Studio development environments.

Polyspace® analyses are often carried out on a dedicated server and users can follow the status of ongoing analyses from the work station. Polyspace® uses the multicore characteristics of machines to accelerate verifications.

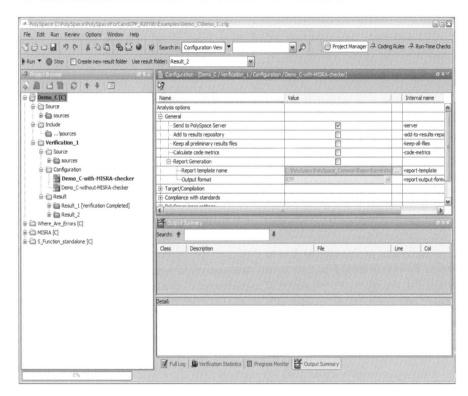

Figure 3.6. *The project view of Polyspace®*

3.7. Robustness verification or contextual verification

Polyspace® users can carry out so-called robustness or contextual verifications. Robustness verification helps to show that the software functions correctly in all of its conditions of use, whereas contextual verification shows that it works correctly in the nominal conditions of its use.

The verification processes can include both types of verification. For example, developers can precociously carry out robustness verifications on their files in the development cycle while they are writing their code. Later, the team can carry out contextual verifications on larger software components. In addition to this, quality objectives can involve the verification of coding rules and define minimum quality thresholds to be reached.

3.7.1. *Robustness verifications*

The objective of robustness verification is to show that the software works correctly in all conditions, including "non-standard" conditions for which it has not been designed. This can be seen as "worst case" verification.

This is the type of verification carried out by default with Polyspace®. In this case, Polyspace®:

– assumes that the inputs of functions are not bounded and can take on all of the values permitted by their types;

– initializes global variables with all the values permitted by their types; and

– automatically stubs the missing functions by assuming that their outputs are not bounded and that they can take on all the values permitted by their types.

The benefit of this approach is to make sure of the behavior of the program in all cases. Its disadvantage is that it can produce more non proven results (therefore colored in orange by Polyspace®). The developer or the tester must then inspect the orange parts of the code, in line with his quality objectives.

3.7.2. *Contextual verification*

The objective of a contextual verification is to show that the software functions within its predefined conditions of use. This limits the verification domain to specific values for certain variables. The realization of contextual verifications with Polyspace® will reduce the number of unproven results.

Various techniques are made available to the user to help him or her define the verification context of his or her application. The user can:

– use the DRS (*data range specification*) module to specify the ranges of function inputs and global variables, thereby limiting verification to these cases;

– write a main program by hand to model the call sequence of its functions, rather than basing it on the main program automatically created by Polyspace®;

– provide manual stub functions that emulate the behavior of missing functions, rather than basing it on stubs that are automatically created by the product.

3.8. Examples of Polyspace® results

The following examples demonstrate the efficiency of abstract interpretation with Polyspace®.

3.8.1. *Example of safe code*

Let us consider the function presented in the context of Figure 3.7.

```
1     int where_are_errors(int input)
2     {
3     int x, y, k;
4
5     k = input / 100;
6     x = 2;
7     y = k + 5;
8     while (x < 10)
9           {
10              x++;
11              y = y + 3;
12              }
13
14    if ((3*k + 100) > 43)
15          {
16              y++;
17              x = x / (x - y);
18              }
19
20    return x;
21    }
```

Figure 3.7. *Example of safe code*

The objective is to identify run-time errors in the function *where_are_errors()*. This function carries out various mathematical calculations, contains a loop, *while*, and an instruction, *if*.

We can note that all variables are initialized and used.

In line 17, a division by zero can occur if $x = y$.

Given the control structures and mathematical operations on x and y, is it possible that x equals y?

```
where_are_errors.c                              _ □ ✕

1        int where_are_errors(int input)
2        {
3        int x, y, k;
4
5        k = input / 100;
6        x = 2;
7        y = k + 5;
8        while (x < 10)
9                {
10                x++;
11                y = y + 3;
12                }
13
14       if ((3*k + 100) > 43)
15                {
16                y++;
17                x = x / (x - y);
18                }
19
20       return x;
21       }
```

Figure 3.8. *Polyspace® result on safe code (for a color version of this figure, see www.iste.co.uk/boulanger/static.zip)*

As shown in Figure 3.8, Polyspace® has proven that this code does not contain any run-time errors. This is due to the fact that line 17 is only executed if the condition $(3*k + 100 > 43)$ is true. Knowing that the value of y is dependant on that of k, Polyspace® establishes that at line 17, when x is equal to 10, y will always have a value that is greater than 10. Consequently, there can be no division by zero on this line of code.

This result is obtained without having to run the code, write test cases, instrument the code or debug the code. Polyspace® identifies all the places in the code where a runtime error could occur. These places are underlined (see Figure 3.6).

In our example, knowing that no execution error can occur, all of the code is underlined in green. In line 17, for example, the fact that the division operator is underlined in green proves the absence of overflow and division by zero at this point in the program.

3.8.2. *Example: dereferencing of a pointer outside its bounds*

In the example of code in Figure 3.9, the table *ar* has been allocated for 100 elements. The pointer, *p*, points to the first element in table *ar*. The *for* loop increments from 0 to 99 via the index, *i*.

In the loop, the pointer, *p*, is also incremented. At the output of loop *for*, the index, *i*, points to the hundredth element of table *ar*. The desire to store data (value 5) causes a run-time error.

```
1    void out_of_bounds_pointer(void)
2    {
3
4    int ar[100];
5    int *p = ar;
6    int i;
7
8    for (i = 0; i < 100; i++)
9            {
10            *p = 0;
11            p++;
12            }
13
14    *p = 5;
15
16   }
```

Figure 3.9. *Example of code with an out-of-bounds pointer*

Figure 3.10 shows the results of the verification of this code with Polyspace®. We can note the instructions underlined in green in lines 8, 10, 11 and part of line 14.

The indications provided by Polyspace® in these places mean that no run-time errors can occur, hence the text is green. Conversely, Polyspace® identified in line 14 that data were written in a memory zone via pointer *p*, and shows that this operation causes a run-time error by underlining it in red.

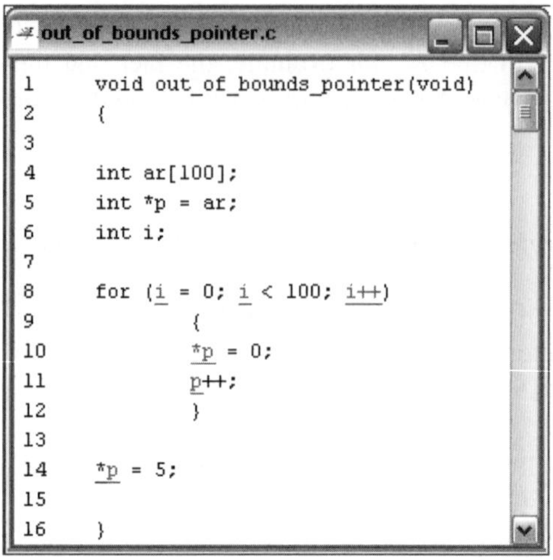

```
out_of_bounds_pointer.c                    _ □ ✕
1        void out_of_bounds_pointer(void)
2        {
3
4        int ar[100];
5        int *p = ar;
6        int i;
7
8        for (i = 0; i < 100; i++)
9                {
10                *p = 0;
11                p++;
12                }
13
14        *p = 5;
15
16       }
```

Figure 3.10. *Polyspace® results for an out-of-bounds pointer (for a color version of this figure, see www.iste.co.uk/boulanger/static.zip)*

3.8.3. *Example: inter-procedural calls*

In the example in Figure 3.11, *d* is a pointer to an integer incremented with 1 at the beginning of the function *comp()*. It is then used as a denominator of a division to determine the value of the *advance* variable, to then be recursively passed as a parameter of the same function, *comp()*. Verifying whether the division of line 6 will cause a division by zero requires an inter-procedural analysis to be carried out in order to determine which value will be passed in the parameter of the function *comp()*.

In the example, function *comp()* is called twice in the *bug_in_recursive* function. In the event where *comp* is called with 10 as the parameter, **d* is a variable incremented from 11 to 49. In this case, there is no division by zero in line 6. When *comp()* is called with -4 as the parameter, **d* is a variable incremented from -3 to 49. At the fourth call of *comp()*, **d* is worth 0, which causes a division by zero in line 6.

A syntaxical verification cannot detect this run-time error. Abstract interpretation (see the result given in the context of Figure 3.12) with Polyspace® enables us to prove that this code is exempt from run-time errors except in lines 6 and 21. Division by zero is shown by an orange color in line 6 because the division operation is correct when *comp()* is called in line 18 and incorrect when *comp()* is called in line 21.

This example illustrates the unique ability of *abstract interpretation* to carry out an interprocedural analysis that takes into account the effects of pointers for distinguishing calls of functions that are problematic from those that are not.

```
1    void comp (int* d)
2    {
3
4    float advance;
5    *d = *d + 1;
6    advance = 1.0/(float)(*d);
7
8    if (*d < 50)
9    comp (d);
10
11   }
12
13   void bug_in_recursive (void)
14   {
15   int x;
16
17   x = 10;
18   comp ( &x );
19
20   x = -4;
21   comp ( &x );
22   }
```

Figure 3.11. *Example of code with interprocedural calls*

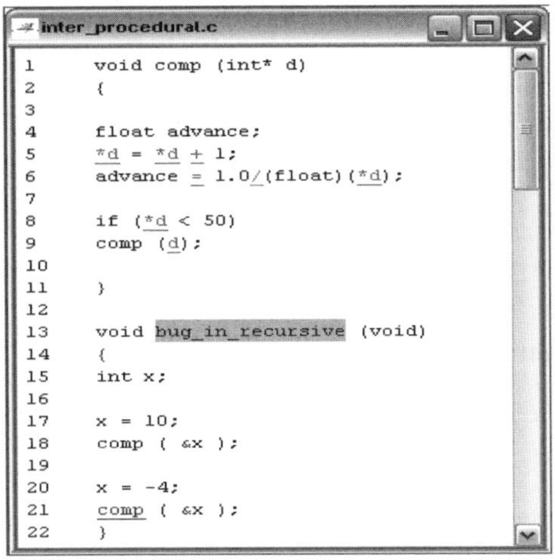

Figure 3.12. *Polyspace® results on the interprocedural analysis of a recursive function*

3.9. Carrying out a code verification with Polyspace

Code verifications with Polyspace® can be carried out in various contexts. They range from individual verification of functions or files, to the verification of more or less luminous components.

The software to be varified may have been written by hand, produced automatically by a code generator or be a mixture of generated and handwritten code. In the latter, case we speak of "mixed code".

Figure 3.13 presents an example of a Polyspace® result on code automatically generated from the *Real Time Workshop Embedded Coder* code generator from MathWorks®. The family of Polyspace® products includes the *Model Link* product, which enables us to connect Polyspace® to certain code generators, facilitating its use in *model-based design* environments. The *Model Link* product facilitates both the launching of Polyspace® *based* on modeling environments and the review of results by enabling a return to models from the Polyspace® results.

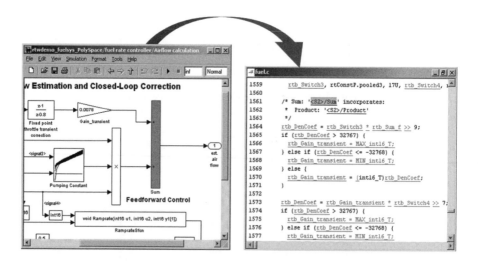

Figure 3.13. *On the left: model of a system in Simulink.*
On the right: code generated from a code generator and colored by Polyspace®
(for a color version of this figure, see www.iste.co.uk/boulanger/static.zip)

With the growing complexity of embedded systems, we note that here is increasingly widespread use of techniques based on models (so-called *model-based design* techniques) with automatic production of code by a code generator. In this approach, control algorithms are mainly modeled and simulated using *block diagrams* and state machines. The code is then automatically generated from these models and deployed onto embedded microprocessors in target machines. The code produced can nonetheless be a mixture of generated code and manual code.

In critical systems, the state of the art regarding V&V techniques recommends using simulation and verification, both for the model and the code. Verification of the code is of particular importance in mixed environments, i.e. those that produce applications containing manual code and code produced automatically.

Automatically generated code can contain references to encapsulated manual code (for example for performance purposes). Conversely, generated code can also be integrated into manual code, for example in an environment of software development. This mixed (manual and automatically generated) code must be verified for the code, as opposed to the verification for the model, to ensure the robustness of the system. This is due to the possible presence of a run-time error in the manual code that cannot be detected in the model. A run-time error can propagate itself from the manual code to corrupt the part of the code that was generated automatically.

Other considerations are worth taking into account in mixed code environments:

– errors linked to the use of data from incorrect calibrations;

– signals that do not respect the bounds provided in their specifications;

– transitions between incorrect states;

– memory corruptions; and

– mathematical operations that produce divisions by zero or overflows. Mixed codes that contain this type of error cannot be considered robust.

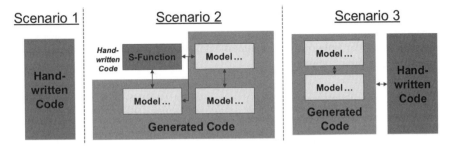

Figure 3.14. *Three scenarios in which Polyspace® can be used*

Figure 3.14 gives examples of scenarios in which Polyspace® can be used. The first is an environment where the whole code is written manually. The second is a mixed code where manually written code is encapsulated in an *S-function* to be integrated into the model. The third scenario is a mixed code where the automatically generated code is inserted in an environment of software development.

3.10. Use of Polyspace® can improve the quality of embedded software

Modern development and test processes take into account a large variety of development methodologies. The personal preferences and experiences encountered, good or bad, often dictate the processes implemented by the development teams. Tools are often integrated with each other with the help of scripts.

At the heart of these *processes*, however, there are are often development and test methods that enable quality software to be produced that is ideally free from errors. The verification of coding standards, of software that is precocious in the development *process*, that quality metrics are reached, and the identification of portions of code that do not contain errors are all stages that will increase the quality of critical embedded software.

3.10.1. *Begin by establishing models and objectives for software quality*

Although the systems they develop are becoming increasingly sophisticated, software development teams must meet rigorous software quality objectives, either dictated by the company itself or imposed by its clients or national regulation authorities. For these objectives to be reached, and ideally to reach zero defaults, it is necessary to define a quality model. This model establishes specific objectives linked to software quality, with metrics and thresholds to be reached. These objectives provide a mechanism through which teams can communicate their objectives and the state of their developments, both internally and with people who are external to their company.

3.10.2. *Example of a software quality model with objectives*

The *Software Quality Objectives for Source Code* [NIS 96] document describes an example of software quality models comprising well-defined objectives. It was written by different automobile constructors and parts manufacturers in partnership with MathWorks®. This quality model includes a list of objectives linked to software quality, of which most implicitly require the use of a tool for the static analysis of code.

Conformity with these objectives is evaluated according to the following criteria:

– a quality plan is in place;

– there is a detailed design;

– complexity code metrics have been defined and verified;

– the respect of coding rules has been demonstrated (for example, respect of MISRA-C [MIS 04]);

– the code does not include an unreachable code branch;

– the code does not include a construction that does not end (infinite loop, for example);

– systematic run-time errors have been corrected;

– potential run-time errors have been corrected or justified;

– data flow analysis has been carried out.

On the basis of these criteria, the document defines six objectives for software quality (known as *software quality objectives* or SQOs). SQO-1 only recommends reaching a restricted subset of criteria, whereas SQO-6 requires all criteria to be satisfied. The selection of an adapted SQO level depends on:

– the criticality of the project;

– the quality processes used within the company; these can for example require the application of *capability maturity model integration* (CMMI) or *software process improvement and capability determination* (SPICE);

– whether or not standards such as CEI/IEC 61508 [IEC 98], ISO 26262 [ISO 11], CENELEC EN 50128 [CEN 01] or DO 178B [RTC 92] are needed.

Table 3.2 details the different criteria applicable to SQO objectives. Certain criteria have associated thresholds, the crossing of which signifies that the SQO objective has been reached. For example, to reach SQO-1 the table shows that we need to have defined a *quality plan*, written a *detailed design* and verified code complexity metrics. To reach SQO-2, it is necessary in addition to this to respect an initial set of coding rules, to have corrected systematic execution errors and to have verified that there are no more constructions that do not end in the code. To reach SQO-3, it is also necessary to show that the code does not comprise unreachable code branches (dead code).

3.10.3. *Use of a subset of languages to satisfy coding rules*

General-purpose languages, such as C and C++, have been designed to develop a large variety of applications, from bureaucratic applications to critical embedded applications.

With extensions like C99, or extensions linked to compilers such as Visual C++ and GNU, these languages have evolved to support constructions that are increasingly distant from the original language. The counterpart of the flexibility brought by these evolutions is an increased difficulty in the verification of complex applications.

The more complex languages are harder to verify, be it by hand or with an automatic tool. To simplify this verification, most standards such as CEI/IEC 61508 [IEC 98], CENELEC EN 50128 [CEN 01] and ISO 26262 [ISO 11, Table A.3] limit the use of a language to a restricted subset. To meet these standards, a development team must only use language constructions that are authorized by the standard. For example, the quality model illustrated in Table 3.2 recommends certain coding rules of the MISRA-C:2004 [MIS 04] to be respected.

As well as making the code easier to verify, coding standards also tend to make the code easier to read, maintain and carry on other targets. Generally, the adoption of a coding standard does not require that all the rules of this standard are verified.

The quality model described above defines two subsets of rules of coding standard MISRA-C:2004 [MIS 04]) The first subset, which is required for objectives SQO-1 to SQO-4, includes rules such as:

– 8.11: The static storage class specifier shall be used in definitions and declarations of objects and functions that have internal linkage.

– 8.12: When an array is declared with external linkage, its size shall be stated explicitly or defined implicitly by initialization.

– 13.3: Floating-point expressions shall not be tested for equality or inequality.

– 20.2: Dynamic heap memory allocation shall not be used.

The second subset, required for levels SQO-5 and SQO-6, includes rules such as:

– 8.7: Objects shall be defined at block scope if they are only accessed from within a single function.

– 9.2: Braces shall be used to indicate and match the structure in the non-zero initialization of arrays and structures.

– 13.1: Assignment operators shall not be used in expressions that yield a Boolean value.

– 20.3: The validity of values passed to library functions shall be checked.

3.10.4. *Use of Polyspace® to reach software quality objectives*

The elimination of certain types of execution errors is a fundamental part of numerous software quality models. In the SQO model described in Table 3.2, all the potential execution errors to correct or to justify increase as the SQO objectives become more rigorous. The *Polyspace Metrics* dashboard, based on a Web interface, provides specific views enabling us to follow quality objectives according to different thresholds defined by the SQO model.

Criteria	*Software quality objectives* (SQO)					
	SQO 1	SQO 2	SQO 3	SQO 4	SQO 5	SQO 6
A quality plan is in place	X	X	X	X	X	X
There is a detailed design	X	X	X	X	X	X
Code complexity metrics have been defined and verified	X	X	X	X	X	X
Adherence to an initial set of coding rules has been demonstrated	X	X	X	X	X	X
Adherence to a second set of coding rules has been demonstrated					X	X
Systematic execution errors have been corrected		X	X	X	X	X
Code does not include a construction that does not end		X	X	X	X	X
Code does not include an unattainable branch code			X	X	X	X
Potential execution errors of an initial subset have been corrected or justified				X	X	X
Potential execution errors of a second subset have been corrected or justified					X	X
Potential execution errors of a third subset have been corrected or justified						X
Data flow analysis has been carried out						X

Table 3.2. *A quality model comprising criteria required to reach predefined objectives*

To reach the SQO-2 quality model, the code cannot contain systematic run-time errors or a construction that does not end. To achieve this, the Polyspace® results must not contain a red error. To further increase software quality and reach the SQO-3 level, the code must not include unreachable branches, which implies that Polyspace results must not contain grey code.

Due to the fact that the unproven code (code colored in orange by Polyspace®) is not always proven as being a problem (it may, for example, only be a problem in certain circumstances), the SQO model establishes different thresholds to define the number of operations of this type that can remain uncorrected and non justified in the code for objectives SQO-4, SQO-5 and SQO-6.

For example, SQO-4 requires that 80% of potential divisions by zero are proven to be safe or justified. If Polyspace® automatically proves that 70% of these operations are safe (colored in green), then reaching SQO-4 requires an additional manual review to demonstrate that at least 10% of these operations are safe or justified.

For the SQO-5 objective, the threshold increases to 90%. For SQO-6, it is 100%. The SQO software quality model authorizes intermediary code deliveries between constructors and suppliers comprising non-proven code. If the final quality objective is SQO-6, then the final delivery must not have divisions by zero that have not been proven safe or justified.

The implementation of a software quality model with well defined objectives is one of the good practices recommended during the development of critical embedded applications. Polyspace® can be used to reach criteria defined by these models by verifying the conformity of the code to coding rules, by identifying execution errors and branches of dead code, and by enabling teams to quantify potential run-time errors in their applications.

As the complexity of onboard software increases, an increasing number of constructors and parts manufacturers are basing their practices on tools such as Polyspace® for the management of their SQOs.

By respecting well identified *processes* and by applying automatic tools, these companies are able to better identify the parts of their applications that do not contain errors and better concentrate on the parts that need to be improved.

3.11. Carrying out certification with Polyspace®

Critical software must often be certified. Verification activities must conform to the recommendations of certification standards, such as DO-178B [RTC 92] or CEI/IEC 61508 [IEC 98]. These standards often mention verification activities such as the verification of coding rules, the detection of execution errors or the detection of design errors.

The improvement of quality, to prove the absence of certain classes of errors, is perfectly at home in these standards. For example, this can enable us to reduce or eliminate other verification activities, such as tests at the limits.

3.12. The creation of critical onboard software

Critical software errors, such as run-time errors, can be introduced in the design or coding phases during software development. It is possible that these faults are not detected with traditional dynamic test methods used during phases of unitary tests and integration. Code verification techniques based on abstract interpretation provide an aid for these points in the development process.

These techniques enable the development teams to know which parts of their code do not have run-time errors, and guides them in identifying the parts of the code that do have or risk having errors. The use of these techniques is part the global V&V phase and allows for an incremental improvement in quality. Their use represents an important step in the context of a software development process that targets zero default software.

3.13. Concrete uses of Polyspace®

Since its creation at the end of the 1990s, Polyspace® has been used in a large number of projects in varied domains, ranging from aeronautics to defense, medical and industrial machines to automobiles.

The projects have involved the verification of software written in C, C++ and Ada languages for codes written manually, generated automatically or a mixture of manual and automatically-generated code. Verification has included unit-by-unit analysis (for example, a verification by C files or C++ classes) to guarantee the robustness of the units verified, or the verifications of integrated software components to guarantee their reliability in their call context.

This section presents examples of practical uses of Polyspace® for varied applications. Subsections 3.13.1 to 3.13.3 present the use of Polyspace® in three key industries: the automobile, aerospace and medical industries. Subsection 3.13.4 provides general examples of use in varied sectors that are concerned with the quality of onboard software.

3.13.1. *Automobile: Cummins Engines improves the reliability of its motor's controllers*

Electronic engine control is an important component in modern motors. However, developing reliable engine controllers that function without problems in varied conditions is a challenge.

The software development and verification techniques used at Cummins Engines were historically based on manual stages, including code reviews and white box tests followed by component and integration tests. Even though most errors were detected by the system tests stage at the latest, the complexity of the software made the identification of these errors very difficult, and possibly only at the cost of important *debugging* efforts.

To take into account this complexity, Cummins created an approach in product lines to favor the reuse of software. For the design of engine control systems, Cummins developers used the *Simulink* and *Stateflow* products from MathWorks®. The automatic generation of code reduced the development time and costs.

For software verification, Cummins engineers decided that it was not enough to focus on component tests and system tests. They needed to increase the efficiency of unitary tests and improve the global process of software tests. They considered the example of a constructor who was encountering undue motor stops as a result of a software error in the motor controller. This same constructor had spent three weeks unsuccessfully trying to isolate the problem. The idea to use Polyspace® as a diagnostic aid was then put forward. Polyspace® detected a problem on an array index that could be decreased in a Stateflow state diagram until reaching a negative value, causing a reinitialization of the controller (see Figure 3.15).

In Figure 4.15, the operation in the Stateflow graph can lead to access to an element of an array outside its bounds:

```
if (status == error_type_2) {
    error_table[index]+1;
    status_table[index++];
}
```

Cummins also used Polyspace® on other motor control software that was in the development phase, which enabled staff to identify run-time errors early in the their development process. In particular, Polyspace® detected data overflow for certain variables of the program. Some of these results were occurring on manual code but also on automatically generated code when the two types of code were integrated into the complete system.

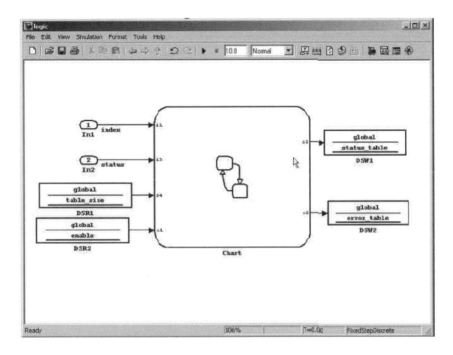

Figure 3.15. *Example of Stateflow design*
where an index can be decreased until it becomes negative

3.13.2. *Aerospace: EADS guarantees the reliability of satellite launches*[2]

EADS Launch Vehicles is part of EADS Astrium Space Transportation, and its mission is to launch satellites into orbit. The reliability of launches is a critical aspect for all space missions.

EADS develops part of the code internally and integrates the code developed by subprocessing companies. If guaranteeing the quality of the code developed internally is difficult, the evaluation of the quality of the code developed by other

2 See [MAT 10a].

companies is even harder. To reduce the risk of the presence of run-time errors, EADS used Polyspace® for the Ada programming language to verify a few 100,000 lines of code developed internally and by subprocessing companies. The objective was to verify the totality of the source code and to detect run-time errors as early as possible in the development process. In particular overflow errors, the use of non-initialized data and conflicts of access to variables shared between several tasks were verified.

Before using Polyspace®, the EADS engineers needed to define, write and execute numerous test cases in order to run as much code as possible with the aim of detecting errors. With Polyspace®, the code was analyzed exhaustively without having to be run. This enabled engineers to locate operations in the code that systematically produced errors, and others that could lead to problems in certain conditions.

3.13.3. *Medical devices: a code analysis leads to a recall of the device*[3]

The sophistication and complexity of onboard software present in medical devices is increasing. Modern *pacemakers* can have up to 80,000 lines of code on board and infusion pumps more than 170,000 lines. These devices must function with maximum reliability and safety.

The Federal Drug Administration (FDA) is the American governmental body tasked with the surveillance of medical devices. It has published several directives and recognized several standards addressing good software development practices. More recently, the FDA established a software laboratory with the Center for Devices and Radiological Health, one of the missions of which is to identify software coding errors in devices that could be subject to recall. One of the investigation techniques retained by the software laboratory is to examine the source code in order to identify the possible cause(s) of problems in medical devices.

A famous example of a software problem that is feared in medical devices is the one that concerned Therac 25. This device diffused a dose of radiation that was too high for numerous patients. The real-time operating system did not support the notion of messages exchanged between the different threads of the program but used global variables instead. Insufficient protection of these global variables caused an erroneous value during the use of the device. The program contained another error that caused the overflow of a whole 8-bit counter. These errors caused the diffusion of radiation doses that were 30 times higher than the prescribed dose.

---

3 See [MAT 10b].

Governmental regulation agencies like the FDA and certain domains of industry recognize the value of sound verification techniques (that are able to prove the absence of certain errors in software) and use tools based on these principles.

During the Embedded Software Reliability Workshop session at the 2010 International Symposium on Software Reliability Engineering conference, the FDA presented the results of the use of tools such as Polyspace® for the verification of onboard software in medical devices. The title of the presentation was "Applying static analysis to medical device software". The static analysis tools used reported 127 potential problems.

These potential problems were classed in the following way:

– 28 dereferences of NULL pointers;

– 36 readings of non-initialized variables;

– 29 illegal transformations of data (*cast*);

– 20 branches of unattainable code (dead code).

For the FDA, static analysis showed the lack of good design and development practices for software onboard this device. The results were integrated into the report submitted to the Office of Compliance and the device was subject to recall.

3.13.4. *Other examples of the use of Polyspace®*

Polyspace® has been used by numerous companies in various industries. The first users were those for which quality and reliability were important criteria. Here are other examples are described more briefly.

3.13.4.1. *Tackling sudden acceleration problems*

In 2010, drivers reported to Toyota that their vehicles were prone to sudden accelerations. A company called Exponent carried out an in-depth evaluation of the software driving control of the gas. Polyspace® was used in this process. The preliminary conclusions were reported to the American Governmental Committee for Energy and Commerce in May 2010. In this report, Exponent mentions (14):

> "Polyspace® provides the ability to prove mathematically if a certain class of run-time errors does not exist in the source code and to identify parts of the code where those errors exist or the proof cannot be completed. Polyspace®'s analysis is equivalent to running every possible test scenario, but does it in such a way that no test cases, instrumentation or real execution of the source code is required. This

allows for an exhaustive testing of the software that would otherwise have require several million hours of drive testing to identify.

The Polyspace® analysis was carried out for critical modules which were identified as controlling the opening angle of the gas command. The analyses carried out have for the moment detected no run-time error at the language level."

3.13.4.2. *Use of Polyspace® on ADA code*

NATO's Hawk Management Office is responsible for the improvement programs of the ground-to-air Hawk missile. Polyspace® was used to verify part of the code onboard the missile, which was written in Ada.

In an application that is as complex as a missile, the use of dynamic test cases is not enough to exhaustively test all the values which could cause a run-time error. The use of these conventional techniques would not have enabled NATO to satisfy the project's calendar constraints in the search for potential run-time errors. By using Polyspace®, the project team was able to eliminate error-prone constructs in the code that could lead to execution errors.

3.13.4.3. *Ensure the reliability of diesel engines*

Delphi Diesel Systems develops diesel injection systems for all types of vehicles. The major preoccupation in the context of this development is the very high amount of calibration data that need to be incorporated. A typical application of around 200,000 lines of code contains thousands of calibration data. These are constants that can be modified *after the fact* by calibration teams, which then affect the behavior of the entire application. These characteristics make testing these applications extremely complex. By using Polyspace®, Delphi Diesel Systems are able to detect run-time errors in software onboard injection systems during the unitary test phase, all the while eliminating robustness tests.

3.13.4.4. *Verification of software in airbag opening systems*

Elesys is developing an airbag suppressor system that detects the weight of the passenger and activates or deactivates the airbag accordingly, to avoid injuring children. In the past, Elesys based itself on code reviews to identify potential problems.

The Elesys engineers then used Polyspace® to carry out an exhaustive analysis of their code. Polyspace® analyses all functions and operations by taking into account all the possible values for variables. The team is now focusing its reviews on places where Polyspace® detected red and orange operations that under certain conditions systematically lead to a run-time error.

3.13.4.5. *Validation of control–command software in nuclear power stations*

L'Institut de Radioprotection et de Sûreté Nucléaire, the French radioprotection and nuclear safety institute, carries out specialized evaluations of nuclear and radiological risks. The IRSN was formed from the union of the IPSN (protection and nuclear safety institute) with the OPRI (protection against ionizing radiation office).

The IRSN has, in particular, used Polyspace® to exhaustively validate applications for verifying neutrons in 900 megawatt power stations. The use of Polyspace® has enabled it to verify the absence of run-time errors, such as divisions by zero, non initialized variables and overflows.

3.13.4.6. *Verification of Nissan motor control software*

Nissan and its parts manufacturers spend a lot of time ensuring the robustness of software during vehicle test phases. In the past, Nissan has encountered software problems linked to the growing complexity of onboard systems. Nissan now uses Polyspace® on software provided by its parts manufacturers and finds around five problems per project, each project comprising around 30,000 lines of code or 100 K of ROM.

3.14. Conclusion

This chapter gave us the chance to present the Polyspace® tool, discuss its implementation and give a few examples of industrial applications.

3.15. Bibliography

[BES 10] BESSEY A., BLOCK K., CHELF B., CHOU A., FULTON B., HALLEM S., HENRI-GROS C., KAMSKY A., MCPEAK S., ENGLER D., "A few billion lines of code later: Using static analysis to find bugs in the real world, Communications of the ACM, vol. 53, no. 2, pp. 66-75, 2010.

[COU 96] COUSOT P., "Abstract interpretation: Theory and practice", *Model Checking Software, Computer Science,* vol. 2318, pp. 1-3, 2002.

[DEU 96] DEUTSCH A., *Static Verification of Dynamic Properties*, SIGDA, 1996.

[IEC 98] IEC, IEC 61508: Functional safety of elecrical/electronic programmable electronic safety-related systems, International Standard, IEC, 1998.

[ISO 11] ISO, ISO/FDIS26262, Road Vehicles – Functional Safety, ISO, 2011.

[JSF 05] JOINT STRIKE FIGHTER, Air Vehicle C++ Coding Standards for the System Development and Demonstration Program, Document No. 2RDU00001, Rev C, December 2005.

[MAT 10a] MATHWORKS, Polyspace Code Verification Products, MathWorks, 2010 (available at: www.mathworks.com/polyspace).

[MAT 10b] MATHWORKS, Using Polyspace to Implement the "Software Quality Objective for Source Code Quality" Standard, MathWorks, 2010.

[MIS 04] MISRA, MISRA-C:2004, Guidelines for the Use of the C Language in Critical Systems. Technical Report, The Motor Industry Software Reliability Association, October 2004.

[MIS 08] MISRA, MISRA-C++:2008, Guidelines for the Use of the C++ Language in Critical Systems. Technical Report, The Motor Industry Software Reliability Association, 2008.

[MIS 10] MISRA, The Motor Industry Software Reliability Association, www.misra.org.uk, 2010.

[NIS 96] NIST, Reference Information for the Software Verification and Validation Process, National Institute of Standards and Technology, 1996.

[RTC 92] RTCA, *DO-178B/ED-12B,* Software Considerations in Airborne Systems and Equipment Certification. Version B, RTCA, 1992.

[WAG 06] WAGNER S., *A Literature Survey of the Software Quality Economics of Defect Detection Techniques*, ACM Press, 2006.

Chapter 4

Software Robustness with Regards to Dysfunctional Values from Static Analysis

4.1. Introduction

This chapter describes how to demonstrate software robustness with regards to dysfunctional values. To this end we use a static analysis tool based on abstract interpretation.

Our approach is original in at least two ways:

– it introduces the use of a formal method during the software development phase instead of the specification phase. The standard EN 50128 [CEN 01a] recommends the use of formal techniques (A.2 point 1 on page 48 and A.4 point 1 on page 50) such as B, Z during design and specification phases, and static analysis during software verification phase. We propose to implement static analysis during the development of the program;

– it implements static analysis in a non-trivial way. Static analysis is generally used to detect targeted errors: runtime errors, memory errors or numerical errors. We propose to use a static analysis tool to verify the consistency between the specified functional domains and the source code of software, but also to calculate the value domains of unspecified inputs.

In section 4.2, we position our approach with regards to standards associated with critical systems. In section 4.3, we explain the need for the software robustness proof method described in section 4.4. Section 4.5 explains how to use static

---

Chapter written by Christèle FAURE, Jean-Louis BOULANGER and Samy AÏT KACI.

analysis to automate one part of our method: the computation of the "required control". In section 4.6, we present the application of the robustness verification method to Thales railway interlocking product PING. We give further perspectives on the method in section 4.7 and conclude the chapter in section 4.8.

4.2. Normative context

A failure in an unsafe critical system (transportion, aircraft, railway, nuclear domains), can put the life of one or more people in danger. For this class of systems, standards require the full demonstration of the absence of failures. Their design is therefore subject to meeting very strict technical frames of reference (standards, trade documents, state of the art).

Electrical/electronic systems have been used to execute functions linked to safety in most industrial sectors. The CEI/IEC 61508 standard [IEC 98] presents a generic approach to all activities linked to the safety lifecycle of electric/electronic/ programmable electronic (E/E/PES) systems that are used to carry out safety functions.

In most cases, safety is obtained by the addition of several systems based on various technologies (mechanical, hydraulic, pneumatic, electrical, electronic and programmable electronic). The safety strategy must take into account all elements contributing to safety. The CEI/IEC 61508 standard [IEC 98] therefore provides a security analysis scheme to be applied to security systems based on other technologies (mechanical, hydraulic, etc.) and is specialized to E/E/PES systems.

Due to the large variety of E/E/PES applications and the very different degrees of complexity, the exact nature of safety measures to be implemented is application specific; this is why in the CEI/IEC 61508 standard [IEC 98] there is no general rule but there are recommendations concerning the methods of analysis to be implemented.

Standards provide scales that enable the allocation of a criticality level to each system. In complex systems based on electronic and/or programmed components, the CEI/IEC 61508 standard [IEC 98] defines the notion of *safety integrity level* (SIL). SIL enables us to quantify the safety level to be achieved and has five values:

– 0 (no danger, material destruction);

– 1 (slight injury);

– 2 (severe injury);

– 3 (death of a person); or

– 4 (death of several people).

Figure 4.1 shows that the railway standard CENELEC EN 5012x is a declination of the generic CEI/IEC 61508 standard [IEC 98] that takes into account specificities of the railway domain as well as successful experiences (Sacem, TVM, SAET-Meteor, etc.).

The railway domain is therefore mainly dominated by three standards derived from CEI/IEC 61508 [IEC 98], which cover different aspects of system security:

– the CENELEC EN 50126 standard [CEN 00] describes methods to be implemented during specification and reliability, availability, maintainability and safety demonstrations;

– the CENELEC EN 50128 standard [CEN 01a] describes the actions to be taken in order to demonstrate software safety;

– the CENELEC EN 50129 standard [CEN 03] describes the structure of the safety files.

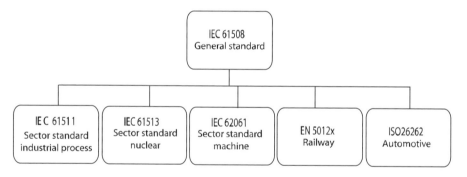

Figure 4.1. *The IEC 61508 general standard and declinations*[1]

Figure 4.2 presents the architectural levels covered by each railway standard: system and subsystem.

Software development depends on a specific criticality level called *software* SIL (SSIL), which varies from level 0 (no danger, no impact) to level 4 (critical, causing the death of several people). The SSIL level is reached by mastering the software quality through the application of a pre-established and systematic development process. This standard proposes a classic lifecycle in V and requires the

---

1 ISO 26262 standard [ISO 09], as shown in Chapter 9 in [BOU 09]. It is also worth noting that standard CEI/IEC 61513 cannot really be linked to standard CEI/IEC 61508 if we consider the history of standards in the nuclear domain.

implementation of techniques such as: application of formal methods during specification and design, traceability of requirements, unit tests, test coverage, etc.

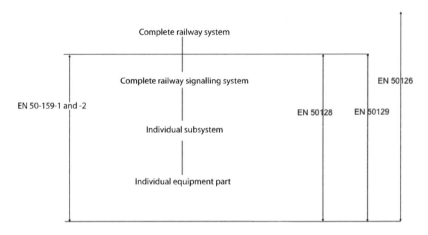

Figure 4.2. *Standards applicable to railway systems*

If a highly recommended measure or technique (Highly Recommended as defined in [CEN 01a] on page 46 of EN 50128) is not applied, this choice must be explained in detail and justified. It is necessary to show that, thanks to the global process implemented and/or to the use of other techniques, this measure or technique is not necessary.

We must notice that for railway systems, and particularly for railway software, it is mandatory to have an independent evaluation (see CENELEC EN 50128, [CEN 01a, Chap. 14]). Software evaluation is carried out by an entity that is independent of the development and known as an *independent safety assessor* (ISA). During the independent evaluation of the software, the conformity to the standard is verified: each non-conformity is studied and the corresponding justification is either validated or rejected by the ISA.

4.3. Elaboration of the proof of the robustness method

Let us consider the common context of a SSIL 3-4 application for which certain high recommendations (HRs) have not been followed. An objective lies behind each recommendation in a standard. We have elaborated a method for reaching this initial objective without applying a chosen subset of HRs. We demonstrate the objectives coverage by showing the relevance and completeness of the software robustness with regards to dysfunctional values.

Table 4.1 lists three choices that are commonly made during software development but which lead to the violation of a subset of HRs [CEN 01a]. The first column presents the development choice, the second contains the recommendation not followed because of this choice and the third associates a reference to this recommendation. This index is used in the remainder of this chapter.

Development choice	High recommendation (HR) not followed	Reference
The chosen programming language is C, which does not offer strong typing	Use of a stronlg typed programming language (Table A.4, point 7, p. 50)	HR-1
The software is integrated in *big-bang* mode, i.e. all the modules (or large packages) are directly integrated with no observable intermediate values	The integration of software modules shall be the process of progressively combining individual and previously tested modules of the software into a composite whole (or into a number of composite subsystems) in order that the module interfaces and the assembled software may be adequately proven prior to system integration and test (section 10.4.17, p. 24)	HR-2
Unit tests and integration tests do not allow the demonstration that the software meeds the recommendations given in the standard	A Software Module Test Report shall be produced and shall include the following features: a statement of test coverage shall be provided for each module, showing that all source code instructions have been executed at least once (section 10.4.14-ii, p. 24)	HR-3
	Test Case Execution from Boundary Value Analysis (Table A.13, point 1, p.55)	HR-4

Table 4.1. *Correspondence between common development choices and HR recommendations [CEN 01a] that are not followed*

Not following the HR-1 recommendation may lead to weaknesses in robustness since static typing is not carried out. To make up for this absence of automatic verification, developers add (dynamic) value control in the source code. To be comparable to static typing, this value control must guarantee that all data handled remain in their functional domain[2] throughout the executions and must be

_____

2 The functional domain is a set of values that are specified as acceptable for a variable. C language is not strongly types. In C, scalar types are stored in memory spaces that are bytes

systematically integrated into the application source code. This can only be ensured by an *a posteriori* verification of the presence and correctness of control points set in the piece of software. We use static program analysis to carry out part of this verification.

In the left-hand column, Figure 4.3 presents a without value control source code written in C, and in the right-hand column contains the same piece of code that integrates the value control: the value of the variable *state* is controlled between its computation by *compute_state* and its use by *use_state*. The functional domain *{FREE, BUSY}* of the variable *state* is defined by its enumerated type. In the controlled piece of code, if the value of the *state* belongs to this domain, the execution continues without modification. If this is not the case, the execution is modified by the call to the ERROR function.

typedef enum {FREE,BUSY} EVT;	*typedef enum {FREE,BUSY} EVT;*
...	*...*
EVT state;	*EVT state;*
state = compute_state(...);	*state = compute_state(...);*
	if ((state == FREE) || (state == BUSY))
	{
... =use_state(state);	*... =use_state(state);*
	}
	else
	{
	ERROR(state);
	}

Figure 4.3. *Example of value control on the state variable*

Lack of HR2 progressive integration and its effects on tests HR-3 and HR-4 could be dynamically covered with unit tests and out-of-bounds integration tests. But the number of tests required for the combinations of all possible values of a set of variables is roughly the product of the cardinals of their functional domains: these tests are frequently too numerous to be carried out during the project time allocated. We use *static analysis* to propagate *functional domains* from the production of software inputs to the *value control* when it is present in the source

---

multiples, or even bit fields that enable the representation of 2^n values where n is the number of bits. These types are used for all variables, whatever their functional domain is, and even the enumerated types are in fact processed as *int*. For this reason, the domain of values associated with the type of variables is much larger than their functional domain.

code and to data consumption in general. If a control point verifies a domain that is different from the one calculated by propagation, it means that it is possible to produce dysfunctional values based on correct inputs or that the control is stricter than expected. If the control verifies the domain calculated by propagation, however, it means that for all possible executions the data produced belong to the expected domains. This therefore completes the limit tests, proves that the execution is inside the control present in the piece of code, and that the control is no more restrictive than expected.

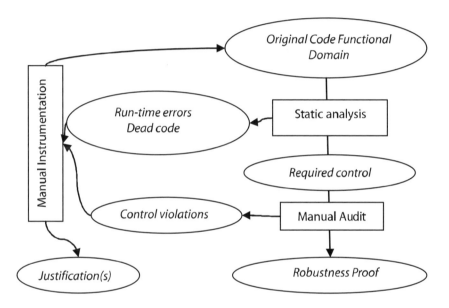

Figure 4.4. *Robustness verification method*

Finally, we consider the piece of software as being robust with regards to dysfunctional values if it implements value control and if the correctness (consistency with regards to functional domains) of this control is established.

We have elaborated a specific method by which to verify software robustness implemented as the value control. This method, presented in Figure 4.4, uses static program analysis but also requires manual processing. It is made up of two main stages:

– a static analysis that calculates the required control from functional domains;

– a manual audit that shows the compliance of the value control.

It is worth noting that here static analysis does not mean direct use of a static analysis tool, but a combination of manual and automated stages.

At each stage, this method detects inconsistencies between the original source code and the specified functional domains: execution errors are detected during the first stage, and non-conformities are identified during the second stage. Table 4.2 associates the objective to be proven by our verification method, and the errors thus detected, to each recommendation: if an error is detected, the corresponding objective is not achieved and the recommendation is not covered. The conformity of the control is therefore only proven if all the automatically detected errors and all the non-conformities that result from the audit are instructed. In other words, if they are corrected in the source code or in the specified domains, or are justified. The errors instruction stage is therefore essential in the method, but is not described in this chapter as it depends on the target application.

Reference	Objective to be proven	Errors to be instructed
HR-1	The production of data outside their functional domains is detected by a control violation	Run-time errors Control violations
HR-2	Modules do not produce erroneous data based on the input's correct values	Run-time errors
HR-3	Non-executable statements of the program are detected	Dead code
HR-4	The bounds of a module's input are attainable and reached by modules that consume them; and an input that takes its value outside its functional domain is detected as incorrect by the function that consumes it	Run-time errors

Table 4.2. *Errors to be instructed*

Furthermore, this method enables us to implement additional recommendations from standard [CEN 01a]:

– LR-5 *defensive programming* (Table A.3, item 1, p. 49);

– LR-6 *programming by assertion* (Table A.3, item 5, p. 49);

– LR-7 *use of static analysis* (Table A.5, item 3, p. 51);

– LR-8 *analysis of values at the limits* (Table A.19, item 1, p. 58).

4.4. General description of the method

This section informally defines the notions of *required control* necessary to ensure the robustness of the software, and the *effective control* which is effectively set in the source code. Software robustness with regards to dysfunctional values is defined as the consistency between the required control and the effective control. This chapter presents the principal aspects of required and effective controls computation on the source code, as well as the verification of robustness.

4.4.1. *Required or effective value control*

Briefly, value control [FAU 09] is implemented in the piece of code by control points that verify that the value of the variable at the chosen program point belongs to its functional domain.

If the control carried out is successful, then the variable is functionally correct and the execution continues. If it fails, an error is raised and the software carries out a predefined security action.

The security action is based on the security rules that are applicable to the target software and can correspond to different behaviors: putting the software in its final state (fallback position in railway); correcting the current state and continuing the execution; or restoring a previous state and restarting the execution.

The action chosen is generally similar for all control points, since it is defined by the security rules that can be applied to the target software.

if (correct_control)
{
    /* do nothing */
}
else
{
  Signal_Fault(state);
}
	if (correct_control)
	{
	    /* do nothing */
	}
	else
	{
	  Signal_Fault(state);
	  FALLBACK_POSITION;
	}

Figure 4.5. *Example of control points with different security actions*

Figure 4.5 presents two examples of security actions:

– in the left-hand column, the execution continues after having signaled the error by *Signal_Fault*;

– in the right-hand column, the software goes into the fallback position after having signaled the error *Signal_Fault*.

The addition of a control point to a piece of software requires knowedge of:

– *its location*, which is determined by the constraint "verifying the value before use", which is translated in terms of source code by "before the consumption statements". As the value is only known after its production, the control point must be located between its production and its consumption. This corresponds to a set of possible locations within the program but leads to one location when the location strategy is applied;

– *its functional domain* can be part of the specification. If this is not the case, it is calculated by hand from the specified functional domains and the piece of code that is executed.

We define *Required control* as the control necessary to ensure the robustness of the software. As its location is chosen as a point between production and consumption, the required control point is described by the quadruplet (*input, value domain, production locations, consumption locations*) where *input* is the name of the input variable or its memory access path, *value domain* is a description of the correct values for the input between each *production* and the corresponding *consumptions* and a location is described by a triplet (*file name, line number, column number*). It is worth noting that the production and consumption locations are potentially situated in different functions and files.

	typedef enum {FREE,BUSY,UNK} EVT; *...* *EVT state;*	
1: 2: 3: 4: 5: 6:	*state = compute_state(...);* *if (condition)* *{ ...=use_state_1(state);...}* *else* *{ ...=use_state_2(state);...}* *...=use_state_3 (state);*	(*state,{FREE,BUSY},{1},{3,5}*)

Figure 4.6. *Example of a required control point*

Figure 4.6 presents original code in the left-hand column: the input is *state*, its functional values are {*FREE BUSY*} and the locations are described by the line numbers {1, 2, 3, 4, 5} to facilitate reading. The required control (*state,{FREE,BUSY},{1},{3, 5}*) presented in the right-hand column means that a control point must be established to protect statements 3 and 5 from an error in the value calculated by line 1. The value control performed before the statements {3, 5} ensures that the value passed to statement {6} is always correct, so no control point is necessary between lines 5 and 6.

We define *effective control* as the control that is effectively present in the source code of an application. An effective control point is described by the triplet (*input, effective value domain, effective location*). The location of the effective control point is the result of a choice from the set of locations between each production and the corresponding consumptions. This choice is not generally left to the developer, but is directed by a location strategy that is globally chosen for a piece of software or a whole project. The two extreme location strategies are:

– the "as early as possible" strategy, which leads to an effective control point being set just after the production statement;

– the "as late as possible" strategy, which leads to several effective control points being placed just before all the consumption statements.

Figure 4.7 presents two examples of controlled code according to these two extreme strategies:

– "as early as possible" left-hand column (one control point); and

– "as late as possible" right-hand column (two control points).

1:	state = compute_state(...);	1 :	state = compute_state(...);
	if ((state == FREE) ||	2 :	if (condition)
	(state == BUSY))		{ if ((state == FREE) ||
	{		(state == BUSY))
2:	if (condition)	3 :	{ ...=use_state_1(state);... }
3:	{ ...=use_state_1(state) ;...};		else { ERROR(state) ;};
4:	else		}
5:	{ ...=use_state_2(state);...};	4 :	else
6:	...=use_state_3(state);		{ if ((state == FREE) ||
	}		(state == BUSY))
	else {ERROR(state) ;};	5 :	{ ...=use_state_2(state);... }
			else {ERROR(state);};};
		6 :	...=use_state_3(state);
	{(state, {FREE,BUSY}, 1)}		{(state, {FREE,BUSY}, 3),
			(state, {FREE,BUSY}, 5)}

Figure 4.7. *Examples of effective control points*

To verify that a piece of software is robust with regards to dysfunctional values, it is therefore necessary to calculate all the required control points, and then verify that they are all encoded (presence and correctness) by one or more effective control points, depending on the chosen location strategy.

Even if control must be set during development, the complexity of the development cycle, modifications in software or specification can lead to incoherencies in the control of the software. It is therefore always necessary to verify *a posteriori* the correctness of the effective control with regards to the required control.

Figure 4.8 presents an erroneous encoding of the required control point presented in Figure 4.6. The effective control point is erroneous for two reasons:

– the first consumption (line 3) is protected in a too restrictive a way, since the correct value BUSY of *state* is rejected and leads to an error and

– the second consumption (line 5) is not protected from incorrect values of *state*.

1:	*state = compute_state(...);*
2:	*if (condition)*
	{ if (state == FREE)
3:	*{ ...=use_state_1(state);... }*
	else { ERROR(state) ;};
	}
4:	*else*
5:	*{ ...=use_state_2(state) ;... };*
6:	*...=use_state_3(state);*

Figure 4.8. *Example of an erroneous effective control point*

4.4.2. *Computation of the required control*

All the required control points can be manually calculated from the source code of the application and the specified functional domains, thanks to the three following steps described below:

– identification of software and function inputs;

– location of production and consumption; and

– computation of functional value domains.

4.4.2.1. Identification of software and function inputs

The identification of all the software and function inputs is done by an analysis for each function. The inputs of the software are the variables associated with the calls to functions that aquire data from the environment such as getc, fget, etc. The inputs of a function are parameters, static variables, variables that contain values produced by the called functions or that are consumed directly or indirectly by the function. In some cases, inputs are not implanted in the form of variables, but are components of variables (structure fields, array components). More generally, an input is a memory zone described by a path built from the name of a variable and accessors (to array components, to structure fields) defined by the language.

4.4.2.2. Location of production and consumption

The location of the production and consumption of an input requires a complex interprocedural analysis to follow variables (paths) that are renamed via function calls. The production of global or local variables is realized by calls to functions that access the environment (getc) or any other function of the application. The consumption of a value corresponds to an explicit computation based on that value: we consider that passing a parameter or storing a value in another variable are not true consumption.

If the input is a scalar object, the production/consumption is atomic. However, if the input is composite, as in a structure or an array, the production/consumption is partial and multiple: the production/consumption points must be collected for each input component.

4.4.2.3. Computation of functional value domains

The functional value domains cannot be calculated based on the source code alone. The functional domains are know from the specification for the software inputs: the values are produced by the environment and belong in general to a restricted value domains.

On the contrary, the domains of function inputs are often unknown, particularly in the case of *big-bang* integration. They must then be calculated by a combination of reverse engineering of the source code of the program, and expert knowledge. In particular, these domains can be calculated by propagating the specified functional domains throughout all the statements of the software by mental execution.

4.4.3. Verification of effective control

To verify the effective control already present in a target code, it is necessary to calculate the required control points, as previously described, then examine the piece of software to verify whether each required point is implemented in the source code. An effective control point (*var, dom, loc*) encode a required control point (*var*, dom*, prod*, conso**) if it applies to the same variable *var==var** with the same functional domain *dom==dom** and if its location satisfies the location strategy *loc*∈ strategy(*prod*, conso**).

The general algorithm for the verification of control points is as follows. For each required control point (*var, dom*, prod*, conso**), we look for effective control points that control the value of the variable *var*:

– if no effective point exists, then a non-conformity is added:

(*var, dom*, prod*, conso**) ? *None*

– for each effective control point (*var, dom, loc*), we verify that the location *loc* is correct with regards to the location strategy and for locations of production *prod* and consumption *conso*:

- if the location is incorrect, then the following non-conformity is added:

(var, dom*, prod*, conso*) ? (var, dom, loc) | NC(prod, conso, loc);

- if the location is correct, then the domains are compared,

a) if *dom =/= dom**, then the following non-conformity is added:

(*var, dom*, prod*, conso**) ? (*var, dom, loc*) | NC(*prod, conso, loc, dom*),

b) if *dom == dom**, then the following partial conformity is added:

(*var, dom*, prod*, conso**) ?(*var, dom, loc*) | PC(*prod, conso*);

– then the conformities are analysed to evaluate their coverage:

- if all the production and consumption points are associated with an effective control point, then a total conformity is added:

(*var, dom*, prod*, conso**)?TC,

- if not, certain production and consumption points are not associated with effective points and we add a non-conformity:

(*var, dom*, prod*, conso**)?PC.

Once all of the required points have been studied, the results are:

– the required points that are not implemented in the source code; and

– potential non-conformities.

Finally, these potential non-conformities are instructed and can lead to a correction of the source code or the specified functional domains, or to a justification.

4.5. Computation of the control required

The control required for software is long and difficult to compute as it demands interprocedural analyses on complex data, such as value domains. The tools based on static analysis (by abstract interpretation) automatically carry out such analyses, but do not directly verify control points, calculate the required control points or collect the effective control points. We have developed a method to calculate the required control that uses the functionalities of static analysis tools as they are.

Static analysis tools simulate all executions of the target application in a symbolic execution and verify dynamic properties. This symbolic execution requires the abstraction of concrete values into abstract values (lattice elements), and the computation of fixed points to cover the recursion often present in programs (loop, recursive function). These tools compute abstract values of each variable at each program point. The abstract value of a variable, v, represents all the values v can take during all possible executions of the program. From these abstract values, tools verify properties such as the absence of run time, numerical or memory errors.

Our method requires the following functionalities from the static analysis tool:

– detection of run-time errors;

– computation of a subset of dead code;

– *observe_value* operator enabling the extraction of the value of a variable;

– *assume_value* operator whose semantic is assert and then assume (see section 4.5.2);

– computation of the software call graph;

– computation of the data dictionary.

Our algorithm for computing required control points from the source code and the functional domains operates in two main stages, as presented in Figure 4.9:

– stage 1 it identifies inputs and localizes their production and consumption points; and

– stage 2 it calculates the value domains at the production points.

These two stages apply static analysis to meet different objectives.

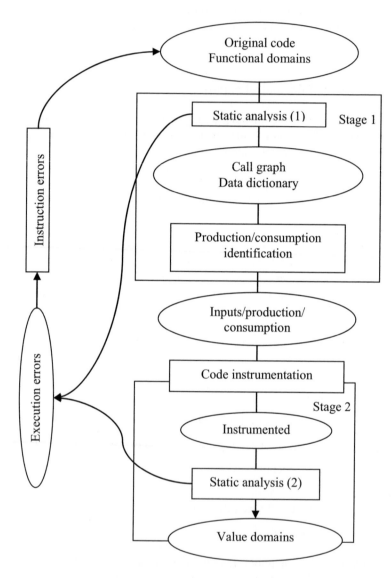

Figure 4.9. *Computation of the required control*

During the first stage, which is explained in section 4.5.1, the static analysis tool is used to calculate the call graph and data dictionary of the original code. During this computation, the tool also verifies the absence of compilation and run-time errors. These errors must be instructed before being the other results can be used.

This is represented in Figure 4.9 by an arrow going from the run-time errors to the original code. Once the errors have been corrected, the static analysis tool produces the data dictionary and the call graph of the application.

During the second stage, explained in section 4.5.2, static analysis is used to compute unknown functional domains and thus complete the definition of the required control points. The errors detected during this stage must also be instructed before using the resulting domains.

4.5.1. *Identification of production/consumption of inputs*

Stage 1 begins with the static analysis of the original code, which aims to calculate the call graph and data dictionary for global and static variables. This information is used to calculate software and function inputs, locations of production and consumption as described below:

– *Software inputs*: the calls of the input functions of the language (getc, scanf, fscanf, etc.) are found in the call graph. These call locations are also the location of the production of input values for the software. By examining the source code at these locations, the assigned variables (software input variables) are determined. We thus obtain the software inputs and their production places. Then, the consumption locations are found throughout the chains of function calls.

– *Function global or static inputs*: the data dictionary contains the list of the application's global or static variables. If it also contains their production and consumption places – either direct or indirect – there is nothing left to calculate. If not, it is necessary to find direct uses in the source code and then follow the call graph to find all the indirect access points.

– *Function parameters*: if the data dictionary contains function parameters, and their direct or indirect input or output, there is nothing to calculate. If not, the list of the function parameters is obtained by looking at their definition. To calculate the subset of inputs parameters, it is necessary to determine all their accesses. We consider that the production place of a parameter is situated before the execution of the first statement of the function. The consumption places are calculated by following their value throughout calls to function (and therefore potential renaming). This computation is done entirely by hand if the static analysis tool does not give information regarding the function parameters.

If a new kind of input is dealt with, it is necessary to define how to identify in the piece of software their occurances and their production/consumption. The rest of the method is applied without change.

4.5.2. *Computation of value domains*

Stage 2 of the method described in Figure 4.9 aims to calculate the value domains of the intermediate inputs from the specified functional input domains. Doing so, tt also verifies the consistency between the specified functional input domains and the source code of the target application.

This stade begins by a manual phase to instrument the source code, followed by a static analysis of the instrumented program, which calculates the unspecified functional domains. The instrumentation phase places constraints on the inputs that have a specified domain, and observation points for those that do not. The specified domains are translated into constraints by using the *assume_value* operator so that any violation of the constraint leads to halting of the execution (a common semantic of the *assert* operator), otherwise the execution continues by taking the constraint as an hypothesis (assume semantic). These constraints are placed as early as possible after the production of the input value. The observation points are translated thanks to the *observe_value* operator placed in the source code at production locations, i.e. at the beginning of procedures for parameters and global (static) variables. The location strategy "as early as possible", used for setting constraints and observation points, minimizes the instrumentation volume and only requires knowledge of the production places.

In the second column in Figure 4.10 we can see an example of source code and in the third column its instrumented version. The observation of the variable *in* is posed before statement *1* and the constraint on the variable *line* is set after statement *1*.

1:	gets(line);	observe_value(in);
		gets(line);
		assume_value(line);

	...	...
2:	state = compute_state(line,in);	state = compute_state(line,in);
3:	if (condition)	if (condition)
4:	{x=use_state_1(state);...}	{ x=use_state_1(state); ...}
5:	else	else
6:	{ x=use_state_2(state);...};	{ x=use_state_2(state) ; ...};
7:	y=use_state_3(state);	y=use_state_3(state);

Figure 4.10. *Computation of the required control point*

Static analysis of the instrumented code propagates specified value domains for the inputs towards observation points. The result of the analysis contains the list of domains calculated for unspecified inputs. The calculated domains approximate all of the values reached from specified domains by symbolically executing the source code and by collecting the constraints related to the correct executing of this piece of code (division by zero, for instance). This approximation is due to the abstraction used by static analysis to take into account all possible executions (sound). For example, if the domain [3..4] ∪ [5..7] is calculated, it may be over approximated in [3..7] by using the interval lattice.

Furthermore, static analysis automatically verifies the consistency between the domains of the software inputs and the instrumented code. Run-time errors, dead code or violations of the control signal incoherencies between the source code and instrumented constraints. These errors are instructed to be corrected or justified. Their correction. can require the modification of the source code or the specified functional domains. It is sometimes difficult to return to the error found at the violated constraint if the influence of the latter is not immediate. It is only once all these errors have been instructed, as shown in Figure 4.9, that the calculated functional domains are correct and therefore exploitable.

4.6. Verification of the effective control of an industrial application

The computation method for the required control described in section 4.5 has been applied to verify the value control of a real application, the development of which did not follow recommendations HR-1, 2, 3 and 4, but implants the value control as previously defined in section 4.4.

4.6.1. Target software

The software for Thales railway interlocking products (PING SSIL3-4) implements a rail root-management system. This product contributes to the safety of the root-management functions of railway signaling posts, to the control and command of elements of the track (switches, signals, etc.) and to the control–command exchanges with external systems, as Figure 4.11 illustrates.

This software integrates the control of the values of its inputs. Function inputs are parameters, static variables or global variables. In this context we consider that values produced by called functions are also function inputs. The location strategy chosen for this supplementary kind of input implies that the control point should be placed in the function that consumes the value "at the latest" before consumption. On the contrary, software inputs need to be protected by a control point placed in the function, which produces the value "as early as possible" after production.

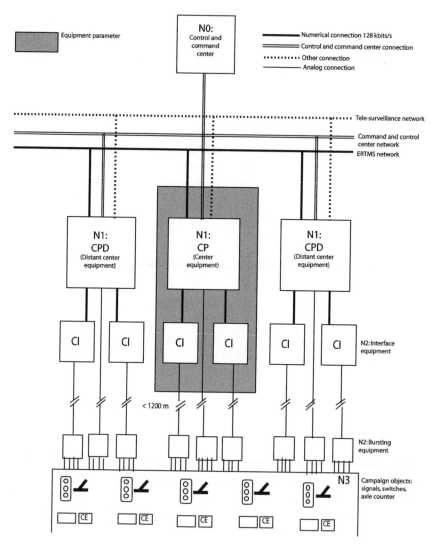

Figure 4.11. *Architecture of the Thales interlocking product*

The general form of the value control is given in Figure 4.12. The call to the *Fatal_fault* function logs the errors detected by the value control: the logged message is constructed from the name of the *module* and the *fault_message* dependent on the control point that has been violated. The call to *FALLBACK_POSITION* commands the restrictive behavior of the system.

```
if (Nbr_variables_safety >= MAX_VARIABLES_SAFETY)
  {
    Fatal_fault (module, fault_message);
    FALLBACK_POSITION
  }
  /* else Nominal processing */
```

Figure 4.12. *Example of a control point present in Thales interlocking product*

Unfortunately, the use of the *Fatal_fault* function is not limited to the control of values but is used to process error cases different in general. Furthermore, the macro *ASSERTION* that defines a control point is not only used to pose the effective control points. The presence of all these patterns leads to a lack of uniformity in the source code. Therefore the search for effective control points, which theoretically could be done automatically by applying pattern-matching in the source code, must be carried out manually.

The functional domains are specified in a table that associates the full variable name or memory access path (together with the module and function names) and the value domain. In our case, domains are only given for what is called software inputs above and is described as set of values *{FREE, BUSY}*, intervals [3..12], or value properties *non_null(p)*, *sizeof(s)==4*.

4.6.2. Implementation

We have chosen Polyspace[®3] as the static analysis tool because it is the tool used by the industrialist who developed the source code and because it offers all the functionalities we are looking for.

Polyspace[®] is a static analysis tool based on abstract interpretation, the aim of which is to detect run-time errors as well as non-deterministic behaviors in the source code of application swritten in C, C++ or ADA. A run-time error is a program state perfectly identified in the standard of the target language as a construction leading to an *unspecified, undefined or implementation-defined behavior*. The tool calculates the target program points that could cause one of these behaviors and gives each of them an error status: impossible (green), potential (orange), certain (red) or unattainable (gray) code. Polyspace® produces the association list of these program points and their error status. Furthermore, it calculates a subset of dead code: the statements never executed and procedures never called.

---

3 The MathWorks, see Chapter 3 of this book.

Polyspace® offers the two operators that are essential to the method:

– Observation points (*observe_value*): this is translated into an Inspection PoinT (IPT) on the variables at the chosen points. The command *#pragma Inspection_Point var1 var2* asks the tool to show the possible values (abstract values) of variables *var1 var2* at the point in the program where it is set. The calculated value domains are added to the analysis results. It is worth noting that the inspection points only be set only be on scalar-type variables, which restricts the possibilities of observation: in particular, the structures and arrays cannot be globally observed but should be observed component by component.

– Constraints (*assume_value*): each constraint is translated into assertions. The semantic of the statement *assert(test)* for Polyspace® is: if the test is verified at the point where it is set, the rest of the execution is restrained to the values for which the test is true, otherwise the execution is stopped. The status of the assertions (definitely violated, never violated or potentially violated) is also present in the results but does not directly prove the control: in particular, the fact that the assertion is never violated (green) proves that the control domain is included in the domain calculated by Polyspace® but does not prove that the two domains are equal. The manual audit described in section 4.4.3 remains, therefore, essential to meet the verification objectives.

Polyspace® makes the intermediate results necessary to the application of our method available to the user:

– unexecuted functions (dead code);

– functions call graph; and

– data dictionary.

4.6.2.1. *Preliminary analysis of the application*

The first stage of the static analysis of a source code is its "compilation" by the tool. To enable the compilation, we have taken into account the specificities of this application and configured Polyspace®, as described in Table 4.3.

Moreover, the Polyspace® compilation is stricter than the one carried out by common compilers, since it systematically verifies the respect of the ANSI/ISO C standard [ISO 90]. Thus, certain modifications have been brought to the application's source code to correct the aspects that do not conform to ANSI C. Once this configuration is finished, the analysis of the application by Polyspace® is possible.

At this stage, the results show that the interruptions are not simulated. In particular, infinite loops were wrongly detected. We have deleted these cycles, which only delay the execution of the rest of the statements without changing their behavior. Then the analysis was correct but too expensive in terms of time.

Polyspace® options	Specificity of the application
-target i386 -OS-target no-predefined-OS -I APPLICATIONS/WATCOMC_Includes	Compiler WATCOMC
-dos	The delimiter "\" is used instead of "/" in processed included file names
-discard-asm	The assembly piece of code automatically skipped and stubbed
-D INTERRUPT= -D __far= -D FAR=	The "interruptions" and "far pointers" are skipped

Table 4.3. *List of options necessary for the compilation*

We have then simplified the source code to enable a more efficient Polyspace® analysis. To reduce the number of pointers computed, we redefine functions without functional contribution (message logging), by associating a nohup semantic to them. We also replaced the *Fatal_Fault, Fallback_ Position* and *Pseudo_ Fatal_Fault* functions with definite stops of the execution. We also defined the function *ALLOCATE_MEMORY* to the standard *malloc* functions. By doing this, we divide the number of aliases calculated by Polyspace® by a factor of 5.8. Furthermore, we redefined the macro *ASSERTION*, which implants the control points, to a call to the *assert* function recognized by Polyspace®. During this preliminary work, were are able to detect and correct three run-time errors in the source code of the application.

Such adaptations are often necessary to make static analysis practicable at the source level because not all existing compiler extensions can be imbed in the analyzer and because some source code characteristics, such as the number of aliases, limit the efficiency of static tools.

4.6.2.2. Instrumentation and analysis of the instrumented code

In our method, the instrumentation of the source code has two goals: add the specified constraints and to add the observation points. These two kinds of modifacations are controlled independently thanks to the *Active_constraint* and *Active_observation* macros that are activated by the compilation options *–D Active_ constraint* and *–D Active_ observation*.

Constraints are implemented in the form of C functions, grouping the assertions together for the same variable. Figure 4.13 presents the translation of the functional domain *[0..NB_ TYPE_CARTE-1]* of the *typeCarte* variable according to the specification in the *constraint_ typeCarte* function. Certain specified functional domains are not translated into constraints because they are too complicated to be propagated by Polyspace®. Examples of unused specification domains are constraints on least significant bit [0.. 255] or most significant bit [0.. 4] of bit fields values, or on IP address structure 192.168.[0.. 255].[0.. 255].

```
void constraint_typeCarte(E_TYPE_CARTE typeCarte)
{
#define TMP_typeCarte typeCarte
  assert(TMP_typeCarte >= 0);
  assert(TMP_typeCarte <= NB_TYPE_CARTE - 1);
}
```

Figure 4.13. *Example of a constraint function*

The constraint functions are duplicated when the constraints must be set at several points in the program. In general, the constraints are set once between production and consumption – just after production for the sake of simplicity. However if there is a *Cast* operation between production and consumption, the constraint is set once just after production and a second time before consumption, if it can be translated on the casted value. This reinforces the effect of the constraints, because it enables Polyspace® value propagation otherwise stopped by the casts, especially if they concern components of structured objects (array component, structure field). Figure 4.14 presents the use of the *constraint_typeCarte* function in the *GetIdCarte* function.

```
1:   T_idCarte DIP_GetIdCarte(E_TYPE_CARTE typeCarte)
2:   {

     #ifdef Active_observation
       OBS_DIP_GetIdCarte(typeCarte)
     #endif /* Active_observation */

     #ifdef Active_contrainte
       contrainte_typeCarte(typeCarte);
     #endif /* Active_contrainte */

3:     DIP_ASSERTION(typeCarte < NB_TYPE_CARTE);

5:     return gLesIdCarte[typeCarte];
6:   } /* FIN DIP_GetIdCarte */
```

Figure 4.14. *Instrumentation of the GetIdCarte function*

The observation points are implemented as macros that expand in Polyspace® *Inspection_Point* for the software inputs and its functions. It is worth noting that Polyspace® only enables the observation of scalar inputs. This limits the possibility of observation on structured objects. Figure 4.14 presents the use of the observation macro *OBS_DIP_GetIdCarte* in the *GetIdCarte* function of the original application.

The instrumented code is then analyzed by Polyspace® using the maximal precision options (-O3 -to pass4) as well as the options required by the analysis of the original code presented in Table 4.4.

Polyspace® options	
-target i386	-D INTERRUPT=
-OS-target no-predefined-OS	-D __far=
-I APPLICATIONS/WATCOMC_Includes	-D FAR=
-dos	-O3
-discard-asm	-to pass4

Table 4.4. *Polyspace® analysis options for the instrumented software*

The analysis of the instrumented code generates run-time errors if the specified domain is not consistent with the source code. Three kinds of errors can be automatically detected: functional constraint violations; value control violations; and run-time errors. The violation of a functional constraint appears as red *assert* in the function constraints definition file. For example in Figure 4.13 if the *GetIdCarte* function is called with an erroneous value (*typeCarte* $\geq NB\_TYPE\_$ *CARTE or <0*) the assertions contained in the function *constraint_ typeCarte* (see Figure 4.12) is violated. The violation of an original code control point also appears as a red assert or dead code. In the example in Figure 4.13, if the control point in line 3 is poorly defined (*typeCarte > NB_TYPE_CARTE*) a violation appears. Finally, a general run-time error can appear. For example, in Figure 4.13 an out-of-bounds access line 5 can be detected if the *gLesIdCarte* variable size is declared to be too small with regards to the control implemented (for example, size(*gLesIdCarte) < typeCarte)*.

The analysis of the errors is simple for constraint errors, but a lot more complicated for other types of errors. The correction of the source code with regards to these errors is quite hard without functional expertise on the application. Once these incoherencies have been corrected in the source code or the specified functional domains, the results of the analysis can be used for the audit. The domains calculated at the inspection points serve as a reference domain for the unknown functional domains.

4.6.2.3. *Source code audit*

The aim of the source code audit is to verify that the effective control points implement the required points. The general algorithm for verifying the effective control points, presented in section 4.4.3, can be simplified by the instantiation of a strategy for setting control points (chosen location), as described hereafter.

In particular, the source code traversal algorithm can be specialized. Each executable function f, is covered according to a traversal algorithm adapted to the kind of input that is controlled:

– for parameters, local statics or globals variables: it is necessary to follow the execution backwards from each consumption in f to the beginning of the definition of f;

– for output parameters and global variables of a function g called in function f: it is necessary to follow the execution forward from the call to g of the definition of function f is reached;

– for software inputs: it is necessary to follow the execution forward from the call to the input function that produces the value until the function that contains the consumption of this value is reached. It is complex research due to its inter-procedural nature.

However, the conclusion algorithm on compliance is the same:

– if no effective control point is found, it means that the production is not verified and we add it to the list of potential non-compliances;

– if at least one effective control point is found, the verification is carried out in two successive stages;

- for each effective point we verify that the controlled domain is indeed the one calculated by Polyspace®:

i) if the domains are not equal, then we add it to the list of potential non-compliances, and

ii) if the domains are equal, we move on to the next stage,

- we verify that the protection offered by these control points is ensured for all possible executions by the computation of the paths covered in the source code:

i) if the effective points protect all possible paths, we add them to the list of non-compliances;

ii) if this is not the case, we add them to the list of potential non-compliances.

The non-compliances thus obtained are instructed one-by-one. The errors are corrected in the source code or in the specified functional domains, and the other errors are justified. This process is beyond the scope of this chapter.

4.6.3. Results

4.6.3.1. Direct results

We have applied the method to two successive versions of the Thales railway interlocking product.

The Thales root-management software V45.05 implemented in 92 Klines of C is made up of 66 files and 717 functions. The functional domains of 95 inputs were specified, which enabled the development of 95 constraint functions in a file of 2,397 lines of C code. We have placed the constraints at 196 program points and the observation on 1,509 scalar inputs, the functional domains of which are unknown. The Polyspace® tool automatically detected one inconsistency between the source code and the specified functional domains. Static analysis of the constrained code led to eight source code corrections and one correction of the functional domain in the specification.

The manual verification of the control required the examination of 2,644 effective control points and showed that 71% of points were correct, 18% were non-conforming and the status of the remaining 11% had to be established by the industrialist as it required functional knowledge about the application.

The Thales root-management software V49.03 implemented in 122 Klines of C is made up of 87 files and 1,409 functions. The specified functional domains of 358 inputs led to the development of 358 constraint functions (containing 1,800 constraints) with 8,099 lines of C code. We placed the constraints at 225 program points, and observed the value of 4597 scalar inputs, the functional domains of which were unknown.

The Polyspace® tool automatically detected around 20 inconsistencies between the source code and the specified functional domains, which led to the correction of 22 functional domains in the specification. The validation of results is ongoing and the manual audit has not yet begun.

Software verification is therefore not finished, but the increase in the number of constraints processed visibly improved the quality of calculated domains. More than 84% of domains were specific (different from the domain associated with the data type), whereas for the previous version only 48% of calculated domains were precise.

This enables us to say that the manual compliance audit of the control points present in the source code with regards to the required control points will be more rapidly performed.

4.6.3.2. *Indirect results*

The application of this methodology reinforced vertical traceability (see Figure 4.16) of the V model development cycle (see Figure 4.15), in particular the data refinement from systems and subsystems towards the lowest levels of software application.

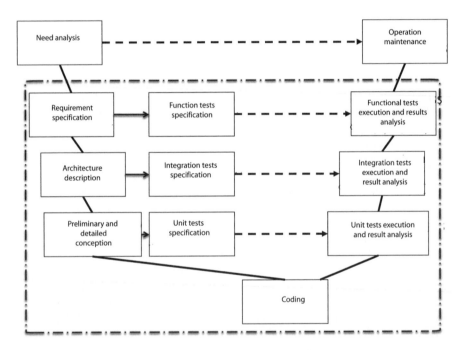

Figure 4.15. *V development cycle*

Indeed, manually verifying the consistency of the functional domains handled by the software from values provided by systems and subsystems is arduous, complex and error prone due to the multiplicity of potential production and data consumption and to data cross-dependencies that can invalidate the established domains.

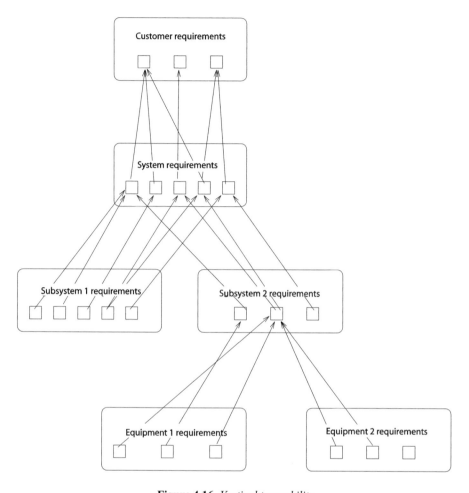

Figure 4.16. *Vertical traceability*

The horizontal traceability application of our method (see Figure 4.17) also statically shows the partial or complete achievement of objectives:

– HR-1 (statements coverage): the Polyspace® underlying technology detects unattainable code and classifies it as a non-compliance;

– HR-2 (progressive integration of software modules): the application of the methodology establishes whether or not the bounds of the output domains can be effectively produced by the modules;

– HR-3 (strong typing): the application of the method shows whether or not the use of data outside their functional domain is detected by a control violation; and

– HR-4 (tests based on a value limit analysis): the application of the methodology establishes whether or not the module input bounds are correctly handled by the modules that consume them; and that an input that takes a value outside its functional domain is detected as incorrect by the function that consumes it.

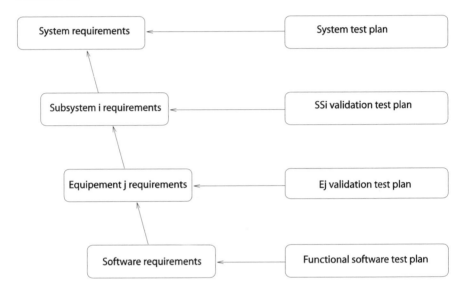

Figure 4.17. *Horizontal traceability*

4.7. Discussion and viewpoints

This chapter describes the verification of value control present in the source code that ensures the robustness of software with regards to dysfunctional values. This value control deals with random faults (disturbed environment, hardware failure, etc.) but also takes into account systematic failures (bugs in the application). The implementation of effective control, and the consistency between control and application, are difficult to ensure manually.

The method that we put forward enables us to semi-automatically perform an *a posteriori* verification of the control. Our method can be extended to implement effective control from the "required control". The method for computing the "required control" presented in this chapter is general and can be applied to systematically add control in software. In this case, the original code does not contain a control point and the final verification stage is replaced by the addition of the control to the source code: each required point is implanted in one or more effective points according to the location chosen strategy.

A large portion of manual operations necessary for the computation of required control are difficult to carry out on software programs of industrial size and complexity without errors. The description in section 4.5 (applied in section 4.6) clearly reveals automation possibilities: function inputs can be calculated by an interprocedural analysis known as *in-out* computation. Similarly, software inputs can be automatically detected and the production and consumption locations can be computed as *def-use* chain. Moreover, the instrumentation necessary for the computation of the required control can be automatically generated from the source code and the functional domains. Finally, the required points can be entirely automatically calculated by combining all of these methods.

It is necessary to remark that a large proportion of this information is produced as intermediate results because they are useful for the verification of the absence of run-time errors. This information is, however, not accessible in general. This is true for Polyspace®, as well as numerous other static analysis tools that "know" a lot of things about the source code they are symbolically executing but do not show this information to the user. To our knowledge, no static analysis tool would have enabled the automation of all the computations that we carried out manually.

The verification or automatic setting of control points is much harder to automate due to the necessary liberty left to the developer to define the best compromise between respect of the location strategy and minimization of the number of control points set. The full automation should require the definition of a restrictive location strategy. From a restrictive location rule, the instrumentation of the software or the verification of the software could be entirely automated. We are currently studying this automation in a static analysis platform offering basic functionalities and allowing the development of new modules.

4.8. Conclusion

Verification of the robustness of industrial applications, such as the Thales interlocking product, would have been impossible to carry out by hand. The computation of unknown functional domains cannot be done by hand in a precise enough way. We have shown that it is possible to use static analysis of programs to make this verification possible.

Static analysis tools based on abstract interpretation are generally used to demonstrate the absence of run-time, memory or numerical errors and calculate abstract values to do so. We have used this functionality to propagate the functional domains of the software input data to the internal inputs. This way, the consistency between the source code and the inputs' functional domains is automatically proven: if no runtime error or non-executable statement is found, consistency is ensured. Furthermore, we have shown that it is possible to specify all the control points ensuring software robustness. This enables the definition of a verification method: if a required control point is not implemented or is badly implemented in the source code of the software, then its robustness is not ensured.

As expected, these two activities enable the demonstration of the robustness of industrial software conforming to the CENELEC EN 50128 standard [CEN 01a]. To limit the manual implementation time, we could apply the method by automatically adding the control and by operating the verification during development. It should then be possible to carry out verification of the control in an incremental way by conserving the successive audit results. One final verification remains necessary on the automatic instrumentation tool, and a differential audit to the previous results is needed.

One strength of the method put forward is that it can be carried out by people without functional knowledge about the application, since the relevant information is automatically extracted from the source code. Another strong point of our method is the complex use (non press button) of static analysis tools, of which there are few examples in the literature. This type of use will be increasingly important in the future as it provides greater confidence in the audit results because part of the information is automatically calculated the method, itself can be audited.

Our method implies the use of a static analysis tool. Any tool or combination of static analysis tools that have the functionalities listed in section 4.5 can be used. We have used Polyspace® to verify a railway application and plan to carry out the same verification with another tool, such as Astrée[4] or Frama-C[5], to compare the precision of results.

4.9. Bibliography

[BOU 09] BOULANGER J.-L., *Safety of Computer Architectures*, ISTE Ltd, London and John Wiley and Sons, New York, 2009.

[CEN 00] CENELEC, NF EN 50126, Railway Applications – The Specification and Demonstration of reliability, Availability, Maintainability and Safety (RAMS*)*, CENELEC January 2000.

---

4 www.absint.com/astree/index_fr.htm.

5 http://frama-c.com/.

[CEN 01a] CENELEC, NF EN 50128 Railway Applications – Communications, Signalling and Processing Systems - Software for Railway control and Protection Systems, CENELEC, July 2001.

[CEN 01b] CENELEC, EN 50159-1, Railway Applications – Communication, Signalling and Processing Systems – Part 1: Safey-related Communication in Closed Transmission Systems, CENELEC, March 2001.

[CEN 01c] CENELEC, EN 50159-2, Railway Applications – Communication, Signalling and Processing Systems – Part 2: Safey-related Communication in Open Transmission Systems, CENELEC, March 2001.

[CEN 03] CENELEC, NF EN 50129, Railway Applications – Communication, Signalling and Processing Systems – Safety Related Electronic Systems for Signalling, CENELEC, 2003.

[COU 77] COUSOT P., COUSOT R., "Abstract interpretation: a unified lattice model for static analysis of programs by construction or approximation of fixpoints", in *Conference Record of the 6thAnnual ACM SIGPLAN-SIGACT Symposium on Principles of Programming Languages, Los Angeles*, pp. 238-252, ACM Press, New York, 1977.

[FAU 09] FAURE C., "Computer Aided Extrinsic Robustness Verification". *Extended Abstract*. SAFA Annual Workshop on Formal Techniques, 2009 (available at: www-sop.inria.fr/oais/SAFA/abstracts09/safa09-Faure.pdf).

[IEC 98] IEC, IEC 61508 – Functional Safety of Electrical/Electronic/Programmable Electronic Safety-related Systems, IEC, 1998.

[ISO 09] ISO, ISO/CD-26262, Road Vehicles – Functional Safety, ISO, 2009 (unpublished).

[ISO 90] ISO, Programming Languages – C. International Standard ISO/EIC9899:1990 (E), ISO, 1990.

Chapter 5

CodePeer – Beyond Bug-finding with Static Analysis

CodePeer is a source code static analyzer, a software tool that analyzes source code written in a specific programming language (Ada here) and computes properties of this source code without executing it. CodePeer occupies an interesting position, halfway between the traditional focuses of source code static analyzers, namely static checking and code understanding.

After discussing this positioning and the original techniques that make it possible, we provide a quick tour of CodePeer capabilities in finding various kinds of errors and in computing and displaying properties that are of interest to the user. In the last part, we detail CodePeer's inner workings, going through each phase of the analysis and illustrating the techniques on a small code example. CodePeer is the result of an active collaboration between SofCheck[1] and AdaCore[2].

5.1. Positioning of CodePeer

5.1.1. *Mixing static checking and code understanding*

Like static checkers, CodePeer issues warnings when it detects possible run-time errors. More generally, however, it aims to find functional errors by computing non-

Chapter written by Steve BAIRD, Arnaud CHARLET, Yannick MOY and Tucker TAFT.
1 www.sofcheck.com.
2 www.adacore.com.

trivial properties of the code and relying on a user to check that they match the expected behavior.

A simple example demonstrates this principle well. Suppose you have a procedure that computes the standard deviation over a set of data. Due to a bug, this procedure can return the value -1 in some cases. Mathematics tells you that this is incorrect, as a standard deviation should always be positive. An easy bug to detect, you would say, but a static analyzer has no way of telling that the procedure was intended to compute a standard deviation (even if the procedure is called "standard_deviation"!). Hence, a static analyzer will not issue a warning unless it can detect a problem in the caller of this procedure due to the use of the erroneous negative value. In contrast, while doing this propagation of values in the callers, CodePeer will also generate a readable annotation expressing that the procedure may return -1. If a user sees this annotation as part of a code review, he or she will easily diagnose a bug. Alternatively, if CodePeer generates an annotation that the procedure always returns a non-negative value, the reviewer will easily be able to check this is correct and move on with his or her code review.

This interplay between static analysis and code review is not new. A user has always been required to inspect the warnings issued by a static checker and to fix the program when there is an actual error, which amounts to a special case of code review. This has led to the formalization of rules for static analysis as part of the code review process, such as those that Brian Chess and Jacob West from Fortify Software discuss in their book on static analysis [CHE 03]. They consider warnings issued by static analysis tools to be clues that a non-trivial safety or security argument has to be made by a human reviewer, based on the fact that "static analysis tools often report a problem when they become confused in the vicinity of a sensitive operation". CodePeer aims to provide greater support for static analysis as part of the code review process by generating useful, user-readable information about the program that a user can then exploit.

The simplest code-understanding capabilities that are needed for code review are the requirement to be able to navigate and visualize program dependencies, whether they are dependencies between procedures (call-graph) or dependencies between data (def-use chains). CodePeer is integrated in various integrated development environments (IDEs) that already provide these features. Thus, CodePeer focuses on deeper code understanding capabilities provided by static analysis, which are inherently related to its static checking capabilities.

In general, the idea of static checking is to determine the correctness of a procedure, P, in a program, starting with the knowledge that it is intended to compute a mathematical function f. So the goal is that for any input x given to P, it should return $P(x) = f(x)$. Attempting to prove that $P = f$ over the entire domain of P

is only feasible for trivial programs, not least because most real-world procedures are "partial functions" – that is, they are not defined on certain inputs. For comparison, a "total function" is one that is defined and gives a well-defined output for any valid input. For example, function $g(x) = x > 2$ is a total function because it is defined for all x. Even implementing something as simple as $g(x)$ as a "real-world" programming-language procedure will generally result in a partial function. This is because it will not perform correctly when x is outside a particular range, as determined by the representation of x.

Most programming-language operations are partial functions. The process of building useful real-world software is then the challenge of building a reliable program out of partial functions. In order to help build reliable real-world programs, CodePeer focuses on showing that the partial function corresponding to each programming-language operation never receives input from outside its domain of applicability, rather than attempting to completely prove the correctness of the entire program. If it is shown that no operation making up a program will ever receive input outside its domain of applicability, then the outputs produced are more predictable from the inputs and a smaller number of points in the input domain need actually be tested for correctness, since the results from the remaining inputs can more reasonably be interpolated.

CodePeer's solution to this problem is to compute a contract or summary for each procedure of the program, which is a safe approximation of the partial function implemented by the program procedure. This contract is propagated to the caller of a procedure during the analysis, which leads to the generation of warnings when possible violations of the contract are detected, and it is displayed to a user to help with code review. A contract consists of inputs and outputs, object allocations and memory management, pre- and post-conditions, external calls and associated presumptions, test coverage and software test vectors, all of which are detailed in section 5.2.

5.1.2. Generating contracts by abstract interpretation

Static checking grew out of theorem proving, which required a formal specification of the goal outputs of a software component as a function of its inputs. Such a formal specification can be hard to create. One possible simplification, instead of checking that a procedure does exactly what it is supposed to do, is to check that it does nothing that is obviously incorrect. For example, we want it to check that there are no buffer overflows (indexing an array out of its bounds), null pointer dereferences, numeric overflow (using a number that is too large for its available number of bits so it "overflows" or "wraps around" into a different number), etc. Even with such simplifications, however, existing static-checking algorithms may be cumbersome to use and might not easily lend themselves to automation.

An alternative to theorem-proving-like methods is the model-checking approach that grew out of hardware testing. In model checking, a finite-state model of a program is created and an exhaustive state search is performed to prove that no requirements are violated. While such an approach is well suited to use on hardware, it may be problematic with respect to software because there are so many more states. For example, a standard memory cell is 32 bits, which in itself allows for 4 billion distinct states. Similar to theorem proving, the model-checking approach requires explicit statements of requirements.

While heavyweight formal methods have shown much promise in academia, they are not as frequently used in industrial software projects due to some of the issues discussed above and other problems that appear when applying formal mathematical approaches to real-world programs. Static checking can verify the absence of errors in a program, but often requires written annotations or specifications, which can be hard to produce. As a result, static checking can be difficult to use effectively because it may be difficult to determine a specification and tedious to annotate programs.

These difficulties with heavyweight formal methods, even when applied to specific properties like run-time errors, have led to the rise of lightweight formal methods based on abstract interpretation, in which automation is paramount. Abstract interpretation is a theory of abstractions of programs that comes from earlier work on data-flow techniques. Tools such as CodePeer, which are based on abstract interpretation, compute an abstraction of the program that makes it possible to compute efficient approximations of the desired program properties.

The focus on generating contracts that are both machine-readable and human-readable in CodePeer led to an original architecture that is halfway between static checkers focused on bug-finding and those focused on verification of the absence of run-time errors.

Static checkers focused on verification of the absence of run-time errors, exemplified by tools like PolySpace[®]'s Verifier[3] or AbsInt's Astrée[4], typically work in a top-down manner by iterating along the call-graph. They compute a safe approximation of the state at every program point, starting from the state where nothing is known at the program entry point.

---

3 www.mathworks.com/products/polyspace/.
4 www.absint.com/astree/.

Static checkers focused on bug-finding, exemplified by tools such as Coverity's Prevent[5] and Microsoft's PREfix, typically work bottom-up by iterating along the call-graph. They compute path summaries that approximate the effect of following certain paths during the execution of a procedure. These path summaries are propagated from callees to callers in the call-graph, so that they represent specific paths across procedure calls.

Tools that compute a safe approximation issue a warning when the approximation computed contains erroneous states (e.g. a state where a divisor is null). Tools that compute path summaries issue a warning when a path summary leads to an error (e.g. a division by zero). Thus, the former inherently suffer from false alarms (a.k.a. "false positives") where the tool issues a warning while the code is correct; while the latter suffer from the opposite – absence of guarantees (a.k.a. "false negatives"), where the tool does not issue a warning while the code is incorrect. In practice, all tools suffer from "false positives", which they tame by ranking the warnings according to severity and likelihood. Warnings that are both more serious and more likely to be genuine errors are presented to the user first.

Both kinds of tools seldom present additional information to the user, for different reasons:

– Verifiers compute a lot of information in the form of state invariants, which they can display as conjunctions of formulas relating variables of the program that hold at specific program points, but this raw information is hardly user-readable.

– Bug-finders compute information that is only valid on some selected paths, which is much less useful than information that is valid for all paths.

CodePeer strives to compute user-readable information by computing a safe approximation of the state at every program point, like verifiers, in the bottom-up propagation mode of bug-finders, leading to the generation of procedure summaries correctly approximating the execution along all paths in a procedure. Section 5.3 provides an in-depth look at the specific techniques used in CodePeer.

A major benefit of the bottom-up approach taken in CodePeer is that it works on partially complete programs. There is no need for a driver that gives a calling context to each procedure analyzed, whether manually written or automatically generated. This compiler-like approach also gives scalability, as the analysis of callers relies on the much simpler generated procedure contracts instead of the complete procedure code. Of course, iterations are still needed to reach a safe approximation of procedure summaries for mutually recursive procedures. The bottom-up approach also allows partitioning the original program so that each

---

5 www.coverity.com/products/static-analysis.html.

partition is analyzed separately in a different thread of control. This exploits multicore CPUs for efficiency and allows performance tuning based on the memory and speed of a developer's machine.

5.2. A tour of CodePeer capabilities

5.2.1. Find defects in code

One of the main uses of CodePeer is to find potential defects in source code. CodePeer uses static analysis to track the possible run-time values of all variables, parameters, and record components at each point in the source code. Using this information, it identifies conditions under which an Ada run-time check might fail (null pointer, array out of bounds, etc.), an exception might be raised, a user-written assertion might fail, or a numeric calculation might overflow or wraparound. In addition, CodePeer also detects logic errors or potential inconsistencies in the source code and race conditions in multi-threaded applications.

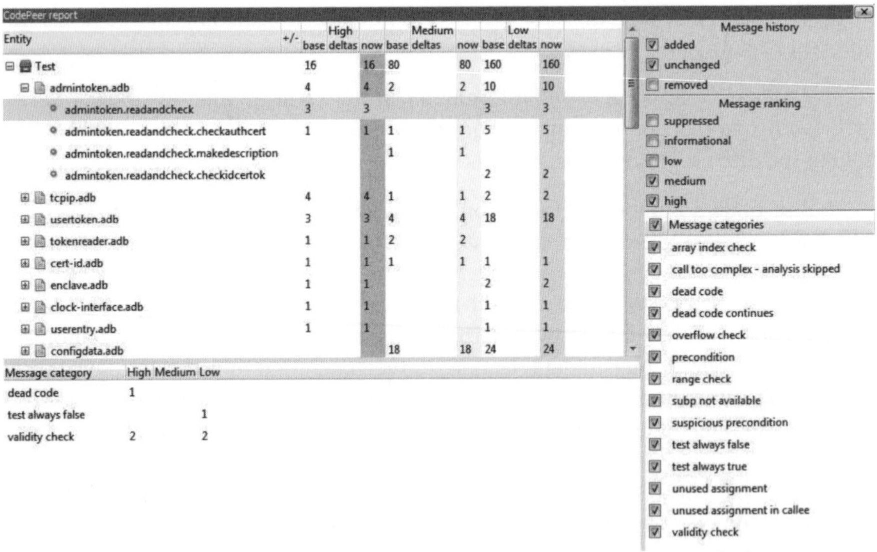

CodePeer report

Entity	+/-	High base	deltas	now	Medium base	deltas	now	Low base	deltas	now
⊟ Test		16		16	80		80	160		160
⊟ admintoken.adb		4		4	2		2	10		10
○ admintoken.readandcheck		3		3				3		3
○ admintoken.readandcheck.checkauthcert		1		1	1		1	5		5
○ admintoken.readandcheck.makedescription					1		1			
○ admintoken.readandcheck.checkidcertok								2		2
⊞ tcpip.adb		4		4	1		1	2		2
⊞ usertoken.adb		3		3	4		4	18		18
⊞ tokenreader.adb		1		1	2		2			
⊞ cert-id.adb		1		1	1		1	1		1
⊞ enclave.adb		1		1				2		2
⊞ clock-interface.adb		1		1				1		1
⊞ userentry.adb		1		1				1		1
⊞ configdata.adb					18		18	24		24

Message category	High	Medium	Low
dead code	1		
test always false		1	
validity check	2	2	

Message history
- ✓ added
- ✓ unchanged
- ☐ removed

Message ranking
- ☐ suppressed
- ☐ informational
- ☐ low
- ✓ medium
- ✓ high

✓ Message categories
- ✓ array index check
- ✓ call too complex - analysis skipped
- ✓ dead code
- ✓ dead code continues
- ✓ overflow check
- ✓ precondition
- ✓ range check
- ✓ subp not available
- ✓ suspicious precondition
- ✓ test always false
- ✓ test always true
- ✓ unused assignment
- ✓ unused assignment in callee
- ✓ validity check

Figure 5.1. *The CodePeer report window details all warnings generated by CodePeer, classified according to ranking and source file.*

The messages produced by CodePeer indicate particular lines of source code that could cause a crash, questionable behavior at run time, or suspicious coding. The kind of check as well as the run-time expression that might not be satisfied (or that

CodePeer is not able to prove statically) is given (such as *array index check might fail: requires i in 1..10*), along with a ranking corresponding to a rough indication (based on heuristics) taking into account both the severity (likelihood that this message identifies a defect that could lead to incorrect results during execution), and the certainty of the message.

5.2.1.1. *Run-time errors*

An important area of CodePeer analysis is the static detection of failures, required by Ada. These are usually only detected at run-time, and only with sufficient testing. In other words, CodePeer will flag all constructs that will or might raise an exception at run-time, such as a null pointer dereference, an array indexing out of bounds, a division by zero, an integer overflow, etc. All Ada run-time checks are exhaustively verified by CodePeer, which also means that if no such messages are generated, it gives a greater confidence in the code. The checks are implicit to Ada, so do not appear explicitly in the source code.

5.2.1.2. *User checks*

Unlike run-time checks, user checks are explicit tests manually introduced in the code that are recognized as such by CodePeer. CodePeer performs the same kind of analysis on these as it does for run-time checks. These are tests of the form:

```
if <condition> then

raise exception;

end if;
```

for which CodePeer attempts to prove that the specified condition cannot occur. Debugging assertions, taking the form of pragma Assert in Aa, are also treated this way.

Note that CodePeer takes the view that an exception should only be raised under exceptional/unexpected situations, and not as normal mode of operation in the application. If the source code does not follow this coding standard, then it is still possible to selectively ignore some or all messages related to user checks emitted by CodePeer.

5.2.1.3. *Uninitialized and invalid variables*

CodePeer attempts to detect as many cases of access to an uninitialized or invalid variable as possible by keeping track of the state of objects. At any point in the code CodePeer computes whether an object or a particular field is known to be initialized, or may be accessed on some path without prior initialization.

5.2.1.4. *Logic errors/warnings*

In addition to run-time checks, CodePeer also attempts to detect many cases of logic errors, which often point to suspicious/possibly incorrect code. Unlike check-related messages, these messages do not always point to a real error if the message is correct. These messages are based on heuristics and hence not meant to be exhaustive. The logic errors are flagged by CodePeer as "warnings" and are classified in several categories, such as dead code (code is determined to be unreachable). Conversely, a test is determined to always be true, and therefore redundant/suspicious. Unused, as well as redundant, assignments (i.e. assignments that have no effect) are also flagged in various contexts, as well as other kinds of suspicious coding.

These messages are computed using the precise understanding of the code produced by CodePeer and new kinds of warnings are regularly added.

5.2.1.5. *Race conditions*

CodePeer detects common forms of race conditions. A race condition might exist if there are two or more concurrent tasks that attempt to access the same object and at least one of them is performing an update. For example, if a *Reader* task makes a copy of a *List* object at the same time that a *Writer* task is modifying the *List* object, the copy of the *List* object may be corrupted. CodePeer identifies race conditions where synchronization (particularly an Ada built-in synchronization construct) is not used or is used incorrectly.

A lock is held during any protected subprogram or protected entry call. Any variable that can be simultaneously accessed by more than one referencing task must be locked at every reference to guard against race conditions. Furthermore, the referencing lock should match the lock used by other tasks to prevent updates during access. If locking is absent, or if one reference uses a different lock to another reference, CodePeer identifies a possible race condition. Note that the identification of a race condition is not guaranteed to create problems on every execution, but it might cause a problem, depending on specific run-time circumstances.

5.2.2. *Using annotations for code reviews*

Whether it is a formal team process or an *ad hoc*, one-person activity, manually reviewing source code is a good way to identify problems early in the development cycle. Unfortunately, it can also be quite time consuming, especially when the reviewer is not the author of the code. CodePeer reduces the effort required to understand source code by characterizing the input requirements and the net effect of each component of the code base. Specifically, CodePeer determines pre- and post-conditions for every Ada subprogram it analyzes. It also makes presumptions about external subprograms it calls whose source code is not available for analysis. CodePeer displays the preconditions, presumptions, and post-conditions associated with each subprogram in a human readable form.

```
1  with Math; use Math;
2

   --
   --   Subprogram: example
   --
   --   Preconditions:
   --      X/Y in -2**31..2**31-1
   --      Y /= 0
   --
   --   Postconditions:
   --      example'Result'Initialized
   --
   --
   --   Subprogram: example'Elab_Subp_Body
   --
   --
   --   Subprogram: example'Elab_Subp_Spec
   --
3  function Example (X, Y : Integer) return Integer is
4    A, B : Integer;
5  begin
6    A := X / Y;
7    B := Sqrt (A);
8    if B > Y then
9       B := 10;
10   end if;
11   return A + B;
12 end Example;
```

Figure 5.2. *Pre-conditions and post-conditions generated by CodePeer in a simple example*

The pre-conditions displayed by CodePeer are implicit requirements that are imposed on the inputs to a subprogram, as determined by analyzing the algorithms used within the subprogram. Violating preconditions might cause the subprogram to fail or to give meaningless results. During code review, the reviewer can verify that the preconditions determined by CodePeer for the code as written are appropriate and meet the underlying requirements for the subprogram.

Early in a development cycle, system documentation might be missing or incomplete. Since CodePeer generates pre-conditions for each module without requiring that the entire enclosing system be available, it can be used before system integration to gain an understanding of subprograms as they are developed. In a mature, maintained codebase, the system documentation might no longer agree with current code's behavior. In either case, CodePeer's generated pre-conditions can be used to verify both the written and unwritten assumptions made by the code writers.

Presumptions represent assumptions made by CodePeer about the results of a call on a subprogram whose code is unavailable for analysis. A separate presumption is made for each call site in the unanalyzed subprogram. Presumptions do not generally affect the pre-conditions of the calling routine, but they might influence post-conditions of the calling routine. These presumptions also allow CodePeer to perform partial analyses, even in the absence of a third-party library or, conversely, allow analysis of a library without necessarily knowing how this library will be used.

Post-conditions are characteristics of the output that a subprogram could produce, presuming its pre-conditions are satisfied and the presumptions made about unanalyzed calls are appropriate. Post-conditions can help a reviewer understand the purpose and effect of code, even in the absence of other documentation. Likewise, post-conditions can be helpful to software developers making use of a subprogram. Comparing post-conditions to either pre-conditions or the context of calling routines can provide a valuable insight into the workings of the code that might not be obvious from a solely manual review.

These annotations, as well as metrics generated by CodePeer such as the number of checks performed and the number of checks passed automatically, can help determine the quality of third-party source code that are sometimes delivered without sufficient documentation or testing.

5.2.3. *Categorization of messages*

CodePeer makes conservative assumptions in order to avoid missing potential problems. These assumptions mean that CodePeer might generate messages that a programmer would decide are not true problems or are problems that would not occur during normal execution of the program. For example, a given numeric overflow might only occur if the program ran continuously for decades. Messages that are not true problems are called false positives.

To help deal with false positives, CodePeer categorizes messages into three levels of ranking, according to the potential severity of the problem and the likelihood that the message corresponds to a real problem. For example, a divide by zero error that it is determined will always occur when the code is executed will be categorized as *high*. An array index check that cannot be proven to be within bounds in all paths might be categorized as *medium*. An overflow that only occurs near the limits of the maximum long integer value might be categorized as *low*, especially if there are intermediate exit points in the loop that would prevent the overflow. These levels are based on heuristics that can be different on different applications, so it is possible for the user to modify these heuristics via an XML configuration file.

In addition to message ranking, CodePeer uses an historical database to keep track of the different analyses performed and to determine which messages are old, new or no longer appear. This capability allows the user to perform an initial analysis of an existing codebase and then use it as a known baseline without necessarily analyzing each message separately. The user can then concentrate on changes in messages relative to this baseline when making changes to the source code, in order to focus on new defects.

5.2.4. *Help writing run-time tests*

As part of the control and data flow analysis of each subprogram, CodePeer identifies which Boolean conditions in a subprogram control the flow of executions. It propagates these conditions backwards to the start of the subprogram as sets of values of individual variables or fields and generates the results as test vectors in textual form, for example:

```
X: {-2_147_483_648..-1, 1..2_147_483_647}, 0

Argument: [+0..+0], (+0..+Inf)

P.Q.S: Out_of_Place, In_Place
```

Here, passing in a value of 0 for 32-bit integer X will force the execution to follow a different path than passing a non-null value for X. This is also the case for floating-point value Argument with value 0.0 vs. non-null value, and field P.Q.S with value Out_of_Place vs. value In_Place.

CodePeer's ability to generate test vectors is not limited to values of memory locations (variables, fields, etc.). It can also generate test vectors based on the values of comparisons, arithmetic operations and Boolean combinations of these, as in:

```
X = Y: false, true.
```

Here, having the same value for X and Y in the parameter will force the execution to follow a different path than when the values for X and Y are different.

The test vector report can help a project achieve higher coverage in run-time functionality tests to complement the full coverage static error detection tests provided by CodePeer.

5.2.5. *Different kinds of output*

CodePeer can be run interactively via an integrated development environment (IDE) as well as in batch mode for integration in scripts that can be run, for example, each night or after each entry in a repository.

CodePeer's results are stored in an historical database, and from this database different kinds of output are generated: text listings that can be incorporated in documents, HTML pages that can be viewed using any web browser, and interactive visualization in an IDE where the source code can be reviewed and modified at the same time.

5.3. CodePeer's inner working

5.3.1. *Overview*

CodePeer's technical core is an intraprocedural bidirectional abstract interpreter inside an interprocedural data-flow analyzer. At the level of an individual procedure, CodePeer computes a safe approximation of the state at each point in the procedure body. This analysis is intraprocedural because it does not involve re-analyzing the procedures called, but instead relies on procedure summaries for procedure calls. This analysis is bidirectional because it repeatedly steps forward and backward through the set of instructions. This analysis is an abstract interpretation because it computes a safe approximation of the possible values for variables and expressions at each program point. It produces a procedure summary to be used in callers. At the outer level, CodePeer iterates its flow analysis on the call-graph of the program until the results converge. This is a data-flow analysis, propagating changes in procedure summaries from callees to callers.

This core, called possible value propagation (PVP), is the third phase of a three-phase process. The first phase is object identification (ObjID) and the second phase is static single assignment and global value numbering (SSA/GVN). Both ObjID and SSA/GVN are interprocedural data-flow analyses that iterate an intraprocedural analysis over a single procedure from callees to callers until convergence.

The ObjID phase involves identifying objects and any potential aliasing between them. This phase identifies all objects inside the procedure and tries to discover the basic relationships between them. During the SSA/GVN phase, "static single assignment" (i.e. tagging every variable reference and introducing additional "pseudo" assignments so that each distinctly-tagged variable has exactly one assignment) and global value numbering (assigning value numbers to each use of a variable and each programming-language expression) are performed. One of the main goals of this phase is to identify and record relationships between different value numbers. Then, value sets associated with each value number, and in turn each reference to a variable, are further refined in the PVP phase. These narrowed value sets may then be used in determining pre-conditions and post-conditions for each procedure. Finally, a user-readable procedure contract (inputs, outputs, pre-conditions, post-conditions, etc.) is derived from each procedure summary, and warnings that would be meaningful to a programmer are generated for possible violations of the contracts and run-time errors.

CodePeer builds on well-known techniques originally used for optimizing the object code generated by compilers and later adapted for static checkers. A large portion of the work carried out on CodePeer was tuning and targeting these techniques with the specific goal of producing machine-readable and user-readable procedure summaries.

The first well-researched area that required adaptation was that of aliasing analyses [HIN 01]. The aim was to determine the possible aliasing between pointers in the program. Extensive academic literature and research papers covering aliasing analyses have been published, although not much has been adopted in compilers and static checkers.

CodePeer performs a local flow-insensitive aliasing analysis in the ObjID phase. This is as much a point-to alias analysis, identifying the objects pointed to by pointers, as it is a may-alias analysis identifying pairs of pointers that may be aliased. The results of this analysis are exploited in the SSA/GVN phase to define value numbers that distinguish the values obtained, depending on the actual aliasing. Finally, the flow-sensitive PVP phase tracks down value sets of all value numbers, including those of pointer type. This is used to refine the value sets of all value numbers.

The second well-researched area where CodePeer has shown some original solutions is that of abstract domains. These define the kinds of relationships that exist between variables that are tracked. Historically, abstract domains are layered by cost and power in non-relational abstract domains that track the value of individual variables, and relational abstract domains that track the relations between pairs or sets of variables. In CodePeer, relations between variables are rewritten as subtractions defining new variables, so that both values of individual variables and relations between variables are tracked in the same abstract domain. This choice allows efficient tracking of values for complex relations between variables that appear in the source program, at the cost of ignoring relations that do not appear in the source program.

Special handling of loops and inductive variables modified in loops introduces some relations that are not present in the source program. For example, in a loop over index I, if variable J is incremented twice at each execution of the loop, CodePeer will correctly infer that $J = 2*I$. The general focus on relations which appear in the source program is reminiscent of predicate abstraction, except that CodePeer not only tracks the value of Boolean predicates, but the range of values of expressions of integer or real type.

The third well-researched area where CodePeer improves on standard practice is that of disjunctive abstract domains, i.e. how alternative values are handled. Most abstract domains used in practice are expressible as conjunctions of atomic formulas, not as disjunctions because disjunctions are much more costly to work with. The base abstract domain used in CodePeer is a disjunctive set of interval values of integer or real type. This domain is used to track both the values of variables and the relations between variables, as seen above. Thus, CodePeer can easily express that "$X - Y = 2$ or ($X - Y > = 4$ and $X - Y < = 7$)" as "$X - Y$ in {2,4..7}". Additionally, CodePeer defines various kinds of value numbers that are precisely tuned to track alternative values, like the ϕ-nodes (pronounced *phi-nodes*, which are common to all static single assignment forms [STA 07]) and κ-nodes (pronounced *kappa-nodes*, which are similar to the γ-nodes of gated single assignment [OTT 90]) described in section 5.3.4. With these special value numbers, CodePeer can express disjunctive properties such as "if $X > 0$ then $Y = X - 3$ else $Y = 0$" that do not fit well in the traditional approach.

Lastly, CodePeer is especially careful in its treatment of calls to unknown procedures, in order to maximize precision while avoiding false alarms. Like most static analyzers, CodePeer allows the analysis of incomplete code, where some procedures are specified but not defined. Calls to such unknown procedures must be stubbed in a way that avoids false alarms, which are typical of stubs that are too shallow (e.g., no-op stub), and degrading precision, which is typical of stubs that are too heavy (e.g., make everything random at each unknown call). Instead, CodePeer carefully selects which objects may have been assigned by a call to an unknown procedure so that objects whose value is known with some precision previous to the call are not modified by the call.

In section 5.3.2, we start with the rationale and challenges involved in translating a source program in a complex programming language such as Ada into a simpler program in an intermediate language called SCIL. In sections 5.3.3, 5.3.4 and 5.3.5, we describe the intraprocedural analysis used in the ObjID, SSA/GVN and PVP phases, respectively. Part of the material presented in this section is subject to a patent application in the United States.

5.3.2. *From Ada to SCIL*

The front end of the GNAT Ada compiler generates an annotated abstract syntax tree. CodePeer's analysis phase expects its input to be represented in SCIL. Thus, a translation step is needed. This translation, performed by a tool called gnat2scil, is similar in many ways to a compiler's generation of a source-language-independent intermediate representation for use as input to code-generating at the back end, but there are interesting differences.

A SCIL program is made up of a collection of modules. Typically, an Ada compilation unit is associated with a single SCIL file containing a single module (a SCIL file, in some sense, plays the role of an object file in a traditional compilation system).

A module may contain declarations of types, objects and procedure bodies. A procedure body may contain the same kinds of declarations and also has an associated statement list. Declarations are static; all "interesting" execution occurs within a statement list. All control flow happens at the statement level (as opposed to within expressions). To generate such code, the translation relies on the compiler choices when disambiguating expressions. For example, the Ada standard does not force a specific order of evaluation between arguments to a call, or between operands of a binary operation. Two different choices may lead to two different executions due to possible side-effects during calls. By making the same choices in the compiler and the analyzer, we can be sure that the code run is the one that is analyzed.

A subprogram's statement list in SCIL consists of a set of basic blocks with two distinguished members: the entry block and the exit block. A basic block consists of a sequence of simple statements (calls, assignments, and checks) followed by a jump, so it can only be entered at one point and only be left at one point – the jump instruction. A jump has a jump-expression of numeric type, an ordered sequence of (statically known, pair-wise disjoint, comprehensive union) sets of numbers, and an ordered sequence of successor basic blocks (basic blocks of the same enclosing subprogram). Typically, the two sequences are of the same length. For the execution of a jump, the expression is evaluated; its value will belong to exactly one of the sets of numbers. If it is the Nth such set, then the Nth basic block on the successor list is executed next.

We may speak informally (as in the preceding section) of the "execution" of a SCIL construct (for example, a subprogram call or an expression's evaluation), but what this really refers to is the dynamic semantics of the program being analyzed. There is no SCIL interpreter (although one could theoretically be written); SCIL is analyzed, not executed.

Supported types in SCIL include scalars, records, arrays, pointers and subprogram types. A SCIL array is always boundless (that is to say infinite) and one-dimensional. It can be thought of as a mapping from mathematical integers to the element type. Ada array objects have bounds, so an Ada array type is usually mapped to a SCIL record type containing as components both bounds information and a SCIL array. Ada multi-dimensional arrays are mapped to arrays of arrays. Variant records (the Ada construct for discriminated unions) are flattened, but appropriate checks are generated when a variant component is accessed. Record extensions make use of SCIL support to identify corresponding components in two different record types.

Ada defines many constructs that may raise an exception at run time. Array indices may be out of range, a de-referenced pointer may be null, the source of an assignment may fail to satisfy the constraints of the target, an arithmetic expression may overflow; the complete list is extensive. For each of these run-time checks, corresponding check nodes are generated in the SCIL, whether explicitly by the front-end of the compiler or implicitly by CodePeer, which has some built-in checks by default such as divide-by-zero and range checks. Additionally, CodePeer generates nodes to check that no uninitialized value is read.

These provide the implicit specification that CodePeer tries to verify. If CodePeer cannot conclude that a given run-time check is guaranteed to succeed, then that fact is communicated to the user. Because Ada defines a very rich and precise set of run-time checks, CodePeer has a very rich and precise implicit specification to work with in analyzing the SCIL generated for an Ada program. Thus, the user is not required to provide any additional explicit specification; this point is particularly important when analyzing legacy code.

The mapping chosen to represent dynamic calls (those subprogram calls where the subprogram being called is not known statically) can affect the amount of information that is available to the analysis phase. It is often useful if CodePeer can infer a fixed set of possible subprograms that a given call might invoke. It might be useful to know, for example, that every subprogram in this set leaves some particular global variable unmodified.

The value of an Ada access-to-subprogram type is represented as an index into an array of SCIL access-to-subprogram pointers. Thus, the contents of this array represent the universe of subprograms potentially designated by a value of this type. At the point of the Ada-type declaration, the array is declared. The index for a given subprogram is based on a collision-free hash of the name of the subprogram. If a given subprogram is used to construct a value of the access-to-subprogram type (for example, via Ada's "Access attribute"), then SCIL is generated to initialize the corresponding element of the array. CodePeer can then see the complete set of all such initializations.

In cases like these, where the representation chosen by gnat2scil diverges substantially from that assumed by the GNAT front end, the complexity of the translation process increases. This is particularly true in the case of tagged types (Ada's "classes"). Dispatching calls to primitive operations of tagged types (Ada's "virtual methods") are handled by generalizing the approach used for access-to-subprogram types. This translation is far from being optimal from an execution point of view. The GNAT compiler creates objects based on pointers to allow quick access to the dispatching function, while CodePeer's analysis is facilitated by using indices and arrays.

5.3.3. *Object identification*

This phase identifies all objects inside the procedure and tries to discover basic relationships between them. These relationships may be used later in restricting the possible object value sets, which, in turn, are used to generate pre- and post-conditions.

An object is a nameable data element whose state/value can be changed (variable, array, record, etc.). A part of an object is also considered an object itself. Determining aliasing of objects involves the identification of whether two distinct object references might refer to the same physical object at run-time. For example, pointer dereference A.X may refer to the same object as pointer dereference B.X if pointer B happens to point to the same object as pointer A. This phase also includes some object value tracking, in a largely flow-insensitive way, to identify the overall range of values for array indices and the possible targets of pointer objects.

The ObjID phase starts with the identification (ID) of all objects. Objects may be elementary – those that do not consist of other objects – or composite. It is important to identify all objects, even those with static values, in order to precisely determine their value sets later. Object IDs are stored in an object ID table that also records such information as enclosing objects or subobjects (if the object is composite); whether it is a new object that will be returned to the caller, the type of object, etc.

Precision is very important in determining aliasing, which takes place after object ID creation. Two references might appear to refer to the same object, but in fact refer to two different ones. For example, array element reference A(I) at line 10 might appear to refer to the same object as the A(I) at line 12 and yet it would not be the same if, for example, line 11 was a statement similar to the following: $I: = I + 1$. On the other hand, some object references that look very different at first sight might, in fact, refer to the same objects at run-time. For example A(I) might refer to the same object as $B(J - 1)$ if A and B refer to the same array object and, earlier in the procedure, there was the following statement: $J: = I + 1$. There are also situations where there are multiple possible values for a particular object. Consider, for example: $A(I): = 3$; $A(J): = 4$; $X: = A(I)$. At this point in the program, it is not clear whether X is equal to 3 or 4, depending on whether J was equal to I or not. Therefore, both possible values are recorded at this point for consideration by the later phases.

As demonstrated, aliasing and assigning unique object IDs must be precise in order to be useful. It is important to not alias two objects that cannot be the same in order to avoid false positives. The aliasing information is passed to phases SSA/GVN and PVP for use in assigning global value numbers or narrowing down object value sets.

Caller-relevant objects are identified both before and after aliasing. A caller-relevant object is one that is "visible" to the caller as it is either received from the calling procedure as part of its input or returned to it as part of its output. Inputs and outputs include both parameters to the procedure and global objects. The possible value sets corresponding to the initial value of an input, or the final value of an output, can be directly converted into the pre-conditions and post-conditions.

"Conservative" object value sets can then be determined, both by being partially conscious of the program flow and following various paths to determine all possible values for the objects and by examining different statements independently of flow. Reconsider the example: $A(I): = 3$; $A(J): = 4$; $X: = A(I)$. In this example, the conservative value set for X might include both 3 and 4 and any other values it might take during the program. If the statement $I: = J$; preceded assignment to X, it would be possible to restrict the possible value set of X to 4. The paths taken to reach a particular value are kept as annotations on the objects and are used by other phases to further narrow the value sets.

When tracking values of objects in the ObjID phase, it is advantageous to distinguish values assigned within the procedure to a caller-relevant object from those assigned prior to the procedure being called. Although this distinction is not directly useful for references made to caller-relevant objects within the procedure, the distinction is useful to the calling procedure, since it generally more precisely knows the values assigned prior to the call. The calling procedure can combine its more accurate information on values assigned prior to the call with the "new values" assigned within the procedure called, to produce an overall value set for the object that has greater accuracy. The objects modified during a call include those directly modified by the callee (Directly MODifable objects (DMOD) in [BAN 79]) and their possible aliases in the context of the caller.

The ObjID phase iterates, if necessary, over the statements within a particular procedure body. Generally, it only needs to iterate over multiple procedures if there is recursion, assuming that the sub-procedures are processed before those that call them. When performing iteration over multiple procedures, each procedure is fully processed before CodePeer moves on to the next procedure. So there might therefore be iteration within the single procedure (in order to perform aliasing and to perform object value tracking) and outside the single procedure.

5.3.4. *Static single assignment and global value numbering*

This phase includes the performance of "static single assignment" (i.e. tagging every variable reference and introducing additional "pseudo" assignments so that each distinctly tagged variable has exactly one assignment) and performing global value numbering (assigning value numbers to each use of a variable and each programming-language expression). One of the main goals of this phase is to identify and record relationships between different value numbers. These relationships are used in value-set propagation in the PVP phase. The relationships between the value numbers are important in tracking possible value sets. A value set of a particular value number may be restricted not just at the point of its definition, but also whenever it is used in the program. By tracking the relationships between the value numbers, it is possible to identify where and how the value set of a particular value number may be affected by changes to value sets of other value numbers. As value numbers are associated with each reference to a variable, the value sets of value numbers can be used directly in computing pre-conditions and post-conditions and in identifying errors in the procedure.

Static single assignment is a technique that converts a program or an individual procedure into one where there is exactly one assignment for each distinctly tagged variable. Such a conversion may be done by "tagging" variables at different assignment points, so that each distinctly tagged variable has only one associated assignment. For example, let us consider the following program:

```
function Example (X, Y: Integer) return Integer is:
   A, B: Integer;
begin:
```

```
A: = X / Y;
B: = Sqrt (A);
if B > Y then:
  B: = 10;
end if;
return A + B;
end Example.
```

The SSA phase will assign different "tags" to variable B in the two assignment statements, as shown in lines 2 and 4 below. The whole procedure is represented internally as follows (the meaning of the ϕ-node is explained later):

```
A₁: = X₁ / Y₁;
B₁: = Sqrt (A₁);
if B₁ > Y₁ then:
  B₂: = 10;
end if;
B₃: = φ(B₁,B₂);
return A₁ + B₃.
```

Having made sure that there is at most one assignment for each distinctly tagged variable, CodePeer can proceed to assign value numbers to all variable values. A value number is an arbitrary identifier. It does not matter what actual value number is used for a particular reference, as long as that value number always uniquely identifies that value. For example, in the program above the value number assignment may proceed as follows:

Expression	X_1	Y_1	A_1	B_1	$B_1 - Y_1$	10	B_2	B_3	$A_1 + B_3$
Value Number	VN1	VN2	VN3	VN4	VN5	VN6	VN6	VN7	VN8

Table 5.1. *Mapping of expressions to value numbers*

It should be noted that there are usually fewer value numbers than there are distinctly tagged variables and multiple expressions may share the same value number. If two expressions have the same value number, they are definitely the same, because static single assignment guarantees that no more than one assignment is made to each tagged variable and value numbers are assigned to individual (tagged) variables and expressions. Therefore, no expression to which a value number is assigned changes throughout the program, and if two expressions have the same value number they are guaranteed to be the same throughout the program, no matter which path is or can be taken. Meanwhile, if two expressions have different value numbers they might or might not be different.

While the attempt is made to assign the same value number to all expressions with the same value, in some cases such assignment is not possible statically. For example, expressions (X + Y) and (Z − S) might or might not have the same value at run time, depending on the particular values of variables X, Y, Z, and S. In this case, these two expressions will have different value numbers, although there is a possibility that their values will be the same. However, if, earlier in the program there is an assignment or condition ensuring that X = Z and Y = -S, the value numbers assigned to the two expressions above will be the same, signalling that their values (and, therefore, possible value ranges) are the same, despite the different variables that are involved and the different mathematical operations.

In order to enhance global value numbering, a mathematical operation is converted to a canonical form to increase the likelihood that it will be given the same value number as an equivalent operation encountered earlier. For example, an ordering is assigned to all value numbers, and all commutative operations are rewritten so that the value numbers of which the operation consists are arranged according to the order imposed.

A computation table is used to store relationships between different value numbers. Table 5.2 is a computation table for the short program above.

VN1	VN2	VN3	VN5	VN6	VN7	VN8
Incoming value of X	Incoming value of Y	VN1/V N2	VN4 − VN2	Literal 10	ϕ(VN4,VN6)	VN3 + VN7

Table 5.2. *Computation table*

Value numbers are stored in the first line and the second line gives their relationship to other value numbers. With every statement analyzed, the computation table is updated with relationships between the value numbers encountered in that statement. These relationships will become very useful in computing possible value sets and annotations for procedures.

As discussed above, the relationships are recorded in a canonical form, after mathematical transformations are performed in order to standardize them. For every assignment, value numbers are assigned to each of the expressions and subexpressions that appear on the right-hand side, and then the value number corresponding to the overall right-hand-side expression becomes the new value number associated with the object referenced by the left-hand side. Similarly, information about relationships between value numbers may also be gleaned from jumps, checks, and other statements and are represented in a mathematical notation.

Note how the conditional test B > Y in our example is also recorded in the computation table. Just as with other logic or arithmetic functions, it is rewritten in a canonical format – for example as a subtraction and membership test: B > Y is rewritten as: "B-Y in {1..infinity}".

As far as determining pre- and post-conditions is concerned, the caller-relevant value numbers in the short example are VN1 assigned to X, and VN2 assigned to Y, which are taken as an input, and VN7, which is returned as the output. In addition to this, any value number that is a function of only other caller-relevant value numbers and static values is considered caller relevant. In this example, all the value numbers except VN5 are caller relevant.

In this process, CodePeer detects those statements that do not influence the caller-relevant variables or their constituents in any way. While such statements are superfluous, they are relatively common in real-world programs, where they may easily get lost among hundreds of lines of code and may appear after a particular procedure has gone through a number of changes. CodePeer records and reports such superfluous statements so that the programmer has a chance to remove them from the source code.

Branches and statements are further analyzed to locate those that, while seemingly useful in that they are involved in computation of caller-relevant value numbers, will never be exercised in practice. This is because in order to reach them, some variables need to take on the values that are outside the range allowed by the procedure pre-conditions, or because such values would be impossible in the scope of the program flow. These unexercised blocks and statements may be relics from earlier versions of the program, or they may be real defects that will require program modification. Identifying these blocks can show the programmer some of the underlying program structure that might not be apparent at first glance.

As part of the static single assignment technique, a special construct called a ϕ-node may be used in assigning a value number to a variable like B. A ϕ-node is an indicator that different paths in the program will lead to this value number representing different combinations of other value numbers. For example, it can be said that in the program above, VN7 = ϕ(VN6,VN4), which means that if the program follows the "then" branch, VN6 should be assigned to variable B, otherwise VN4 remains assigned to variable B.

ϕ-nodes may also be annotated with more information about the particular paths leading to them and their basic-block specific information. Collecting and analyzing information about ϕ-nodes, rather than bypassing those ambiguous statements in static analysis, leads to more precise definitions of value-number relationships and, consequently, to more restricted value sets, which is one of the goals of the analysis.

These refined nodes are called κ-nodes in CodePeer, and are also known as γ-nodes in gated single assignment [OTT 90]. In our example, instead of simply recording VN7 = ϕ(VN6,VN4), CodePeer detects that the "then" branch is only taken when VN5 is strictly positive, which can be expressed as a κ-node:

$$VN7 = \kappa(VN5 > 0 => VN6, \text{otherwise} => VN4).$$

Another problem for value numbering relates to the potential aliasing between distinct object references, especially aliasing-related members of data structures such as, for example, the elements of an array or the corresponding components of a tree structure. CodePeer also uses a κ-node to capture this kind of underlying ambiguity and possible relationships. As indicated above, a κ-node records possible value numbers and associated information such as, for example, which conditions would need to hold for one of those value numbers to be the true assignment.

Once the relationships between the value numbers are computed, which might take several passes through the procedure code, in each of those passes the value number relationships being updated at every point of reference, those relationships are used in the PVP phase in computing possible value sets. In addition to the information in the computation table, other information is passed to the PVP phase, such as earlier aliasing or possible value set information for objects from the ObjID phase, or ϕ-node and κ-node annotations from the SSA/GVN phase.

The goal of the PVP phase is to generate annotations (pre- and post-conditions) and error messages. The SSA/GVN phase decides which value numbers represent pre-conditions and post-conditions. The main data structure produced by the PVP phase is a mapping for each basic block in a procedure, from those value numbers to their possible value sets. A possible value set is a set of values that a particular value number may take consistent with the conditional jumps and without causing any run-time faults.

While the ObjID phase is involved in determining some value sets, those value sets are for objects, not for value numbers, as in the PVP phase (although those value sets for objects may, of course, be useful later in determining possible value sets for value numbers). It is important to determine the value number value sets as precisely as possible within the confines of a particular procedure because more precise bounds on the value sets will produce more precise bounds on pre- and post-conditions.

For example, producing a pre-condition that:

X must be in {0..99}

is more informative than just stating that X may be any integer (especially if the true domain for X is only these 100 values). In fact, it would be misleading to indicate a broader range as a pre-condition than is warranted by the program.

5.3.5. *Possible value propagation*

Value sets associated with each value number, and in turn each reference to a variable, are further refined in this phase. These narrowed value sets may then be used in determining pre- and post-conditions for each procedure. Tracking of value sets is performed by iteratively stepping through the procedure to identify all points at which value sets may change, and by "walking" the expressions to affect value sets of their constituents. The expression of "walking" is accomplished by using the relationships identified and recorded in the SSA/GVN phase. In fact, through these relationships, a value set of a particular value number might be affected through an instruction in which it does not even occur, because it might be related to value numbers that are used in that instruction and whose value sets are changed because of it.

The PVP phase runs in two modes: main mode and error-generating mode. In the main mode the static analyzer iterates over the analyzed procedure until possible value number value sets stabilize. Then the error-generating mode is used to generate errors that would be meaningful to a programmer.

As discussed above, generating value sets for value numbers ultimately helps in determining pre- and post-conditions for the procedure. Value sets for value numbers are used instead of value sets for objects because the earlier phases (ObjID and SSA/GVN) have identified the caller-relevant value numbers. When reporting results to the user, these value numbers are converted back into the variables or expressions they represent. Determining and propagating value sets for value numbers, not just for objects, is one of the key concepts of CodePeer.

While the value numbers do not change during the procedure, value sets associated with them may change from statement to statement, because some statements affect what is known about the values that a value number might represent. For example, the statement $A_{VN1} := B_{VN2}/C_{VN3}$ effectively restricts the value set of VN3 because, in order to not generate a run-time fault, VN3 should not be equal to zero. Therefore, mathematical limitations can affect value sets of value numbers. Similarly, restrictions of the programming language and/or programming environment can affect the value sets. For example, in the expression $A_{VN4}(X_{VN5})$, which references the X'th element of array A, VN5 should be in the range of indices allowed for array A. If VN5 will be outside this range, a serious memory problem might occur (in fact, a number of security breaches are based on such "buffer overflow" errors, where the program allows writing outside the memory structure's bounds).

As CodePeer analyzes program statements, value sets of value numbers shrink based on the mathematical and logical constraints of the operations in which they are used. All such restrictions on values allowed for certain operations are in fact present in SCIL code as checks generated during the translation from Ada described in section 5.3.2, or are inherent in the semantics of SCIL itself.

The value sets do not only shrink, they might also grow, for example at the join points of two basic blocks. The value set of a value number under test is restricted for the different branches of the conditional, but at the join point the value set of the value number under test grows back to incorporate all of the branching possibilities.

The growing and shrinking of value sets is accomplished by performing set-wise operations, such as unions, intersections, etc., on the value sets. For example, if the value set for value number VN1 is {0..30, 40..50} at some point in the procedure and then an operation is encountered that restricts the values of VN1 to {-20..30, 45..60} allowed, the value set for VN1 is computed by taking the intersection of these two sets, resulting in the value set of {0..30, 45..50}. In such a way, encountering statements that allow for a broader value set does not actually broaden the value set because the intersection operation limits the domain to the smallest possible set.

Before the value sets may shrink, they need to be initialized to something. Generally, initialization assigns the broadest possible value set for the variable type corresponding to the value number or to a special value representing an invalid set. Providing an explicit invalid value helps detect a common programming error where an uninitialized variable is used in a computation. Uninitialized variables can lead to hard-to-reproduce errors during execution. There are different initialization rules for different kinds of value numbers:

– incoming from outside: initialized to invalid plus all legal values for that variable type;

– local variable: initialized to invalid;

– global constant: the value set is taken from the final value set for the initialization procedure, if one exists;

– computation (i.e. a value number associated with an expression involving a computation) initialized to the result of set-wise arithmetic of value sets corresponding to the value numbers of the operands involved in the computation.

The value numbers that are caller relevant correspond to initial or final values of objects that are somehow visible to the caller. For a given value number, its "exit-block" value set represents those values of the set of all possible values that "survive" until the exit block, without being "filtered out" by a (run-time) check. For a value number that corresponds to the final value of a caller-relevant variable, this exit-block value set represents its "post-condition" – the values that the variable may have after successful completion of the procedure. For a value number that corresponds to the initial value of a caller-relevant variable, it is one of the key concepts of CodePeer that the exit-block value set represents a "pre-condition" on this variable. In other words, if the initial value of the variable falls outside this exit-block (pre-condition) value set, then this initial value will cause some check to fail prior to reaching the exit block.

Additional values might be identified as causing possible failures of checks along some, but not all, paths through the procedure, and these additional values are identified as a "possible failure set" for the value number. If the initial value of a caller-relevant variable falls within the exit-block value set, then there is at least one path where it will not fail a check. If it also falls within the possible failure set, then there is at least one path where it will fail a check. The set difference formed by removing failure set values from the exit-block value set represents a *soft*, as apposed to a *hard*, pre-condition on the initial value of a caller-relevant variable. If the initial value of the caller-relevant variable violates the hard pre-condition, a run-time failure will occur (on every path to the exit block). If the initial value violates the soft precondition, a run-time failure might occur, depending on the path through the procedure.

In addition to identifying exit-block (and possible failure) value sets for value numbers that correspond directly to initial and final values of caller-relevant variables, it is useful to identify such value sets for value numbers that represent combinations of such value numbers. For example, it may be that the difference or sum of two caller-relevant variables is what is being checked, rather than the individual values. In general, any combination of initial and final values can be of interest. If a value number corresponds to a combination involving only initial values, then its exit-block value set represents a precondition. If one or more final values are constituents of the combination, then the exit-block value set represents a post-condition. A final value may correspond to an initial value, or to a combination of initial values, so the value set of a given value number may represent both a pre-condition and a post-condition. However, in CodePeer, when translated into caller-relevant variable terms, a post-condition will be associated with the variable(s) whose final values are constituents of the combination, whereas a pre-condition will be associated with variable(s) whose initial values are constituents of the combination.

In addition to restricting the value set of the left-hand side of the assignment or equation when using mathematical or logical rules for restricting value sets, CodePeer pushes the computation to the operands and modifies their value sets appropriately. For example, in the expression: $A_{VN1} = B_{VN2}/C_{VN3}$ where the value sets for the value numbers before the computation are as follows: VN1 in {0..100}, VN2 in {-infinity..50} and VN3 in {2..100}, the value set for VN1 may be restricted to {0..25} and the value set for VN2 may then be restricted to {0..50}. If, later in the program, the value set of any of the constituents for this statement changes, the changes will be properly propagated to other constituents.

The computation table from the SSA/GVN phase is used for propagating changes in the value sets to other value numbers because it conveniently stores relationships between the value numbers. Those relationships are directly used in set operations to affect all value sets that can possibly be involved. If the computation table is logically viewed as a directed graph, it may be said that those changes are pushed down to the children of the nodes of value numbers that are actually involved in the computation or statement, and up to their parents.

Mathematical and logical operations are re-expressed as their equivalents for the convenience of computing the value sets and their intersections or unions, for example, the addition of a negation as a subtraction, a comparison as a membership test, etc. As long as mathematical and logical rules are followed, the resulting expressions will contain the same amount of information, which will be pushed down to all possible constituents and relations of those constituents. In such a way, almost every time one value set is modified, modifications to other value number value sets ripple through as a result. Therefore, at every point of use not only might the value set for a particular value number shrink, but also the value sets of related value numbers. Such a rippling effect of modifications helps provide greater precision and results in better-defined pre-conditions and post-conditions which, in turn, provide more help to program developers in writing, understanding and testing their programs.

It can be necessary to carry out several top-down and bottom-up walks through the procedure in order to propagate all possible value-set-affecting conditions. To improve performance, CodePeer only keeps track of the value sets for caller-relevant value numbers and current value sets for value numbers involved in the basic block currently being analyzed.

Once the value sets for caller-relevant value numbers are determined, those value sets can be expressed as pre-conditions and post-conditions and given to the user. In the error-determination phase, value sets for caller-relevant value numbers are examined again to locate any empty value sets – signaling that the program is constructed in such a way that no value for that variable will result in a valid execution.

Additional errors and notifications can be issued if, for example, certain statements can never be reached during execution, or if there are unused branches of code, etc.

5.4. Conclusions

Static analysis tools are gaining popularity for safeguarding against the most common causes of errors in software. The main focus of these tools is on automatic bug-finding – the first stage in a two-phase process where the tool finds bugs and the human then corrects them. CodePeer is a static analysis tool that exploits this synergy between the machine, which can compute many useful properties about programs, and a human reviewer, who is ultimately the one deciding whether warnings or properties uncover program errors.

We have shown the benefits of integrating static analysis with the compiler and the development environment, both in terms of ease-of-use and assurance. We have detailed the inner workings of CodePeer, whose compiler-like modular approach based on subprogram summaries allows fast analysis on multicore machines, and more importantly a natural integration in the developer's workflow. This is in contrast with heavier approaches that require the entire application to be analyzed on dedicated machines during nightly runs.

Feedback from CodePeer industrial users continues to influence the direction for future evolution, including:

– *Exploiting subprogram summaries to perform quick analyses.* AdaCore and SofCheck are working on a persistent representation for these summaries. In this way, a developer will be able to run a very fast incremental analysis on his or her changes by using the the summaries previously computed for the rest of the codebase.

– *Providing better contextual information for the presence of a warning or an annotation.* We are planning modifications of possible value sets so that the path causing an error can be displayed by highlighting relevant code in the graphical user interface (GUI).

– Further refining the ability to generate test vectors for improving test coverage.

For the latest details of CodePeer, visit www.adacore.com/home/products/ codepeer. To watch online demos of how CodePeer works, visit the *Find the Bug Challenge* page at www.adacore.com/home/products/ codepeer/toolset/findthebug/.

5.5. Bibiliography

[BAN 79] BANNING J.P., "An efficient way to find the side effects of procedure calls and the aliases of variables," *Proceedings of the 6th International Conference on Principles of Programming Languages*, San Antonio, 1979.

[CHE 03] CHESS B.,WEST J., *"Static Analysis as Part of the Code Review Process"*, Secure *Programming with Static Analysis*, Chapter 3, Addison-Wesley, 2007.

[HIN 01] HIND M., "Pointer analysis: haven't we solved this problem yet?" *PASTE'01, Workshop on Program Analysis for Software Tools and Engineering*, Snowbird, Utah, 2001.

[OTT 90] OTTENSTEIN K. J., BALLENCE , R.A., MACCABE A.B., "The program dependence web: a representation supporting control-, data- and demand-driven interpretation of imperative languages", *PLDI'90, Proceedings of the International Conference on Programming Language Design and Implementation*, pp. 257-271, White Plains, New York, 1990.

[STA 07] STAIGER, S., VOGEL, G., KEUL, S. WIEBE, E., Interprocedural Static Single Assignment Form in Bauhaus, Technical Report, University of Stuttgart, Department of Computer Science, 2007.

Chapter 6

Formal Methods and Compliance to the DO-178C/ED-12C Standard in Aeronautics

6.1. Introduction

Formal methods have been used by several industrialists in the fields of aeronautics, rail, nuclear energy and integrated circuits design, for around 20 years. By 2005, conscious of the evolution of software programming and verification techniques during the 1990s, aeronautic certification authorities and industrialists began the third revision of the RTCA-EUROCAE standard, which defines the recommended practices to justify the quality of embedded software: DO-178/ED-12 Software aspects of aeronautical systems and equipment certification [RTC 92].

The first version of this document was made public in 1981. Since then, revisions A and B have been published in 1985 and 1992, repectively. Revision C, which is the first one to provide guidance on the use of formal methods, is to be published in 2012.

This chapter will analyze how this type of technology and the latest version of DO-178/ED-12 [RTC 92] contribute to increasing confidence in embedded software

Chapter written by Emmanuel Ledinot and Dillon Pariente.

safety. The analysis is illustrated by two industrial-sized case studies carried out at Dassault Aviation[1].

After a reminder of the main principles underlying the DO-178/ED-12 [RTC 92] standard, and a presentation of the formal methods technical supplement that was added to revision C, this chapter analyzes and illustrates how certain formal methods provide means to meet the quality assurance objectives required by the standard.

6.2. Principles of the DO-178/ED-12 standard

In the regulatory context which rules aeronautical certification, the DO-178/ED-12 ([RTC 92]) document has the status of an AMC (*Acceptable Mean of Compliance*). It is a collection of good practices agreed to by industrialists (aircraft and motor manufacturers) and American and European certification authorities (FAA[2], EASA[3]), as acceptable means to demonstrate that an embedded software has reached the safety level that is required by aeronautical regulation: *Certification Specification* 25.1309.

6.2.1. *Inputs of the software development process*

The safety level is quantified by the CS 25.1309 as the maximum probability that feared events will occur in the aircraft or system. Probabilities depend on the severity of the consequences of feared events for the crew and passengers of the aircraft.

DO-178/ED-12 ([RTC 92]) considers the software as an object whose functioning is deterministic without failures other than those which follow the activation of residual development errors, or failures in the hardware that supports its execution.

Consequently, the objective of the DO-178/ED-12 ([RTC 92]) is to provide practical means to justify that a certain level of confidence has been reached in the non-existence of residual software development faults. This confidence level is rated in a qualitative way by five development assurance levels, from A to E. Each level is characterized by a subset of 72 quality objectives. These five levels of development assurance are not explicitly associated with the levels of probability of feared system

---

1 Other experiments carried out in the past are presented in various articles, including [LED 06] and [PAR 10].

2 *Federal Aviation Administration,* see www.faa.gov.

3 *European Aviation Safety Agency,* see www.easa.eu.int.

events (10^{-9} for catastrophic events, 10^{-7} for severe events, etc.) defined by CS 25.1309.

Risk analysis, system architecture and preliminary safety assessment aim at determining the contribution of the different software items to the aircraft-level feared events. The criticality of software items is computed by means of fault tree analysis (qualitative part only).

The development assurance level (DAL) attributed to each software item is an input of its DO-178/ED-12 ([RTC 92]) development. The higher the DAL, the more quality objectives or development activities are required in terms of:

– verification of the software architecture;

– verification of the compliance of the source code to low level requirements (detailed specification);

– structural coverage obtained by the end of requirement-based testing;

– verification of the verification activities themselves;

– independence of the verification team with respect to the development team;

– redundancy of verification activities to detect the same class of errors;

– verification of software robustness.

Level A requires meeting all of the 72 objectives, level B – 70 out of the 72 with slightly relaxed independence requirements, and level C – 62 out of the 72.

The cost of conforming to DO-178/ED-12 [RTC 92] is very high for levels A and B. It reduces considerably for level C (all the while remaining high) thanks to relieving many planning, documentation, conformance and structural coverage requirements. Level E imposes no quality objective. A level A development may be 300% more expensive than a level C, and 500% more than a level E.

6.2.2. *Prescription of objectives*

DO-178/ED-12 [RTC 92] prescribes software quality objectives that entail carrying out a definite set of development activities. These activities can be organized and scheduled in any development process: V, Y, W, spiral, extreme programming, etc.

Even though it imposes restrictions on the development process, DO-178/ED-12 [RTC 92] is not a reference development process.

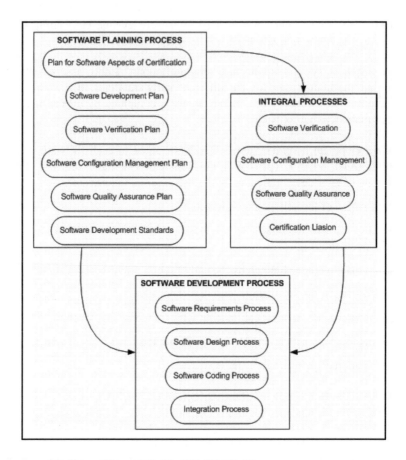

Figure 6.1. *The DO-178/ED-12 processes*

The software lifecycle is broken down into nine "processes" ("process" here meaning an homogeneous group of activities): plannning, requirement capture, software design, programming, integration, verifaction, configuration management, software quality assurance and certification liasion.

Each process is described by:

– some development assurance objectives;

– input data;

– activities;

– output data;

– transition criteria;

– sometimes technical topics to be dealt with (numerical precision, interruptions, memory allocation, etc.).

The 72 quality objectives aim at ensuring that:

– the system requirements allocated to the software item are ensured by the behavior of the executable code when run on the target computer:

    - the executable code's behavior always conforms to the requirements (no unintended functions),

    - no part of the executable code is to remain unactivated after completion of the tests demonstrating that all the requirements have been implemented (no dead code).

Dead code, is in fact code presumed "dead" and is considered as a potential source of unintended functions; so, DO-178/ED-12 requires it to be removed, or else, to explicitly justify why it is left and how one ensures it will never be activated.

Functional and non-functional requirement capture plays an essential role. DO-178/ED-12 requires us to specify software in two stages:

– high level software specification (*High Level Requirements* or HLR) based on reformulating the sytem requirements allocated to the software item;

– software architecture and design leading to the detailed specification called LLR (*Low Level Requirements*). LLR must contain all the information necessary to write source code.

The main quality objective assigned to these two stages of requirement capture is *compliance*: all the system requirements allocated to the software must be faithfully translated in the LLRs, possibly with additional information called derived requirements. Derived requirements cannot be traced to system requirements but have to be traced to design choices.

The core document of version C stipulates that only execution on a target can "demonstrate" software compliance to its high level requirements. A noticeable fact is the absence of requirements regarding functional safety in the standard. Safety requirements are handled as any other kind of requirement.

6.3. Verification process

The aim of the verification process is to detect and report to the development team the existence of faults either in the requirements, the architecture, the source code or in the executable code. These faults have to be corrected by the development team.

The verification process is meant to verify that:

– the system requirements allocated to the software item have been correctly and completely transcribed into the high level software requirements (HLR);

– architecture and LLRs conform to HLRs. If the refinement of HLRs is performed in several steps, conformance has to be verified at each step. There is one exception to the requirement conformance objective when LLRs do not exist because the source code is automatically generated from formalized HLRs:

– source code complies with architecture and LLRs,

– binary code executed on the target computer meets the high level and the low level requirements;

– binary code executed on the target computer is robust, that is to say, is able to appropriately meet the requirements even in the case of abnormal[4] inputs;

– the means used to carry out these verification activities are correct and complete for the software development assurance level.

There are three kinds of verification activity:

– those that deal with the qualities expected of each lifecycle product, considerd in isolation: HLR, LLR, architecture, source code, executable code. These qualities are verifiability, accuracy, consistency, compliance to applicable standards, and compatibility with target hardware;

– those that deal with compliance relations: HLR → system requirements, LLR → HLR, Source → LLR, Executable → LLR, Executable → HLR;

– those that verify verification activities are performed appropriately. DO-178/ED-12 ([RTC 92]) requires verification of verification: verification data has to be documented, reviewed, managed in configuration, and traced to development artifacts. The discrepancies between observed and expected verification results must be explained and resolved in compliance with a planned process.

---

4 The standard does not specify the meaning of the terms "appropriate" and "abnormal conditions".

The verification objectives of the artifacts produced by the development process, considered in isolation, can be summarized in Table 6.1. The references Ax.y are references to these objectives used in the appendices of the standard.

	HLR	**Arch.**	**LLR**	**Source code**	**Integ-ration**	**Param. data.**	**Exec. Code**
Accuracy and Consistency	A3.2	A4.9	A4.2	A5.6			
Accuracy of algorithms	A3.7		A4.7				
Verifiability	A3.4	A4.11	A4.4	A5.3			
Conformance to standards	A3.5	A4.12	A4.5	A5.4			
Integrity of partitioning			A4.13				
Correctness and completeness					A5.7	A5.8	
Compatibility with hardware	A3.3	A4.10	A4.3				A6.5

Table 6.1. *Verification activities and objectives*

– A blank box means the quality objective is not required for the artifact.

– "Arch." abbreviates software architecture issued at the design stage.

– "Param." represents the parameters and the data part of the software.

– "Exec." represents the executable code loaded in the airborne computer.

Numerous objectives apply to several artifacts of the development process, sometimes with very different meanings.

Architecture consistency means absence of control-flow or data-flow dependencies between software items that have different DAL. A component can only use information from components of equal or higher DAL.

Compatibility of HLRs, LLRs and software architecture (objectives A3.3, A4.3 and A4.10) with target hardware has to be assessed on technical issues such as initialization, interruptions, synchronizations and asynchronous calls.

Conformance of software architecture to standards means conformance to design patterns, complexity rules or design constraints defined by system standards such as ARINC 661 ([ARI 10]) for Integrated Modular Avionics (IMA).

Source code is verifiable if all its instructions can be tested without any modification of the source code.

The accuracy and consistency objectives for HLRs and LLRs can be interpreted in the same way as in logic: no contradiction and meaning that is the true intended meaning.

For source code, accuracy and consistency (A5.6) mean absence of run-time errors. A list of technical points to be analyzed is provided to satisfy objective A5.6:

– stack overflow;

– memory usage;

– *overflow* in fixed-point arithmetic;

– resource contention;

– non-initialized variables;

– worst case execution time;

– exception management;

– data corruption due to multi-tasking or interrupt handling;

– cache management.

Quality objectives required in comparing two artifacts are given in Table 6.2, with the same conventions.

	Compliant with	Robust vis-à-vis	Traceable to
HLR => System requirements	A3.1		A3.6
LLR => HLR	A4.1		A4.6
Architecture => HLR	A4.8 (compatibility)		
Source => LLR	A5.1		A5.5
Source => Architecture	A5.2		
Executable => LLR	A6.3	A6.4	
Executable => HLR	A6.1	A6.2	

Table 6.2. *Quality objectives*

The first column is fully marked with objectives that enforce the first of the two main objectives of the standard: to ensure that all intended functions contained in the system requirements allocated to the software are realized in the executable code running on target hardware.

This demonstration is difficult to perform. The traceability objectives of the third column support the justification of compliance throughout the development process.

Theoretically, a downstream product conforms to an upstream product which it derives from if all the characteristics stipulated in the upstream product have been translated or realized in the downstream product, and nothing more. In particular, the downstream product must not introduce unintended functions, that is to say, behaviors that are not explicitly present in the upstream product.

The absence of unintended functions is a critical point to be verified. Formal methods provide new means, more powerful than traceability and testing, to meet this verification objective. They significantly increase the quality of conformity justification.

Since the first version in 1981, any non-traceable development artifact is considered a potential generator of unintended functions because it appears to be not intended to conform to some upstream requirement[5]. It must therefore be eliminated.

Conformity of source code to LLRs is defined by (see [RTC 11] section 6.3.4a) "the source code must be accurate and complete with respect to LLRs and must not implement any non-documented function".

Conformity of source code to the architecture concerns the control flow and data flow dependencies: the source code must conform to that described in the software design document or in a model of the architecture.

Conformity of source code to standards is defined as complying to the coding rules mentioned in the development plan, especially the rules limiting software complexity and enforcing the use of restricted subsets of C, C++, Ada or Java.

Source code traceability to LLRs is defined as "ensuring that LLRs have been implemented in the source code".

Objectives A6.1 to A6.4 are the main conformity criteria to be met: the executable code must conform, i.e. must realize the two requirement levels (HLR and LLR) in a correct and complete way, even in case of abnormal solicitation (robustness objective).

---

5 Or design choice for the derived requirements present in the LLR.

DO-178/ED-12 strives to prescribe only objectives, never means. There is one exception: testing. Testing is a verification mean, like analysis and review.

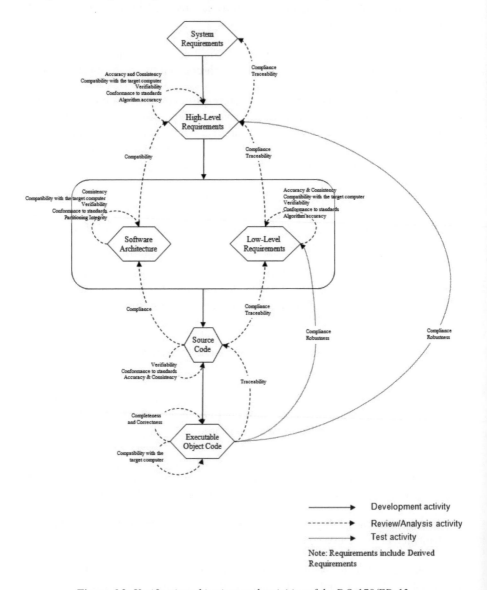

Figure 6.2. *Verification objectives and activities of the DO-178/ED-12*

Test cases have to be defined according to requirements[6]. They must provide a means of justifying that the executable code realizes all the requirements (compliance) and nothing more (absence of unintended functions).

Since testing is an incomplete means of uncovering the discrepancies with respect to requirements and the existence of unintended functions, a metric of software activation was introduced: structural coverage. Structural coverage is a verification termination criterion. It is an *auxiliary* means to gauge the activation effects of the functional testing campaign (external black box approach) on the inner structure of the software item. However, the quality objectives are to ensure complete coverage of the requirements and elimination of unintended functions. High structural coverage is not a quality objective *per se*.

If, thanks to structural coverage measurement (the higher the DAL, the higher the structural coverage), some instructions remain unexecuted after completion of all the tests that ensure 100% functional coverage of HLRs and LLRs[7], there are four possible cases:

– The inactivated instructions meet an intended need, but that need was not stated in the requirements (either high or low level). Then the requirements must be supplemented with some statement of this need and some test cases, activating this code and traced to this new requirement, must be added (see [RTC 11] 6.4.4.3b). Structural coverage therefore contributes to the search for requirement completeness.

– The inactivated instructions meet a formulated requirement, then the test cases of this requirement are incomplete and need to be supplemented with some cases activating them (see [RTC 11] 6.4.4.3a).

– The inactivated instructions belong to a software part that is tagged as non-executed for reasons duly justified in the design document. In some specified cases ([RTC 11] 6.4.4.3d), these instructions can be left in the executable code.

– The inactivated instructions do not meet a need and their inactivation is not justified. They are regarded as a source of potential danger (possible generation of unintended functions), and must be drawn out of the source code, whether actually inactivable or not.

In principle, structural coverage analysis should be performed exclusively on the executable code that is loaded into the airborne computation unit. Section 6.4.4.2 of the core document [RTC 11] specifies that it can also be performed on the assembly

---

6 *Requirement-based testing or functional tests*. DO-178/ED-12 forbids tests whose sole objective is to activate some structural element (conditional, loop, path, instruction etc.).
7 In the sense of traceability between test cases and requirements.

code or on the source code, provided that any instruction from the excutable code is traceable to the instructions of the code on which structural coverage analysis is performed.

Formal methods provide means other than test and traceability to justify conformance of software behavior with requirements, and when doing so they take into account all the values the variables of a program may take at run-time. Though they don't truly execute the program on the target computer[8], they can ensure exhaustiveness of analysis of its dynamics and thus prove non-existence of a kind of unintended functions: the behaviors, however rare they may be, that violate some stated properties. Of course they cannot detect the other kind of unintended function: the behaviors that violate some intended properties that were not formally stated as requirements.

So formal methods have to revisit the role of structural coverage analysis as a way of striving to achieve verification completeness.

6.4. The formal methods technical supplement

Revision C includes three technical supplements dealing with three software development technologies:

– object-oriented programming;

– model-based development;

– formal methods.

It also includes a fourth technical supplement on the qualification of development and verification tools. Three technical supplements add, and sometimes delete, objectives. They substitute the supplement for the core document as soon as the corresponding technology is used.

The rationale and structure of the core document remained basically unchanged after the completion of revision C. Information was added and adjusted locally and it underwent numerous editorial modifications, in particular to better separate the objectives to be met from the activities to reach these objectives.

The application of the *Formal methods technical supplement* (FMTS) is required only when formal *verification* is used. Formal modeling with no formal analysis leads to conforming to the model-based technical supplement only.

---

8 This is the reason they are called "static" methods though they analyze software dynamics.

A language is considered as being formal in the FMTS when its semantic is mathematically defined. In particular, this language can be any programming language whose reference semantics have been mathematically defined. The supplement does not distinguish between the formal verification of model and formal verification of program. The objectives which are set are the same.

The FMTS requires justification of the soundness[9] of the formal analysis method to be used by the applicant. Soundness means that the formal analyzer never concludes that a property is true or proven whereas on the true code or model it is false or not provable. This justification of soundness needs to be provided to the authority even if the analysis tool is not qualified because no certification credit[10] is claimed on that formal verification.

The acceptable means to justify the soundness of a formal analysis method are not specified in the supplement.

6.4.1. Classes of formal methods

FMTS introduces three families of formal analysis techniques, also called proof techniques:

– *Abstract interpretation*: a kind of efficient mathematical set-valued execution of code or model, which calculates for any variable its abstract domain, i.e. a mathematical structure over-approximating all the values it can take during any possible execution, but in a way sufficient to prove a given class of properties[11]. These properties are most of the time non-functional properties such as run-time errors: non-initialized variables, invalid pointers, divisions by zero, numerical overflows, stack overflows, worst case execution times, numerical precision upper bounds, etc.

– *Model-checking*: is also a sort of mathematical execution, more of an enumerative nature. Originally limited to systems with finite states programs, i.e. automatons, it may also be applied to systems with infinite states because of numerical variables, unbounded recursion or dynamic process creation. It can also be applied to source code (software model checking).

---

9 *Soundness*. The word *correctness* is sometimes used to mean *soundness*, sometimes in the meaning of accuracy and completeness. For example for the detection of abstract interpretation of unattainable code, possible superior approximations of attainable instructions can lead to an incompleteness of unattainable instructions. The tool can be accurate without being complete, which is a kind of incorrection.

10 A certification credit is an authorisation to delete, reduce or automate a development or verification activity.

11 For an accurate and formal definition of abstract interpretation see footnote 9.

– *Theorem proving*: originates from mathematical logic and computer-based automated deduction. It uses formulas and symbolic variables which are not instantiated to handle any value that may be taken at run-time by a given program or model variable. These formulas, called verification conditions, are automatically generated from annotations set on parts of the source code or model to formalize the HLRs or LLRs that part is expected to conform with.

The boundaries between these three classes of formal analysis techniques, clearly delineated from the 1970s to 2000, are beginning to fade. To scale-up on codes or models of industrial complexity, the new generation of formal verification tools combine techniques belonging to the three classes.

Consistently with DO-178/ED-12's principle of prescribing objectives only, the formal methods' technical supplement does not require or even recommend any formal method in particular. It neither characterizes their respective domain of use, nor maps their functionalities to the quality objectives they can help to meet.

The FMTS highlights the subset of the 72 objectives that can be addressed by formal methods but in a generic way, without getting into the specifics of analysis, program, model or property classes.

Formal methods distinguish two classes of objects:

– the *properties* expected to be satisfied by the software or model dynamics. They are called specification traits, features or requirements in DO-178/ED-12. They are formulated:

  - by logical annotations when using theorem proving or abstract interpretation,

  - by temporal logic formulas or observers when using model-checking;

– the *behaviors* of programs or models. They can be sequential (functions, procedures, objects) or parallel (processes, tasks, threads, communicating automata, etc.).

The neat distinction between the expected properties (the "what") and the behaviors (the "how") can disappear in certain situations:

– At the stage of high level specification, when HLRs are formalized in logic, set theory or type theory (Z, B, VDM, Coq, PVS, etc.), the formal analysis may aim to demonstrate that certain logical consequences of the formalized requirements are true. In that case, there is no behavior or explicit calculation at stake in the analysis. So to speak, one proves properties of properties.

– Conversely, especially in control-command software, even when using the highest level languages, the requirements may intrinsically look like temporal behaviors: automata, operator networks, pseudo-code, etc. The "what" is then expressed in the same language as the "how". The expected property itself is formulated as a behavior.

Roughly speaking, formal analysis consists of confronting the code's or model's behavior to expected properties, taking into account all the possible execution scenarios while executing nothing.

As they do not execute codes or models, formal methods cannot contribute to meeting the A6.5 hardware compatibility objective. Testing the integrated code on the target airborne computer remains essential to meet A6.1 (conformity to HLR) and A6.5.

The validity of any formal proof depends on the accuracy of the mathematical description of the mechanisms running the language analyzed by the formal tool[12] wrt. to the actual hardware execution. This adequacy issue has to be addressed at methodological and tool qualification levels.

6.4.2. *Benefits of formal methods to meet DO-178C/ED-12C objectives*

The formal methods' technical supplement is structured like the core document. It specifies, section after section, the objectives of the core document which formal methods can help to meet, either partially or in totality.

	HLR	Arch.	LLR	Source code	Integration	Param. data.	Exec. Code
Accuracy and consistency	A3.2	A4.9	A4.2	A5.6			
Accuracy of of algorithms	A3.7		A4.7				
Verifiability	A3.4	A4.11	A4.4	A5.3			
Conformance to standards	A3.5	A4.12	A4.5	A5.4			
Partitioning integrity			A4.13				
Correctness & completeness					A5.7	A5.8	
Hardware compatibility	A3.3	A4.10	A4.3				A6.5

Table 6.3. *Review of Table 6.1 from the point of view of formal methods*

---

12 In other words, the formal language semantics.

The objectives that formal methods may help to address are shown in Tables 6.3 and 6.4.

Formal methods provide the means to reinforce quality verification of specifications (consistency of HLRs and LLRs, accuracy of algorithms) and that of source code (absence of run-time errors, correctness of data, etc.).

In cases where requirements are formalized in logic, the detection of incoherence can take on a strong meaning, in particular by using provers based on disproof procedures.

However, in general, accuracy of formalized requirements is a difficult semantic property beyond the scope of formal methods. Exceptions are cases where the interpretation domain of the requirements (their "intended meaning") can also be formalized and computed.

Even though modeling, especially control-command behavioral modeling, has become common practice in control engineering, the system requirements allocated to software often remain accessible only in natural language textual form. The interpretation domain of such requirements is thus specific to every reader of these texts. The verification of their accuracy ("intended meaning fit") and completeness is intractable with formal methods. It can only be performed by expert review.

	Conforms to	Robust wrt	Traceable to
HLR => System Requirements	A3.1		A3.6
LLR => HLR	A4.1		A4.6
Architecture => HLR	A4.8 (compatibility)		
Source => LLR	A5.1		A5.5
Source => Architecture	A5.2		
Executable => LLR	A6.3	A6.4	
Executable => HLR	A6.1	A6.2	

Table 6.4. *Table 6.2 Applicability of formal methods to verification objectives*

Objective A3.1 is thus rarely tractable with formal methods, except in control-command when a Simulink®, Modelica or SCADE® model, is granted a double (LLR + source code) or even triple (HLR + LLR + source code) status. In this case, A3.1, A4.1 and A5.1 conformance objectives are provable, but qualification of the code generators may be needed.

Usually, formal methods are used to formalize LLRs, to verify LLRs (objectives A4.2, A4.4, A4.7) and to meet objective A5.1 of source code conformance with LLRs. Most often HLRs remain in a textual form, which is desirable for readability of the requirements by people who did not participate in the development process.

FMTS highlights the following benefits:

– *Contribution to making requirements unambiguous*. A formal requirement is definitely more precise than an unformal one. However, it may still contain some sort of ambiguity that may be harmful for correct software implementation. As an example consider the following requirement: design a procedure which for any positive input float x computes an output float y such that $x = y^2$. It is formal and precise, but ambiguous as well since the implementer will be left free to choose the sign of the square root on his own. A formal specification is less ambiguous than a specification in natural language, but complementary verifications are necessary to be sure not to leave input/output choices to the programmer.

– *Possibility of verifying properties against requirements*, these properties can be called upon for consistency, non-ambiguity, correctness, completeness, or (rarely) accuracy objectives.

– *Possibility of demonstrating conformance relationships*, between two requirement levels, or between some behavior and some requirements.

6.4.3. *Verification of the executable code at the source level*

This voluntarily provocative statement targets the somewhat paradoxical situation where the industrialist and the certifier are faced with formal methods: adopt them but be careful on them.

Indeed, in theory they deal with all execution cases, but in practice, they concretely deal with… none.

Like any engineering activity, they remain at a distance from the reality of the final manufactured object. They only take the models. The representativity of these models in relation to the code executed in the certified equipment depends on the validity of their proofs if they are claimed on objects different from those that were analyzed.

Ideally, formal methods would need to be able to analyze the binary in a way which is rigorously equivalent to the behavior of the target processor. Even if there are static analyzers of the binary code, in particular for the computation of worst case execution times and, verification of the executable code is too complex to be envisaged.

For a language such as C, many proofs already require a certain obstinacy. The case study with the Frama-C platform, presented later in this chapter, illustrates this point. Proving properties for a model or source code can be difficult, depending on the complexity of the properties to establish. This is particulary the case as soon as the properties either temporal operators or nonlinear arithmetic.

Reaching the exhaustivity of behaviors thanks to formal methods has a price which can be high, but which for level A software can nonetheless be favorably compared to testing with MC/DC coverage[13] cover. Activating all the cases specified by the MC/DC criteria from functionally relevant test cases, and not constructed according to the boolean expressions to be activated, can turn out to be extremely costly.

MC/DC coverage is the most demanding criteria to measure "the activation energy" injected into the program by only exciting it with a series of use cases. However, a formal method systematically "activates" all the instructions of a code or a model which contribute to determining the validity status of the property to establish.

It then becomes useless[14] to measure which part of the instructions of the code or the model is activated to formally verify that the model or the source code satisfies its requirements, because the answer is systematically 100%.

Using formal methods on level A software can lead to simultaneously increasing productivity and the covering of verification, on condition of accepting to drop functional testing with MC/DC termination criteria.

Maintaining it in addition to a source level formal verification because the "activations" analyzed by formal methods are not the real activations on the processor would be doubly strenuous:

– the cost of exhaustive verification in the source code;

– then the cost of MC/DC coverage on the executable code.

It would then be economically impossible to use formal methods.

To avoid double verification, FMTS introduced the possibility to claim verification of the binary code against LLRs when this verification is performed by formal methods only at source code level. But a demanding condition was added: the property preservation principle must be satisfied. In other words, it is required to

---

13 *Multiple Condition / Decision Coverage.*
14 At first glance, the detection of unintended functions and processes meeting non-formulated requirements is dealt with in the following sections.

justify that the properties proved at source code level are preserved at binary code level by the later stages of compilation, link-edit and load.

This authorization therefore means the suppression of testing to meet the conformity objective of A6.3.

In line with the principle of prescription of objectives, the not means of the DO-178/ED-12, the FMTS does not give eligible means to justify the preservation of property. Section 6.7 of this chapter presents a means for language C.

6.4.4. *Revision of the role of structural coverage*

To avoid making double verification mandatory, i.e. accepting formal verification only when it is performed in addition to testing; one of the major advances of the FMTS is the acceptance of verification exclusively by formal methods in a limited but significant domain: objective A5.1, i.e. verification of compliance of source code with the LLRs. However, testing remains mandatory, whatever use of formal methods is made, for verifying conformance of source code or executable code to the HLRs.

When testing is replaced by formal analysis, the termination criterion of the corresponding verification activity, based on structural coverage analysis, has to be revisited and replaced by another criterion. For instance, using MC/DC coverage, or any lower coverage ratio, as a means to enforce test case completeness, becomes useless since formal methods ensure exhaustiveness of execution cases.

The FMTS performed such a revision. The purpose and modalities of structural coverage analysis have been modified wherever a verification activity is performed exclusively by formal analysis. This revision is the most tricky part of the document. We try, hereafter, to provide some help in deciphering its underpinning rationale. In the following, we consider exclusively the role of structural coverage in the particular setting of LLR verification by sole formal analysis.

Since structural coverage analysis is a termination criteria of part of the verification activities, the related objectives are defined in table A7 "Verification of verification process results". In DO-178B/ED-12B, and in the core document of revision C, there are three objectives related to structural coverage analysis whose applicability depend on the software Design Assurance Level:

– A7.5: MC/DC coverage is achieved.

– A7.6: Decision coverage is achieved.

– A7.7: Instruction coverage is achieved.

– A7.8: Data-coupling and control-coupling coverage is achieved.

The FMTS suppresses A7.5 to A7.8 and substitutes a single objective named *FMA7.5-8: verification coverage of software structure is achieved.* Five activities, to be completed as a whole, have been defined to meet this new and unique FMA7.5-8 objective. They were thought of as means to detect shortcomings in requirement-based verification and to detect dead code. These two contributions of structural coverage analysis remain valuable when replacing testing by formal analysis. Conversely, the third role of structural coverage analysis, i.e. its contribution to detect incompletness of the test cases and procedures (equivalence classes, limit test cases, etc.), had to be discarded since formal methods ensure completeness of the execution cases that are analyzed against the properties that formalize the LLRs.

The five activites that were assumed to contribute to completeness of requirement-based verification and dead code detection to the same extent as MC/DC, DC or instruction coverage analysis, are:

– requirements-based coverage analysis: a formal analysis case must exist for each LLR and include the normal range and abnormal cases;

– complete coverage of each requirement: complete coverage is reached when no assumption is made in the formal verification, or when all of the made assumptions are verified;

– completeness of the set of requirements: completeness is defined with respect to the intended functions, and assumed to be decidable by means of the following criterion (FM6.7.1.3), quoted as is:

- for all input conditions, the required output has been specified;

- for all outputs, the required input conditions have been specified.

The FMTS stipulates that if requirement completeness cannot be *demonstrated*, structural coverage analysis must be performed.

– detection of unintend data-flow relationships: one must verify that the data flow dependencies in the source code are exactly the ones specified in the architecture document or model and in the LLRs.

– detection of dead code and deactivated code: straightforward, but the FMTS stipulates that the detection must be performed by review or an analysis *other than formal*.

The tricky part is the requirement completeness criterion. Why was this criterion assumed to capture its intent as well as amenable to formal demonstration? The underlying idea is that by enforcing a systematic way of formulating the input/output relationship of software items, such that all the execution cases are partitioned in a limited number of cases, should help thinking about all the intended properties and stating all the I/O constraints. *Input conditions* are predicates over the input variables. Though not explicitly stated, these predicates are intended to form a partition of the input domain, thus ensuring orthogonality (no overlap) and exhaustiveness of the execution cases. Ensuring that the outputs are defined for all the cases of a complete set of input cases, and only for them, is advocated as a kind of completeness requirement.

Checking that the formal LLR properties state functional (and non-functional) constraints over a complete set of execution cases, definitely contributes to satisfying a complete set of constraints. But does it ensure that the stated constraints are *de facto* complete with respect to the intended functions?

The great advantage of this criterion is that it is syntactic and amenable to computerized verification using meta-programming over the LLR formulas and theorem provers to discharge the partitioning conditions.

Seemingly, the second oddity is the restriction "other than formal" for dead code detection analysis. One point here is that at least formal analysis usally delivers only lower approximation of dead code. Consistently with the soundness requirement, formally detected dead code is ensured to be truly dead, but many instructions formally tagged as "executable" may be indeed undectable. So dead code detection needs (additional) human expertise anyway.

Before ending this discussion of the FMTS on structural coverage analysis, it is essential to note that even though the FMTS is questionable on these two issues discussed, these intrinsic limits are the same, not to say worse, with testing. Even though powerless to ensure full requirement completeness (see the next section), formal methods definitely and tremendously improve the quality of the LLRs and the verification of source code conformance with the LLRs.

6.4.5. *Verification of the completeness of requirements and detection of unintended functions*

Failing the guarantee of the completeness of requirements, which the intensive test with MC/DC cover does not guarantee either, two compensatory objects offer a perspective of being able to subtract from the costly functional test with MC/DC cover to hold objectives relative to the executable code, on condition of being able to justify:

– that we know how to reach them at the source by formal analysis;

– that the proofs of property are preserved in the executable code.

Are formal methods capable of demonstrating true requirement completeness with repect to the intended functions?

And to what extent can they detect the unintended functions?

Requirement completeness is not an explicit objective of the core document because DO-178/ED-12 assumes that the completeness of the requirements allocated to the software item is ensured by the system engineering process, and taken for granted as inherited.

This objective was added in the FMTS to compensate for the mitigation of structural coverage analysis.

Generally, system requirements, and even HLR, are expressed in a textual form in natural language. The frame of reference of the required properties contained in these texts is not accessible to the calculation for the evaluation of completeness criteria.

The situation is different if the system requirements allocated to the software are formalized and can act as a frame of reference as criteria for the completeness of HLR.

Nonetheless, even in this case, formally proving that the HLR are complete in relation to this frame of reference is a challenge, except if the completeness criteria can be in the form of a theorem to prove, like any other logical consequence of HLR.

Therefore, except for any particularly favorable situation mentioned in section 6.4.2, formal methods are unable to prove the completeness of requirements.

They are even unable to detect a part of unintended functions. Indeed they answer questions that are asked of them, which already are a lot, but cannot infer questions which should have been asked of them.

Thus they detect unintended functions which appear as counter-examples of the functional properties we were hoping to verify, but that the exhaustive analysis of execution cases turns out to be false in some cases which had not been thought of.

However, if the omission has to do with properties which we want to see verified, no formal method can make them appear on the screen, nor can the execution cases which violate them.

Formal methods are capable of finding cases which do not do what we expected, but not those which do what was expected.

6.5. LLR verification by model-checking

This section gives two examples of the formalization of low level requirements with the help of formal models enabling us to generate automatically generated code. In addition to this, models also enable us to verify the expected behavioral properties.

These verifications meet DO-178/ED-12 objectives:

– A4.4: LLRs must be verifiable;

– A4.1: LLRs must conform to HLRs;

– A4.2: LLRs must be continuous and accurate;

– A4.7: algorithms must be accurate.

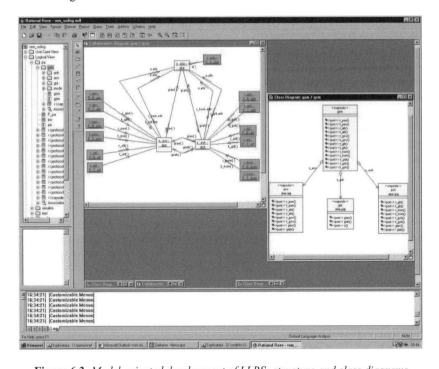

Figure 6.3. *Model-oriented development of LLRS: structure and class diagrams*

In both cases, it is a matter of finite automata that react to pilot commands by selections of modes. Algorithms are sequential logics.

The first example illustrates the model-oriented development of a mode activation software component[15] which is part of flight control software. The modules of this component, their connections and their inheritance hierarchy are defined as structure and UML2 class diagrams (see Figure 6.3).

The behavior of the instances connected in the structure diagrams are defined by synchronous *StateCharts* [HAR 85] translated in Esterel [BER 92]. A compiler processes the structure and behavior inheritance and produces a global Esterel program which is then compiled in C and integrated into the rest of the application.

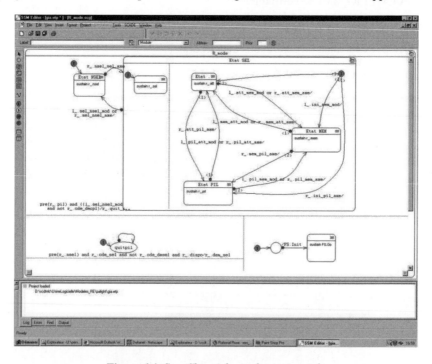

Figure 6.4. *SyncChart inherited generic mode*

The behavior of the component managing the activation logic of guidance modes is defined by around 15 SyncCharts which interact with each other. The resulting global automaton defines the responses to around 50 input events and has several million reachable states (see Figure 6.4).

---

15 Around 10,000 lines of generated C code.

Mutual exclusion of exclusive modes and non-existence of untimely mode activations are the safety LLR properties verified with the *model checker Prover*® integrated into Esterel Studio®.

The development was carried out without certification constraints but by meeting the requirements defined by the C level of the DO-178B/ED-12B. The tools were not subject to qualification.

In the second case, the application corresponds to a modeling stage of a function with a high combinatorial content from the Falcon EASy® avionics: the window manager module.

Modeling was carried out with the same tools as previously. Its aim was to verify the correctness of the detailed specification (LLR) and to define the test cases. It was carried out in parallel to embedded software development by Honeywell.

The application was made up of five modules, one per display unit and one for the coupling logic between the four units.

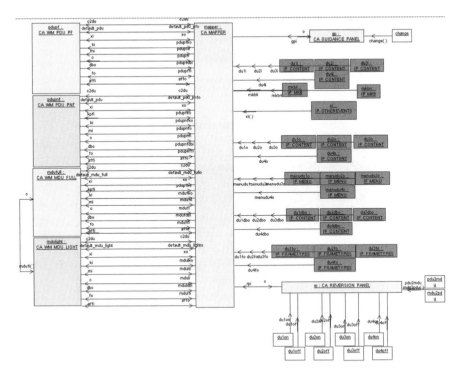

Figure 6.5. *Structure diagram of the EASy® window manager application*

These five modules contain 42 SynchCharts that manage the respond to 167 input signals by emitting 184 output signals. These hierarchical, parallel and communicating automatons decide, according to the pointing interactions of the pilots by means of trackballs and keystrokes, which is the subdivision of the four displays (1, 2 horizontal, 2 vertical or 4 display zones) and the content of each zone (see Figures 6.6 and 6.7).

Figure 6.6. *EASy® cockpit*

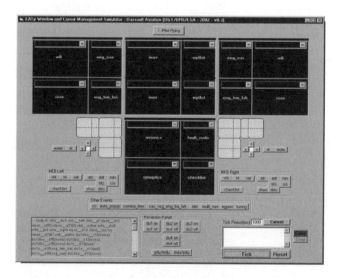

Figure 6.7. *Simulation interface of the flight deck window manager*

As in the previous example, properties verified by *model-checking* on this detailed specification model are safety properties, such as:

– mutual exclusion between contents in certain zones – permanence of certain pages which are essential to the pilot;

– distribution invariants of contents between first and second pilot, whichever their affectation to the left and right seats;

– switch of contents during the switch of primary/secondary roles between left pilot and right pilot:

- absence of display of untimely pages,

- absence of defaults of page calls.

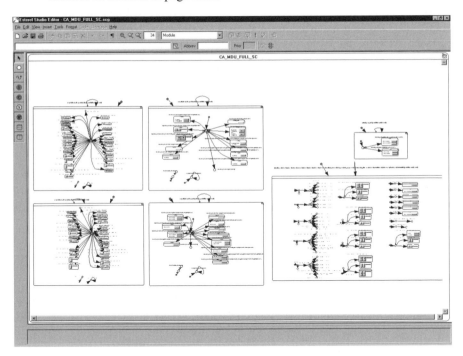

Figure 6.8. *SyncChart of page and window calls*

The reachable state space could not be calculated as a whole. The verification was carried out on different sub-models only comprising the parts which were necessary for proving each property (*slicing* of the model by hand).

Modeling, simulation and verification highlighted 9 ambiguities and 16 cases of incompleteness in textual LLR of this function.

6.6. Contribution to the verification of robustness properties with Frama-C

6.6.1. *Introduction to Frama-C*

Frama-C is a platform dedicated to the static analysis of C source code, developed by the CEA LIST and the INRIA labs. It allows interpretation of a given program in an abstract way, and detects its potential run-time errors (dereferencing of uninitialized pointers, *overflows*, divide by zero check, etc.).

It also allows us to verify functional properties expressed as annotations in the source code. Among the available analysis tools, Frama-C was chosen for its ability to make different static analyses collaborate on the same annotated code. Lessons learnt from past experiences clearly illustrated that this collaboration was highly necessary to scale up when dealing with real-size industrial use cases.

Moreover, this platform offers the capability of developing our own specific extensions (plug-ins) through an extendable API, in order to implement various complementary analyses on the same annotated code. Frama-C is an *open source* software, free to download[16].

Static analysis of source code consists of extracting a certain amount of information from source code, without running it. The techniques implemented in Frama-C which enable this extraction of information are *abstract interpretation* [COU 77] (by the means of the *Value Analysis* plug-in) and *deductive verification* (*Jessie* plug-in, and more recently WP, based on weakest-precondition computation) [HOA 69] [DIJ 75], among the main ones.

Indeed, these plug-ins exploit the results computed by several kernel and basic services provided by the Frama-C platform (see Figure 6.9): abstract syntax tree, proof project management (saving and reloading of analyses sessions), logging of commands (generation of scripts for automatic replay of analyses), computation of inputs/outputs for each function or even each C expression, program dependency graph, control flows, data flows, code reducing (*slicing*), impact analysis, detection of dead or unreachable code, etc.

---

16 Website: www.frama-c.com/download.html.

Frama-C provides correct analyses:

– users are informed of all of the potential run-time errors identified in the source code;

– any formal annotation in the code (users' specifications or alarms generated by any analysis plug-in) is systematically evaluated, and possibly proven correct;

– the dependencies between annotation verifications are tracked in order to detect possible circularity or causality.

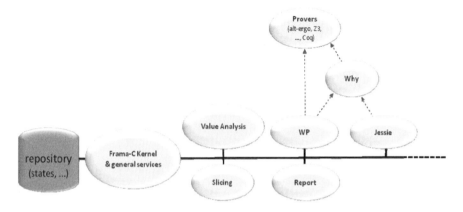

Figure 6.9. *Frama-C's architecture[17]*

As presented in Figure 6.9, the *deductive verification* plug-ins Jessie and WP may use the Why[18] tool (developed at INRIA labs) to respectively generate the verification conditions (VC), and translate them into a few languages accepted by some commonly used theorem provers. Any result of the analyses, from the AST to domains of value computed by abstract interpretation for example, is stored in a repository of analyses, and readable from any other Frama-C tools.

6.6.1.1. *ACSL: an annotation language which is common to all plug-ins*

In the source code, the annotations are written in a common language to all Frama-C plug-ins (all of them interpret the annotations with the same semantics), named ACSL for ANSI/ISO-C *Specification Language*. This communality of language is one of the means allowing the different plug-ins to collaborate. In brief, a plug-in A may need to emit some assumptions onto the code, and then may

---

17 Frama-C provides an API allowing the different plug-ins to share data through a repository (states/results of analyses, project management, dependencies between analyses, etc.).
18 See the website www.why.lri.fr.

generate a new annotation that it can not discharge yet but helps pursuing A's analysis further. If any other plug-in B is able to discharge the annotation added by A, then results computed by A are correct.

ACSL allows "Hoare-like" expression of properties such as pre-conditions, post-conditions, invariants, etc., thus permitting a *design by contract* approach. ACSL can be classified as a behavior specification language, or BISL – *Behavioral Interface Specification Language*, for C code, inspired by the JML language classically used to specify Java programs. A notable difference between ACSL and JML is that the latter can be used for the verification of assertions during run-time, whereas ACSL is solely dedicated to static verification.

```
/*@
  requires \valid(p+(0 .. n-1)) && n>0;
  assigns p[0 .. n];
  ensures \forall integer i;
    0<=i<n ==> p[i]==\at(p[i],Pre) + 1;
*/
void main (int *p,int n)
{
  int i;
  /*@
    loop invariant 0<=i<=n;
    loop invariant \forall integer j;
      0<=j<i ==> p[j] == \at(p[j],Pre) + 1;
    loop invariant \forall integer j;
      i<=j<n ==> p[j] == \at(p[j],Pre);
    loop assigns p[0 .. i];
    loop variant n-i;
  */
  for(i=0;i<n;i++)
    p[i] = p[i]+1;
}
```

Figure 6.10. *Example of an annotated C function*

ACSL specifications are written as particular comments in the C source code. Code annotated with ACSL can therefore be compiled as for a regular program.

The simple example in Figure 6.10 illustrates the annotation of a C function which increments the contents of an array of integers. The annotations are inserted into special C comments starting with the "@" character. Among others, the clauses "requires", "assigns" and "ensures" respectively specify the pre-conditions, effects and post-conditions of the given function, and "loop invariant" and "loop variant" refer to the loop behavior specification, according to the classical Hoare semantics (see [BAU 10a], [BAU 10b] and [PRE 10]).

6.6.1.2. *Abstract interpretation with the Value Analysis plug-in*

This is one of the main plug-ins of the Frama-C platform, from a final user point of view. *Value Analysis* ([CUO 10], [CAN 09], [BON 10]) computes, for each variable in the source code, a set of values necessarily containing those that might be obtained during a concrete program execution. Using this plug-in is facilitated by a high level of automation, and the results obtained for the values of the source code variables are often of a remarkable precision.

However, as usual with common Abstract Interpretation implementations, some C constructs may lead us to broadly over-approximate the set of possible values, and then not be able to conclude on the validity of properties referring to these variables. To palliate this point, *Value Analysis* can reduce the set of possible values by using complementary ACSL assertions (written by the user or generated by other plug-ins), and propagates this new reduced value domain downstream in the code. Of course, the validity of these complementary assertions – which aim at reducing the value domain – will need to be discharged by other plug-ins or analyses.

The results obtained by *Value Analysis* are made available to other plug-ins: all the value domains computed by *abstract interpretation* are stored in the analyses states repository.

During the analysis of C code, *Value Analysis* may add some annotations of its own in the abstract syntax tree of the program. The principle is simple: in certain cases, this plug-in identifies potential run-time errors and then emits assertions (as ACSL annotations on pointer validity, absence of overflows, absence of division by zero, etc.) which allow it to pursue computations further. Then, it will be up to other plug-ins to discharge the annotations added by *Value Analysis*.

In practice, *Value Analysis* has shown its ability to scale up in terms of size of code (several tens of Kloc). The precision[19] and speed in providing useful results make this plug-in a particularly efficient analysis tool.

---

19 W.r.t. the accuracy of the computed interval values for the source code variables.

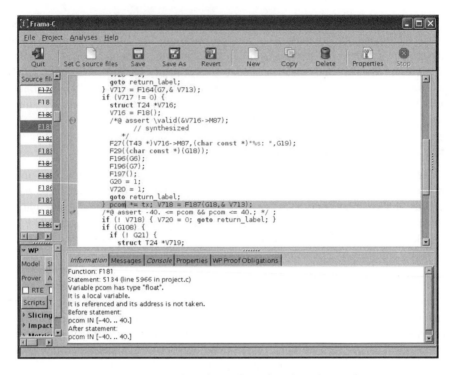

Figure 6.11. *Screenshot after code analysis by Value Analysis*

Figure 6.11 presents the results of *Value Analysis* on a real code. When selecting any variable from the C source code, its possible values computed by abstract interpretation are displayed in a dedicated panel ("information" tab at the bottom of the window, e.g. [-40. .. +40.] interval value related to variable *pcom*).

6.6.1.3. *Deductive verification: Jessie and WP plug-ins*

In Frama-C, *deductive verification* is based on Hoare logic and the computation of the *Weakest-Precondition* (WkP), defined by Djikstra [DIJ 75].

6.6.1.3.1. Notations and principles

Let Q be a post-condition, P a pre-condition, C a source code. Then WkP(C,Q) is a formula such that it is necessary to prove P=>WkP(C,Q) to guarantee the validity of the triplet {P} C {Q}.

This triplet can be read as follows: if P is verified before the execution of C and if C terminates, then Q is guaranteed.

P=>WkP(C,Q) is called *verification condition* (VC), which will be discharged with the help of automatic or interactive theorem provers.

If code C contains a function call for which a contract has been defined, then:

– Let Rf, Af, and Ef respectively be the clauses "Requires" (pre-condition), "Assigns" (effects) and "Ensures" (post-condition) of a called function f;

– Let MLi be the memory state of the control point Li for calling f in the source code C;

– Let "Assigns" (MLx, MLy, Af) be a predicate in which Af is an over-approximation of the set of memory zones modified from the MLx state to the MLy state;

– Finally, let us note X{@MLi} the predicate X for which the parameters are evaluated at the Mli memory state.

With these notations, the WkP at the memory state Mli of a property P after the "return" control point of a function f, is computed as follows:

$$WkP\{@M_{Li}\}(\ f(...) \ , P \ ) =$$
$$R_f\{@M_{Li}\} \wedge (Assigns(M_{Li}, M_{Li+1}, A_f) \wedge E_f\{@M_{Li+1}\} => P)$$

These various notations will be used in the following.

6.6.1.3.2. Implementations

Two plug-ins implement deductive verification in Frama-C: Jessie ([HUB 07], [MOY 09]) and developed by INRIA labs, and WP[20] from CEA labs. In [HUB 07] [HUB 08], details regarding the memory model implemented in the Jessie plug-in (Burstall-Bornat model [BUR 00]) can be found, with the solutions to solve the so called *separation problem*, among other difficult issues met during developments and experiments.

Regarding the CEA's WP plug-in, it integrates a particularly promising and innovating approach. Indeed, several memory models are made available: from the simple representation in the original "Hoare" model (without pointer dereferencing), to low level models which enable the handling of bit-fields, taking into account any target architecture, heterogeneous casts, etc. The swapping from one memory model to another is generally decided by the user; in that case, WP plug-in is in charge of ensuring the whole analyses correction. The expected advantage of using different memory models is very important: it allows us to adapt the modeling to the kind of

---

20 See www.frama-c.com/download.html.

source code under analysis, in order to avoid having to discharge VCs whose complexity would not be justified.

Once the *verification conditions* have been generated by Jessie or WP, they are processed by a certain number of automatic theorem provers (Alt-ergo [CON 07], Simplify [DET], Z3 [MOU], etc.), and if necessary by proof assistants (Coq [BER 04], PVS[21]).

6.6.1.4. *Reducing code by slicing*

Slicing enables us to identify a subset C' of instructions from a given C code, such that any property verified on the C' code is considered as also being verified on C. In Frama-C, the *slicing*[22] selection criteria are numerous. They can be any ACSL annotation (only the C statements possibly involved into the verification of the annotation will be preserved in the sliced code), or the instructions writing or reading a given variable, etc. *Slicing* can be used for many different purposes, such as helping in revewing a code, or also reducing the size and complexity of the original code for facilitating later analyses.

The C' reduced code computed by the Frama-C *Slicer* plug-in can be compiled, and it is guaranteed (at the condition of tool qualification) that, regarding the selection criteria, the behavior of C' is equivalent to that of the original C code: C' is the *useful* part of C with regards to the given criteria.

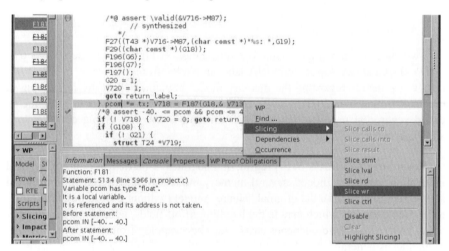

Figure 6.12. *Selecting a source code variable, and then slicing all the statements writing to this variable*

---

21 See www.csl.sri.com/papers/pvs-prover.
22 See www.frama-c.com/slicing.html.

Figure 6.13. *Screen snapshot of code after slicing: the instructions not involved in the slicing criteria are barred in the window, and removed from the new abstract syntax tree*

6.6.1.5. *Other plug-ins distributed with the Frama-C platform*

Many other useful, even essential, plug-ins should also be presented here, in particular those regarding project management, the handling of dependencies between states [SIG 09b], etc. For the sake of readability, we will not discuss them here, but the reader is of course invited to visit the Frama-C website for more details.

6.6.1.6. *Plug-in development*

Frama-C offers a documented API and a guide to the developer [SIG 09a] for the design of user specific plug-ins. The case study described hereafter illustrates how this capability is essential to overcome the issues encountered when dealing with real-size codes. The development of these complementary plug-ins requires a good knowledge of the OCaml language and of the platform architecture.

Finally, let us clarify that Frama-C and its plug-ins [COR 09] can be used in batch mode, or by means of a graphical user interface, under Windows, UNIX and Mac OSX systems.

6.6.2. *Presentation of the case study*

This case study deals with analyses that contribute to meet the robustness objective of DO-178/ED-12 for level A control software, both civilian and military, submitted to certification constraints.

The robustness objective is considered in the LLR of this software. LLR are expressed in the form of SCADE® models[23] from which the C code is automatically generated by KCG, a qualified code generator.

The robustness objective stipulates that the behavior of the program remains the one expected even if it receives input data outside the nominal domain of use.

To meet this objective, the adopted approach is two-fold:

– a system and software analysis which characterizes the conditions in which the data outside the nominal domain would be likely to be passed as input to the SCADE® application;

– an analysis of the propagation of these abnormal data inside the SCADE® model and their effect.

The first analysis leads to the definition of a value interval for each input variable which represents the total variation domain: normal + abnormal.

The second analysis is the subject of this case study.

Currently processed by a manual review of SCADE® models, these analyses of interval propagation in a model can be automated by the abstract interpretation of code generated from the model, by considering, thanks to the qualification of the code generator, that the behavior of the model on the one hand, and the behavior of the C code on the other, are equivalent.

Model design is subjected to such a constraint that reviewing the modeling remains somehow "simple and humanly" feasible. However, the gain obtained when using Frama-C is the exhaustivity of analysis and the possibility of replaying it automatically, which can lead to a reduction of certain recurring costs. The works reported in this case study deal with operational avionics codes, but the analyses were carried out in an R&T environment, for which complementary Frama-C plug-ins were developed to reach acceptable productivity conditions.

To establish that robustness is indeed guaranteed – i.e. nothing unacceptable can occur when the model inputs have abnormal values – we prove by static analysis, therefore by considering all values that can be taken by all input variables of the code, that the whole behavior is the same as when running within the nominal domain.

---

23 SCADE® is distributed by the Esterel-Technologies company. See www.esterel-technologies.com.

Running in nominal domain is characterized by the respect of a series of pre-conditions set for functions which are internal to the model, specifically library functions. The model is robust if none of these pre-conditions is violated for inputs of the abnormal model in any of the calling contexts.

To guarantee the robustness objective, the models are designed in such a way that any changes of values internal to the model remain inside the hypotheses imposed as the domain of validity for the model, even for extreme input values. Static analysis proves that this is the case. It is a matter of an integration proof, and not a unit proof.

The size of the analyzed codes is in the range of n x 10 Kloc. Models have around 200 C functions. These codes also include hand-coded low level functions. C code has some classical nested structures, pointers, loops, *bitwise* expressions, linear and non-linear arithmetic over floating numbers. However, they don't have function pointers, complex pointer arithmetic, or recursive function calls.

Several tens of pre-conditions, main elements of the robustness criteria, are set on the library functions. To illustrate the kind of property sought, let us take the example of a function computing the square root using the Newtonian method, for which it is necessary to ensure that whatever the calling context in the SCADE® model, the input parameter value is always positive or null.

Frama-C Value Analysis plug-in gives useful results regarding numerical accuracy with single or double precision floating variables. In some cases, when a higher level of numerical accuracy is needed, the Fluctuat analyzer [GOU] can also be used, though on a quite restricted number of lines of code to preserve rounding error computations from the impact of unavoidable abstract interpretation over-approximations. In the other cases, the approach described in section 6.9.6 is also implemented to minimize analysis costs.

6.6.3. *Analysis process of the case study*

In this section, the process that was adopted is described step-by-step. It highlights an iterative approach, in which the phases of annotation (handwritten or automatically generated) are often intricate with static analyses (abstract interpretation, deductive verification), as long as the total amount of properties is not verified.

The progression of the analysis is measured by the number of annotations which remain to be proven. At the beginning, this number corresponds to the pre-conditions set in the functions of the model to express hypotheses made on their input domain for a nominal behavior. This number of pre-conditions is about one hundred for the SCADE® models concerned with this case study. Then, this number of annotations increases rapidly to reach several thousands. Indeed, many plug-ins, like *Value Analysis*, generate their own complementary annotations as mentioned before.

Once again, collaboration strategies of different static analysis techniques are made possible within the Frama-C platform, and this unique ability has turned out to be essential to scale up in the integration proof for the class of code and sought properties considered in our case study. This is presented in the following.

6.6.3.1. *Appropriation of the code*

In this study, the team verifying the code is different from the one that developed it. An appropriation phase is therefore necessary before beginning verification analyses.

It consists of characterizing important information which will enable us to identify more rapidly the possible causes of non-conclusive analysis results:

– Total number of functions in the code, their complexity, the kind of instructions used (arithmetic, conditional expressions, identifying complex algorithms, etc.)?

– Iteration loops (number, nested or not, with side-effect or not, etc.)?

– Floating variables and the level of accuracy needed?

Some metrics computed by Frama-C are available, which enable us to obtain some information about the category of the code. The callgraph of the application (see Figure 6.14) generated automatically by a Frama-C plug-in, is one of the precious – and basic – aids provided by the platform.

In practice, and with some experience of the kind of code under analysis, a rapid scan of the application (10 to 20 Kloc per day) is enough to identify the functions which could be more complex to deal with regarding the sought properties: functions comprising nested loops, bitwise arithmetic, pointer arithmetic, non-linear expressions involving floating variables, presence of numerous and/or nested conditionals. In static analysis, like elsewhere, the 20-80 rule applies: 20% of functions of the application often require 80% of the user analysis task.

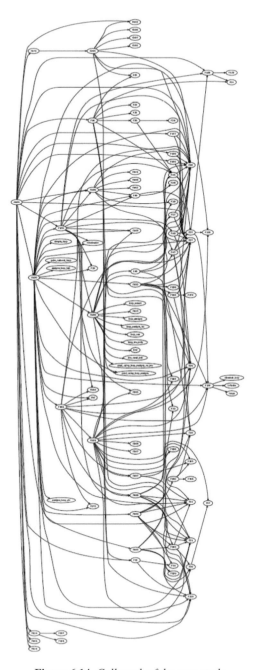

Figure 6.14. *Callgraph of the case study*

In the following, the necessary different steps of analysis are presented in chronological order, and for each of them a graph will show the cumulated number of annotations inserted by the user and by analysis tools (curve in black), and the number of those formally verified (curve in gray).

6.6.3.2. *Chronology of analyses*

The process described here mainly involves *Value Analysis* plug-ins and WP. It consists of a series of 14 steps of analysis and annotation.

In the appendices (section 6.9), one can find more details about the technical aspects of certain steps or additional plug-ins developed for our robustness analyses, in order to reach acceptable levels of productivity. A number of them automate the setting or moving of annotation strategies to minimize manual procedures often tedious and time-consuming.

The first step naturally consists of annotating C code in ACSL to insert the functional sought properties. In this case study, it consists of preconditions, defining the conditions for which the computations would be safely carried out, and that any input variables out of bounds meet the DO-178 robustness objective. At this stage, about 70 properties are inserted into the code. The calling contexts which must verify these 70 preconditions, therefore the total number of functional properties to verify, are about 500.

In this same step, ACSL hypotheses on the input domains at the *main* function entry point are set. These intervals permits us to specify the values of code variables which will be "propagated" downstream throughout the whole application. In the context of this case study, around 90 annotations are necessary. We also define a few ACSL predicates and lemmas (around ten formulas) which will be useful for some complementary analyses based on deductive verification.

The second step consists of launching the *Value Analysis* in order to rapidly obtain a first idea about the whole behavior of the application. *Value Analysis* indeed enables us to obtain many results, information on the code variables, with a minimum user effort, the approach is indeed really "push-button". In particular, numerous computations carried out allow us to know about the effects of each expression and function, and an estimate of the reachable value intervals for the code variables. The options used to tune *Value Analysis* are not given here for readability reasons. This first analysis takes about 15 minutes.

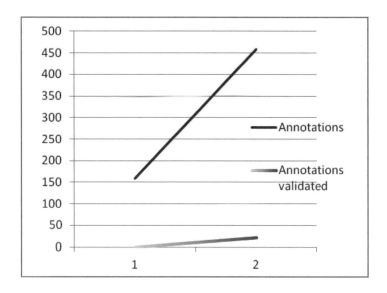

Figure 6.15. *Annotations after the initial pass of Value Analysis*

Value Analysis, during its analysis, adds some annotations to the code itself in order to pursue as far as possible its computations. Typically, for our case study, it emitted around 300 new *run-time error* assertions (for instance, related to pointer validity, etc.).

At this step, *Value Analysis* has not validated a large number of properties inserted by the user or generated automatically (see Figure 6.15). But the code variables are now "valued" with a domain of values expressed as an interval. We can therefore carry out a quick manual review of the analyzed code by means of the Frama-C GUI in order to identify the expressions in the code which are at the origin of possible non-conclusive over-approximations computed by *Value Analysis*.

The third step consists of manually adding precisely new assertions to these expressions for which the intervals computed by *Value analysis* are considered as being too large. These annotations aim at reducing these over-approximations, and they will be verified later on by *deductive verification*.

As an example, let us take a C function which computes a linear interpolation between several points taken from a given matrix. Computing this interpolation requires handling nonlinear arithmetic expressions. These expressions are classically largely over-approximated by approaches and tools like *Value Analysis*, which in many cases lead to non-conclusive evaluation of properties to establish, and are propagated downstream in the computation flow.

Regarding this precise example, complementary annotations which are required, express that the result of the interpolation is necessarily between the smallest and the greatest values of the input matrix. These annotations can also introduce an over-aproximation, and this is the case here: the user could consider other hypotheses to better specify the possible interpolation values case by case. However, the first "weak" hypotheses turned out to be precise enough to verify the sought properties which depended on these interpolations, and they have been themselves formally verified.

For the codes of our case studies, about 40 annotations must be added to tighten the intervals required to be more precisely estimated, expressed as post-conditions (*ensures*).

With these *ensures* clauses, it is generally necessary to add information regarding the effects[24] of related functions (step 4). We had to develop a specific plug-in to automate this step as far as possible (see section 6.9.1).

A Frama-C plug-in, RTE (run-time error), is then called (step 5), which will add new annotations: several thousands of requires, assigns and ensures clauses taken from contracts of called functions, and inserted into calling contexts, as well as several assertions in the code related to the detection of potential run-time errors.

At this step, more than 3,000 annotations have been automatically inserted by the different plug-ins, to which are added the annotations defined manually.

This number is quite high, particularly with respect to the initial 70 functional properties. But an important part of these thousands of annotations will be easily and rapidly proven. It will typically be the case of function contracts which have been copied into their calling contexts.

Step 6 consists of relaunching *Value Analysis* on the current project with all its new annotations (see Figure 6.16).

As we can see from the figure below, about 50% of the annotations have been proven by *Value Analysis*. As expected, most of them are generated by the RTE plug-in.

---

24 The memory locations *written* by the function.

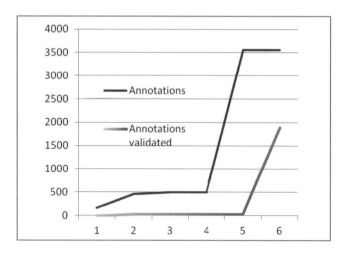

Figure 6.16. *Annotations set and proven at step 6*

Step 7 consists of systematically processing the functions comprising non-linear arithmetic expressions on floating variables. Their outputs generally entail some over-approximation issues with *Value Analysis*. To reduce the interval domains of values while taking into account the calling context, another specific plug-in was developed in-house to automatically add after each *call* statement to "arithmetic" functions, an *assert* annotation which tightens the value domain of their outputs. This plug-in and the different mechanisms involved are presented in section 6.9.4.

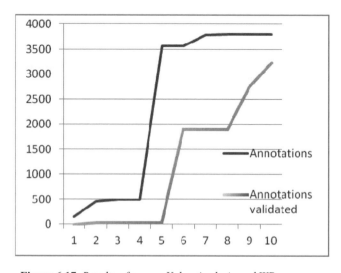

Figure 6.17. *Results after new Value Analysis and WP processes*

At this stage (step 8), some post-conditions defined at step 3 may need a few refinements; followed by steps 9 and 10 consisting in launching *Value analysis* and WP in sequence (see Figure 6.17).

Then about 1,000 annotations remain unvalidated, which could not be proven by *abstract interpretation,* nor by *proof of theorem,* despite the enrichment of annotations during all the previous steps. Even with a significant increase in the *timeout* of automatic provers (from a few seconds to several tens of minutes), these annotations (mostly *ensures* on instructions – or statement contracts) could not be discharged.

To help understanding why these annotations cannot be discharged by automatic provers, it can be useful to analyze them manually with an interactive prover such as Coq. Indeed, this more subtle analysis of formulas generated by WP shows that during the computation of the weakest pre-condition, the nested *if-else* statements yielded a dramatic increase of the size of VCs.

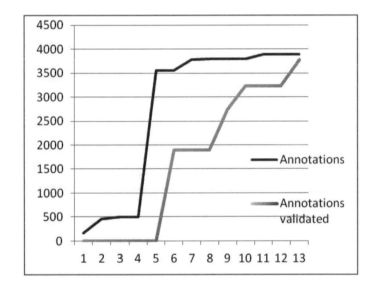

Figure 6.18. *Illustration of the efficiency of proof cuts*

Furthermore, it often occurs that the context of VCs contains thousands of information which has no direct relationship with the goal of these VCs. This information comes from code instructions, but is pointless for the purpose of proof of property which only needed – in our specific cases – on average the last four or five instructions and their annotations.

It then becomes essential to implement proof cut strategies. The implemented cut mechanisms (step 11) are presented in section 6.9.3. These strategies lead us to modifying code annotations. It is therefore necessary to replay the analyses of *Value Analysis* and WP (steps 12 and 13; see Figure 6.18).

We can see now that there are still a few annotations which resist automatic verification. Approaches which are complementary to Abstract Interpretation and theorem proving are then applied case by case:

– the automatic subdivision of intervals to avoid systematic over-approximation of certain arithmetic expressions (see section 6.9.2);

– the verification of certain algebraic ACSL lemmas (added in the axiomatic during step 1) with the help of a symbolic solver (see section 6.9.5);

– the use of an interactive theorem prover;

– the probabilistic estimation of the validity of the annotations, by means of Monte-Carlo simulations, according to a given confidence level (see section 6.9.6);

– validation by expert review for VCs which cannot be demonstrated by the tools available in the platform, and which in our case study are essentially temporal (multi-cycles) properties (see section 6.9.7).

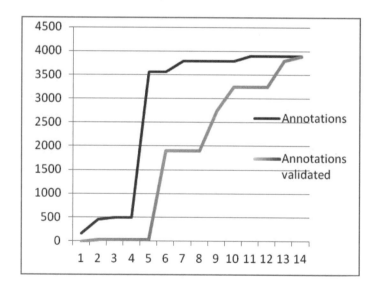

Figure 6.19. *All properties have been proven or reviewed*

In brief, the 14 steps described above show a *spiral* cycle, mainly alternating between phases of annotation and analysis. Their automatic replay is made possible by Frama-C and a few *makefiles*, and covers almost all of the sought properties' validation.

Let us also mention that on these 14 steps, only four were manually carried out (partially or totally, mainly related to the initial and the few ultimate annotations and validations), all the others were processed automatically with the help of the Frama-C plug-ins, and a few other – more specific to our needs – developed in-house.

6.6.4. *Conclusion on the case study*

The proof of functional properties on a whole C application (of several tens of thousands of lines of code) is still a challenge reserved to a few specialists of static analysis, needing complementary techniques and sometimes specific methodology for achievement. But compared with a code review where the robustness properties are ensured "by experts" after days of reviews of source files, the confidence level regarding the quality of verification carried out here is far greater.

Static analysis, despite its unavoidable issues such as systematic over approximations of certain C expressions, enables us to formally verify codes of increasing complexity, for which giving credit to verification only by review might become more difficult to justify.

This case study shows that the Frama-C platform offers the possibility of making several static analysis tools cooperate, in an iterative process of annotation and analysis. This process is guided by a static analysis expert who must identify the origin of over approximations or proof failures, and provide enough information at the right place that the static tools cannot always infer themselves.

6.7. Static analysis and preservation of properties

Be it by model-checking, abstract interpretation or deductive verification, formal methods presented in the two case studies prove LLR properties in the C source, or on models from which the C code is generated.

In the last case, the hypothesis is that C code is generated by a code generator which is DO-178/ED-12 qualified. SCADE 6 KCG[®25] offers this ability, including

---

25 SCADE[®] is distributed by the company Esterel-Technologies. See www.esterel-technologies.com.

programs generated from *synchronous StateCharts* described by means of a language close to the Esterel language from Esterel Studio®.

The qualification of semantic equivalence between LLR in the form of SCADE® models and the generated C source code also supports the following claims:

– conformity of the source code to the model (objective A5.1 of the DO-178/ED-12);

– consistency-accuracy of source code, proved at model level (A4.2, A4.4, A4.7) and preserved by qualified C code generation.

If one cannot justify to the certification authorities that this verification performed at source code level is preserved in the executable code, the demonstration that this executable code conforms to HLR and LLR (including robustness cases) must be done by intensive requirement-based testing.

In the case study using the Frama-C platform, this means that, unless one can justify that the C compiler preserves the properties verified by Frama-C, it is necessary to test on the target the 500 properties of robustness.

For a long time out of reach of industrial and even academic state of the art, this kind of justification becomes plausible at mid-term. As an experiment, the application analyzed by Frama-C and generated by SCADE® was compiled in PowerPC assembly language by a public domain C compiler which guarantees that there is property preservation from source level to assembly language level.

And this compilation does not take more time than with a standard compiler such as gcc[26]. This C compiler, CompCert [LER 09], [LER 10], is a compiler whose "HLR is to offer a means of escaping the double penalty" and the LLR is a formal 3,700-line Coq[27] specification. This formal specification includes, essentially, three parts:

– a mathematical modeling[28] of "theoretical execution" of any C source code, for a subset of C language which is big enough in practice for critical embedded codes;

– mathematical modeling[29] of the execution of the PowerPC assembler (among some other possible targets), representative of the physical execution of binary after linkage of assembler generated by CompCert (semantics of a subset of PPC assembler);

---

26 To find out more visit www.gcc.gnu.org.
27 See www.coq.inria.fr.
28 With all the questions of model validity that go with it.
29 Same comment.

– a logical formula which expresses that whatever the source code S that is compiled by CompCert, the obtained assembler A has the same observable behavior as S, whatever the chosen observation criteria.

The third property, called *semantic equivalence,* is defined for the programs which end and those which do not, as in control program where the main function embeds an infinite loop.

The observable behaviors of the source and its compiled code are traces of calls to observation[30] functions that make visible any inner variables of the program.

The proof of semantic equivalence carried out to demonstrate the correction of the CompCert compiler is valid for any observation criteria used to compare the behavior of the source program S and that of the compiled program A: the setting of the observation functions of S can be adjusted to match the targeted property whose preservation has to be justified.

In the case presented in section 6.6 contributing to the objective of robustness, the observation functions to be invoked are those which make the variables referenced in the 70 preconditions of library functions visible in all the calling contexts.

If these values "computed" by the assembler are the same as those which can be computed by an interpreter which is exactly implementing the mathematical semantics of the C used for Coq proof of CompCert, the Frama-C proofs remain valid for the assembler. This is exactly what the CompCert correctness proof guarantees.

Unless one (legitimately questions the link editor' correctness or the adequacy of the assembler's formal semantics, semantic equivalence and property preservation are ultimately ensured at binary level on the PowerPC target.

The punctilious reader will ask with good reason whether the validity of the principle of property preservation which can be invoked thanks to compilers such as CompCert does not also depend on a justification that the "mathematical execution" of S done by Frama-C is identical, or at least equivalent from an observational point of view, to the mathematical execution of S defined in Coq and used in the 30,000 lines of proof script.

Admittedly, it depends on this. The justification must be defined carefully, by research teams and in the context of the DO-178/ED-12 qualification of these tools,

---

30 Or external, the body of which is not part of the S compiled program.

so that the analysis and compilation tools can be used in a coherent chain that ensures the validity of all the verifications carried out so far.

But now, thanks to a good level of efficiency of this prototype compiler in terms of computation time, of scaling up and efficiency of the generated code, compiling with CompCert, for codes verified by Frama-C, opens up interesting perspectives for the development of critical software under certification constraints.

The CompCert prototype also opens interesting perspectives in the matter of product-based qualification of complex development or verification tools: the Coq proof is a correctness justification of much stronger coverage than a functional test campaign of the compiler with MC/DC structural coverage as performed today for state of the art development tool qualification.

The qualification of compilers is not currently required, and is still not asserted in version C of DO-178/ED-12, whereas it is required for tools generating source code from models as soon as one applies for certification credits to reduce verification activities on the generated source code.

The C, Ada, C++ or Java compilers do not need to be qualified as long as all of the verification activities (objectives A6.1 to A6.5) of the generated executable code are carried out. Indeed, since they are applied to the compilation output, they are also meant to be able to detect compilation errors.

Only one case leads to studying the code generated by a compiler for certification: when the measure of structural coverage is done on the source code and not on the executable code, and when the compiler does not generate a code with traceability towards the source code. This traceability is a means accepted by certification authorities to justify that there is equivalence of structural coverage measures between the source and object levels.

This is why the optimizations which break this traceability are generally deactivated in compilers in order to avoid having to produce this justification of equivalence of structural coverage measure for complex generation patterns.

If CompCert's correctness proof would include a structural coverage preservation property in addition to the semantic equivalence property, one would then have a compiler allowing:

– to use, in certification, optimization options breaking traceability;

– to obtain certification credits on the executable code by justifying the applicability of the property preservation principle stated by the FMTS.

Only the second use requires it to be qualified. Will the correctness proof be truly valued by certification authorities? Will they agree to greatly reduce the qualification tests? These questions are still pending.

6.8. Conclusion and perspectives

The revision C of the DO-178/ED-12 standard marks an important step for the use of formal methods in aeronautics since it officially introduces them in processes eligible for certification, and authorizes a wide use in verification.

Applicable to goals of quality of requirements and conformity, in particular to conformity of the source code with respect to its low level requirements, formal verification is authorized to replace numerous tests, excluding those demonstrating compatibility of the executable code with the target hardware.

This large field of applicability of static analysis methods as a replacement for certain test categories or manual analyses, fields which are rather larger than the current state of technology can cover, is subject to the ability to provide a justification to the correction of formal analyses carried out, and a justification of the preservation of properties demonstrated on source code after compilation when the credits are taken on the executable code based on verifications made at the source level.

This chapter has illustrated verification by *model-checking* of quality objectives on LLR modeled as state machines with parallel hierarchical states, and the verification of robustness properties through LLR expressed on C code with the Frama-C platform.

Finally, a concrete means of proof for the preservation of robustness properties between the source level and the executable level has been presented: the CompCert C compiler whose proof of correctness establishes the equivalence of behavior between a C source and its compiled code, whatever the observation criteria used to compare both behaviors.

"Formal methods are the future of computing, they always have been and always will be". This ironic well known judgment targeting the non-industrial viability of formal methods, even if it remains partly relevant, has also been shown to be faulty during the last ten years in aeronautics, as well as in the rail and nuclear sectors. The evolution of regulation and the number of industrial developments of embedded critical software with formal methods are good evidence of this.

This trend will continue, with the expected progress of static analysis tools and their integration, as transparent as possible, in the modeling and programming environments.

Both for embedded software and development tools (code generators, compilers, static analyzers), formal methods will reinforce the product-based development assurance. In the future, they will enable us to envision a better balance between process-oriented and product-oriented recommendations. So that this reinforcement of the verification of the product itself does not lead to an increase in development costs, the additional required activities of formalization and verification need to be compensated by discarding other activities to obtain a global economic gain over the whole process.

On the descending branch of the V cycle, such a transfer of activity has however taken place. The additional cost of formalization in the model was balanced by the automatic code generation, which can lead, for control program software, to productivity gains reaching 30 to 50% compared to processes separating specification and programming.

For the ascending branch, which represents 50 to 60% of the total development cost for level A and B software, gain perspectives also exist but it is necessary to obtain certification credits on certain verification tasks.

The DO-178C/ED-12C qualification of static analysis tools is therefore a critical point of the economic equation that aeronautics industries have to solve to benefit from the technological progress in the verification domain, since it is a necessary condition to obtaining such credits, in particular for test and formal analysis of the verification activities. But in the meantime one observes a progressive hardening of regulatory requirements for tool qualification.

This hardening is visible with the C revision of the DO-178/ED-12 since it defines a new category of verification tools to cover verifiers, from which we can take important credits such as the removal of test activities. This new category includes qualification objectives which are reinforced with respect to version B, which though justified and appropriate, can nonetheless constitute a barrier to the industrial use of formal verification in a certification context.

For the Frama-C platform presented in this chapter, Airbus, CEA and Dassault Aviation are working together to reach its DO-178C/ED-12C qualification in the best conditions in terms of cost, time and acceptance by the certification authorities.

6.9. Appendices

This section presents the main complementary techniques and in-house developments addressing a few tool issues or difficulties met during our experiments. Indeed, they apply to an earlier release of Frama-C. Since our case studies were completed, more recent releases of the static analysis platform have showed real improvements that could alleviate or even remove some of these complements.

6.9.1. *Automatically annotating a source code*

Several Frama-C analyses require prior annotation of the code. This is in particular the case for *deductive verification*. Several required annotations can be automatically generated: it is quite easy to produce the clauses required with regards to the validity of pointers handled in a given code for example, it is also easy to identify the memory zones which are written by a function, or also generate simple loop invariants and variants.

To reach the desired productivity in verification by static analysis (for example 0.5 to 1 h.m for the case study presented before) the implementation of this systematic annotation has been automated by developing a dedicated plug-in. For each of the C functions, it implements a "minimalist" contract, that is to say:

– pre-conditions (*requires* clauses) on the validity of pointers and arrays;

– effects of functions (*assigns* clauses);

– simple loop variants and invariants (that can immediately be deduced from a loop *for* without effects on the iterator inside the loop body).

This plug-in can in addition use the results of the *Values Analysis* (it accesses the repository of states that is available to all plug-ins), and thus generates more accurate annotations as it benefits from previous control and data flow analyses.

From past experience, it is often costly for the user to manually insert these annotations. For certain classes of programs, a code of 10 Kloc could require up to 3 K lines of annotations. However, this activity can be automated quite easily, and the execution time required is less than 10 minutes (several days of work would be necessary to write the same annotations).

The example hereafter illustrates the work done by this plug-in.

Original code:

```
void copy(int *o,int *d)
{ int i, n=g(o,d);
```

```
    for(i=0; i<n; i++) { d[i] = o[i]; }
}
```

After computation of the value domain returned by *Value Analysis* for function g(), the plug-in annotates the C code as follows:

```
/*@ requires \valid_range(o,0,4)&&\valid_range(d,0,4);
    assigns d[0 .. 4]; */
void copy(int *o,int *d);

void copy(int *o,int *d)
{ int i, n=g(o,d); // Value Analysis return {5} in n

/*@ loop invariant 0<=i<=5; loop assigns d[0 .. 4];
    loop variant 5-i; */
  for(i=0; i<n; i++) { d[i] = o[i]; }
}
```

Of course, all the annotations necessary for the verification of the expected behavior of the *copy* function are not generated. Promising works exist in research labs, for an even more powerful invariant generation; their integration is forecast in future releases of this internal plug-in.

6.9.2. *Automatically subdividing input intervals*

In presence of nonlinear arithmetic over floating variables, it is not rare for *abstract interpretation* in Frama-C to largely over-approximate the value domains for the outputs of a given function.

This phenomenon also appears when the same variable is present at different places in the same expression: unless *abstract interpretation* benefits from efficient relational domain or *ad hoc* heuristics, each of these occurrences of the same variable will be considered *de facto* as a new independent variable.

The expression:

$$y = x - x;$$

with x in [-1; 1] is a typical example. Many implementations of *abstract interpretation* will give as a result: y in [-2; 2], which is not wrong, but far from the expected – i.e. accurate – result.

The user can choose to add an annotation just after the instruction such that:

//@ y == 0;

and easily verify that this annotation is valid by proof of program.

But in many other cases, the added annotation to reduce the computed domain by *abstract interpretation* is not easy to verify by formal methods. This is the case for nonlinear expressions such as:

```
//@ assert -10.0<=x<=10.0;
y = x * x;
//@ assert y>=0.0;
```

Proving that the second *assert* is valid can indeed present a few issues for automatic provers if they do not benefit from an axiomatization based on real or floating numbers. *Abstract interpretation* will be more likely to find the result in [-100.0; 100.0].

However, *Value Analysis* has the ability to independently take into account the terms of a disjunction and to propagate them separately. In the code, the disjunction is "materialized" by an ACSL annotation. The union of the computed domains is therefore provided once all of the separate propagations have been realized.

Let us take the previous example and include a disjunction in the first annotation.

```
//@ assert -10.0<=x<=0.0 || 0.0<=x<=10.0;
y = x * x;
//@ assert y>=0.0;
```

Now, the second assertion is validated by *Value Analysis,* as the propagation has this time been carried out for each of the two terms of the disjunction, and in both cases the second assert obtains the *Valid* status.

This principle has been generalized in the in-house development of a plug-in which generates the necessary disjunctions until the sought property is validated. In other words, in the limit of a number of iterations fixed by the user, this plug-in subdivides the input interval as a disjunction until the *Value Analysis* is able to validate the sought property for each of the terms of the disjunction it generated itself.

Let us take, for instance, the following code which computes an approximate of the *cosine* with the help of a Taylor series:

```
//@ requires -pi<=x<=pi;
float my_cosine(float x)
{ float y, x2 = x*x;
  float x4 = x2*x2;
  y = 1 - x2/2 + x4/24 - x4*x2/720;
  //@ assert -1.0<=y<=1.0;
```

```
        return y;
    }
```

For this kind of code, the plug-in generates 1,600 subdivisions of the input interval, before *Value analysis* is able to demonstrate the sought assertion "//@ assert -1. <= y <= 1. ;". In this case, the computations take less than 40 seconds. This generation of disjunctions is said to be "lazy": only the intervals which have invalidated the sought property are subdivided at the following iteration, which enables us to scale up in terms of computation time and necessary memory space.

One of the main limits of this approach, however, is its inability to deal with functions with several inputs to subdivide: the Cartesian product of subdivisions of each of these input parameters rapidly causes a high consumption of memory space. In this case, one would rather use other complementary techniques, such as the one presented in section 6.9.6.

6.9.3. *Introducing cut strategies for deductive verification*

With *deductive verification,* the computation of the weakest precondition (WkP) can sometimes lead to the generation of huge verification conditions (VC) that automatic provers may not be able to discharge. This occurs when the C function analyzed contains for instance numerous assignments, or also when the code has a large number of nested conditional statements (if/else).

Of course, techniques have been implemented by our academic partners in such a way to alleviate some of these difficulties. But not everything is solved at this time. In particular, implementations allowing us to compute WkP in a quadratic manner [RUS 05] in the presence of if/else statements, process some families of code efficiently, but up to a certain size limit of the code.

In this case study, the properties to demonstrate by *deductive verification* can most often be proven with the help of a few instructions which precede the annotation. In this case, there is no need to compute the WkP backwards up to the entry point of the given function. And even when certain preconditions of the analyzed function would be necessary, these can be "recalled" (i.e. copied) into the code below within a reasonable range from the annotation to prove.

This observation has led us to implement a certain number of strategies of proof cuts when using *deductive verification*. First of all, by annotating the if/else statements which were not necessary for the proof, by means of statement contracts: there it is a matter of statement specification on a block of if/else, such as, during the computation of the WkP, only the specifications will be embedded in the WkP formula, and not the contents of the two if/else branches. A second WkP will of course need to be computed, but only for the annotated if/else block.

Using this cut strategy – i.e. statements masked by local contracts – enables us to drastically reduce the complexity introduced by numerous if/else conditions, or in fact any other kind of C statements.

The code annotated below illustrates a new case in which we assume that the assertion P, to be proven correct, only requires a few instructions of the function f(), for instance the contract of the function f5() with the label L5:

```
        void f(...)
        {
L1:         f1(...);
L2:         f2(...);
L3:         f3(...);
L4:         f4(...);
L5:         f5(...);
L6:      //@ assert P;
        }
```

By taking the notations defined previously in this chapter, we can write first of all:

– WkP in L5:

$$WkP\{@M_{L5}\}(\ f5(...)\,,P\ ) =$$
$$R_{f5}\{@M_{L5}\} \wedge (Assigns(M_{L5}, M_{L6}, A_{f5}) \wedge E_{f5}\{@M_{L6}\} => P)$$

– WkP in L4:

$$WkP\{@M_{L4}\}(\ f4(...)\,,WP\{@M_{L5}\}(\ f5(...)\,,P\ )\ ) =$$
$$R_{f4}\{@M_{L4}\} \wedge (Assigns(M_{L4}, M_{L5}, A_{f4}) \wedge E_{f4}\{@M_{L5}\}$$
$$=> WkP\{@M_{L5}\}(\ f5(...)\,,P\ ))$$

– and so on until the entry point of the function f().

Without cut strategy, we can easily imagine the size and the complexity of the WP once at the entry point of function f(). However, as mentioned previously, to prove P, it is only necessary to use the contract on f5():

$$E_{f5}\{@M_{L6}\} => P$$

which is a lot simpler to prove.

The approach will therefore consist of masking all the different calls to functions f1 to f4 by contracts on these instructions; in this case simple "ensures\true" clauses are sufficient:

```
      void f(...)
      {
L1:         /*@ ensures \true;*/ f1(...);
L2:         /*@ ensures \true;*/ f2(...);
L3:         /*@ ensures \true;*/ f3(...);
L4:         /*@ ensures \true;*/ f4(...);
L5:         f5(...);
L6:         //@ assert P;
      }
```

The behavior of the function is not modified by these annotations, these "ensures" clauses simply enable us to "mask" the original contracts at the function call points. And these "ensures" will of course be discharged in a trivial way.

In the absence of "assigns" clauses on these functions f1 to f4, the corresponding calls are considered (by default) as being able to affect any memory zone, but this is not important: to prove P, only the contract on f5 is necessary, and this is indeed what we have in the computation of the WP once these annotations are added:

– WkP in L1:

$$WkP\{@M_{L1}\}(\ \{all\ f's\ statements\}\ ,\ P\ ) =$$
$$R_f \wedge (Assigns(M_{L1}, M_{L6}, A_{f5}) \wedge E_{f5}\{@M_{L6}\} => P)$$

For a function generated by Scade®/KCG of a previous case study which included 20 function calls, numerous affectations and 30 if/else statements, the computation of WkP with Jessie plug-in generated 19,456 VCs of which a large part appeared as particularly difficult to discharge automatically. Once the cut strategy was implemented, the computation of WkP only generated 2 VCs to discharge, which were proven correct in less than 10 seconds by most of the automatic provers.

In the same way, a plug-in was developed, generating ACSL contracts on the if/else selected by the user through the Frama-C's GUI, to alleviate this manual annotation task.

6.9.4. *Combining abstract interpretation, deductive verification and functions which can be evaluated in assertions*

In our different case studies, some C functions implemented nonlinear computations over float variables, or for instance handled large size arrays. And the properties expressed on these arithmetic expressions or these arrays led to complex VCs, sometimes impossible to discharge by automatic theorem provers.

For instance, proving that a given array's values are correctly sorted, or that the min and max values of this array do belong to a given interval, are properties difficult to prove automatically with available provers, as soon as the array is of a large size and given in extension.

A way to cope with this issue, is to take advantage of the ability of the ACSL language to define *ghost code*, that is to say code which does not impact on the embedded C code, but which enables us to evaluate some pure C functions in annotations, in other words additional symbols interpreted by all of the Frama-C plug-ins.

To illustrate this mechanism, here is a simple example: the function "max_array" hereafter returns the maximum value of an array. It is added by the user in the analyzed C code, then used as a *ghost function* in order to facilitate the proof of a sought property on the function f.

```
//@ ensures \result == Max(t,i,j);
float max_array(float * t,int i,int j) { ... }

void f(float t[100])
{
...
//@ ghost float V = max_array(t,0,99);

//@ assert V <= 1.e+12;

//@ assert Prop(t) <= 1.e+12;

...

}
```

The variable V above is a *ghost* variable; it is initialized with the value returned by "max_array" which takes as parameters the array t, and returns the max value of this array (this value is typically computed by *Value Analysis* when interpreting function max_array). This max value of the array can thus be exploited if needed in any annotation downstream in the code.

To make the verification possible, it is also necessary to define an axiomatic to establish the logical relationship between the predicate *Prop* and the *ghost function* "max_array". It is worth noting that the contract on "max_array" can also be formally verified, since this function follows a recurrence reasoning which is independent of the size of the array, and therefore not subject to the scaling up issue encountered with automatic provers.

Large parts of these ghost codes and annotations are automated thanks to dedicated plug-ins developed in-house.

6.9.5. *Validating ACSL lemmas by formal calculus*

Adding *lemmas* which aim to facilitate, even make possible, the verification of properties by automatic theorem provers is a common practice in proofs of programs, in particular to prove nonlinear arithmetic properties for instance.

These "arithmetical" lemmas are generally good candidates for verification by means of formal calculus engines. Indeed, tools such as Maxima[31] are able to process the kind of calculatory theorems useful to Frama-C proofs, at the cost of a translation carried out by another dedicated plug-in. The principle is simple: all the lemmas contained into the code in the form of ACSL annotations are translated into Maxima formulas. All the possible ACSL syntaxes for writing lemmas are not taken into account by this plug-in at this moment: only the lemmas in the form of Horn clauses are taken into account. Once the lemmas are translated, they are submitted to Maxima, and the result of the symbolic calculator is imported in a Frama-C state.

The main benefit is the great simplicity of use, more adapted to the culture of operational teams than the use of an interactive prover such as Coq assistant. For sure, the confidence level in the "proof" carried out in this way is not as high as when using Coq, but it is enough in this experimental context, at least to rapidly be reassured regarding the correction of formulas inserted in the ACSL axiomatic of the annotated code. Unless one foresees a proper qualification of the Maxima tool, which is not currently planned, the lemmas will need to be reviewed later, even demonstrated by experts with the help of interactive provers such as Coq.

As an example, here is a lemma that is representative of those used in the case study presented in this chapter:

```
/*@ lemma qr7_7a:
    \forall real u,yi,ys,xi,xs; (xi<=u<xs) &&
(yi<ys)
    ==> yi<=(((u-xs)*(yi-ys))/(xi-xs))+ys; */
```

---

31 To find out more, see www.maxima.sourceforge.net/documentation.html.

and its translation which is automatically translated in Maxima language by our specific plug-in:

```
assume(xi <= u);assume(u < xs);assume(yi < ys);
(yi <= ((u-xs)*(yi-ys))/(xi-xs)+ys), pred;
maybe(%);
```

Then finally, the result obtained by Maxima:

```
(%i2)  assume(xi<=u)
(%i3)  assume(u<xs)
(%i4)  assume(yi<ys)
                       (u - xs) (yi - ys)
(%i5)  ev(yi <= ys + ------------------,pred)
                          xi - xs
(%o5)                         true
```

6.9.6. *Combining static and dynamic analysis*

Our experience has shown that the formal verification of a certain number of properties and functions required a much greater cost than for others. In most cases, these properties and functions which are difficult to process concern numerical algorithms which have a certain complexity and which might require – at least – the use of the interactive Coq prover, which indeed would be quite time-consuming and is of course not intended to be carried out by non-expert users. Seen from a callgraph point of view, in most cases it is a matter of leaf-functions.

Generally speaking, the reason why static analysis can be preferred to testing activity is the exhaustive input domain from which the verification is done. The test is not exhaustive by definition, but it has the advantage of being able to be executed on the target, its results can therefore have the expected numerical accuracy.

However, testing often suffers from unrealistic computation-time on an entire application, and sometimes from a difficulty for the user to define realistic scenarios on smaller subsets of its application, in particular on the leaf-functions of the callgraph: the operational input domains of library functions are generally not precisely known, at the opposite of the operational input domains of the application.

These considerations have guided us to search for a means to take advantage of each of the two approaches, static analysis and testing. Briefly presented, it is a matter of automatically generating tests aiming to validate some sought ACSL properties which resist static analysis, and particularly on library functions which are richer in complex numerical algorithms.

Tests have to be representative of the global behavior of the application. To partly meet this constraint, tests are then generated according to value domains computed by *Value Analysis* from the main function to the entry point of the function under test. To do this, a dedicated plug-in (called GENA-MC; see Figure 6.20) is in charge of:

– determining the input domains of values of the C function under test, using the results computed by *Value Analysis*;

– calling the library R^{32} for random generation and the computation of a few probability laws;

– generating the calling context of the leaf-function to be tested (the sought property is translated into a C if/else statement);

– launching the compilation and execution of test scenarios (Monte-Carlo simulations);

– catching the result obtained by tests and storing it as a Frama-C state (testing is therefore considered as another, complementary, decision procedure).

These tests are carried out on a machine having the same representation of numbers as on the target, which contributes to the analysis of numerical accuracy. As they are mostly leaf-functions, the computation time remains reasonable (one hour on average for 10 billion Monte-Carlo simulations), thus authorizing a probabilistic coverage with a high confidence level, such as "Six Sigmas" or even more.

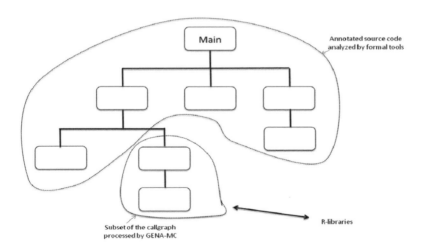

Figure 6.20. *Coupling of formal and probabilistic approaches*

---

32 To find out more, see www.r-project.org.

Basically, the properties which are supposed to be true but difficult to discharge by static analysis can be declared as valid after one hour of massive Monte-Carlo simulations in uniform distribution law on domains, with a probability of 1 and a confidence interval for this property of about 1.e-6 to 1.e-5.

Also, note that these intensive tests remain guided by requirements, as values of input domains used during tests are obtained from a propagation by *Value Analysis* of input domains of the whole application[33].

This plug-in enables us to rapidly conclude on some verifications, with a high confidence level which might be favorably compared to justifications by means of expert manual reviews.

6.9.7. *Finalizing*

Once all the resources reviewed in the previous sections have been exhausted, there might still remain unproven annotations. In our case study, they all deal with some temporal properties. These very few properties concern C functions which use cycle memories (values preserved over several cycles or "ticks"). The notion of cycle applies here to a complete execution of the application. And it should be therefore necessary to define some recurrent properties (invariants, and other inductive definitions) related to the sought properties. This task was beyond the scope of this case study.

However, to address this kind of property, ongoing research works (in the context of the French ANR U3CAT 2008-2012 research project) aim at assisting the user during the annotation and analysis of code, partly based on model-checking of source code, that we will not detail here.

For the purpose of our case studies, these properties were commonly validated by human reasoning: the code is critical and therefore leaves no room for doubt. But applying formal analysis to this kind of temporal property with adapted tools constitutes a future and unavoidable challenge.

6.10. Acknowledgements

The authors would like to thank Benjamin Monate (CEA-List) and Claude Marché (INRIA Proval), as well as their respective teams, for their involvement in

---

33 Ongoing developments will also enable us to take into account relationships between variables (such as the *relational domain* available in certain implementations of *abstract interpretation*) as constraints extracted from requirements.

the development of solutions within Frama-C, solutions which are both robust and innovative, and in particular adapted to the rigorous constraints of embedded critical software verification.

Our sincere thanks also goes to Pierre Guyot, Philippe Bourdais and Bruno Stoufflet from Dassault Aviation for their commitment to these activities, both in terms of transfer towards programming teams and R&T investment to bring them to the required level of maturity.

6.11. Bibliography

[ARI 10] ARINC, 661-4 Cockpit Display System Interfaces to User System, 2010.

[ARP 96] ARP4754 Certification Considerations for Highly-integrated or Complex Systems, SAE – EUROCAE, no. ED79, 1996.

[BAU 10a] BAUDIN P., CUOQ P., FILLIÂTRE J.-C., MARCHÉ C., MONATE B., MOY Y., PREVOSTO V., ACSL: ANSI/ISO C Specification Language (v. 1.4), www.frama-c.com/download/ acsl_ 1.4.pdf, 2010.

[BAU 10b] BAUDIN P., CUOQ P., FILLIÂTRE J.-C., MARCHÉ C., MONATE B., MOY Y., PREVOSTO V., ACSL: ANSI/ISO C Specification Language. Preliminary Design (v.1.4), www.frama-c.com/download/acsl_1.4.pdf, 2010.

[BER 92] BERRY G., GONTHIER G., "The synchronous programming language Esterel: Design, Semantics, Implementation", *Science of Computer Programming*, 19, 83-152, 1992.

[BER 04] BERTOT Y., CASTÉRAN P., "Coq'Art: The Calculus of Inductive Constructions". *Texts in Theoretical Computer Science. An EATCS Series*. Springer, Heidelberg, 2004.

[BON 10] BONICHON R., PASCAL CUOQ P., "Une table d'association d'intervalles fusionnable", *Proceedings of 21e Journées francophones des langages applicatifs (JFLA'10)*, February 2010.

[BOR 00] BORNAT R., "Proving pointer programs in Hoare logic", in *Mathematics of Program Construction*, p. 102–126, 2000.

[CAN 09] CANET G., CUOQ P., MONATE B., "A Value Analysis for C Programs", *Proceedings of the 9th IEEE International Working Conference on Source Code Analysis and Manipulation (SCAM'09)*, September 2009.

[CON 07] CONCHON S., CONTEJEAN E., KANIG J., LESCUYER S., "Semantical Combination of Congruence Closure with Solvable Theories", *Proceedings of the 5th International Workshop on Satisfiability Modulo Theories, SMT 2007, Electronic Notes in Computer Science*, ol. 198-2, p. 51-69, Elsevier Science, Amsterdam, 2008.

[COR 09] CORRENSON L., CUOQ P, PUCCETTI A. SIGNOLES J., Frama-C User Manual, www.frama-c.com/download/user-manual-Boron-20100401.pdf, 2009.

[COU 77] Cousot P., Cousot R., "Abstract interprstateion: a unified lattice model for static analysis of programs by construction or approximation of fixpoints", 4th ACM SIGACT-SIGPLAN POPL, p. 238-252, Los Angeles, 17-19 January 1977.

[CUO 10] Cuoq P., Prevosto V., "Frama-C's value analysis plug-in", www.frama-c.com/download/value-analysis-Boron-20100401.pdf, 2010.

[DET] Detlefs D., Nelson G., Saxe J., Simplify theorem prover, www.compaq.com/src/esc/simplify.html.

[DIJ 75] Dijkstra E.W., "Guarded commands, nondetermiNADy and formal derivation of program", Communications of the ACM, 18(8):453–457, August 1975.

[GOU 06] Goubault E., Putot S., Manuel d'utilisation de Fluctuat C : analyseur statique de la précision de calculs utilisant des nombres flottants, CEA DRT/LIST, 2006.

[HAR 85] Harel D., Pnueli A., "On the Development of Reactive Systems", Logics and Models of Concurrent Systems, K. R. Apt (ed.), NATO ASI Series, vol. F-13, p. 477-498, Springer-Verlag, New York, 1985.

[HOA 69] Hoare C.A.R., "An axiomatic basis for computer programming", ACM Press, vol 12, p. 576 - 580, New York, October 1969.

[HUB 07] Hubert T., Marché C., "Separation analysis for deductive verification", in Heap Analysis and Verification (HAV'07), p. 81-93, Braga, Portugal, March 2007.

[HUB 08] Hubert T., Analyse Statique et preuve de Programmes Industriels Critiques, PhD thesis, Paris-Sud University, June 2008.

[LED 06] Ledinot E., Pariente D., Formal verification of manual code: some industrial needs and recommendations, Embedded Real Time Software, www.sia.fr/dyn/publications_ detail.asp? codepublication=R-2006-01-3A3, SIA ed., 2006.

[LER 09] Leroy X., "Formal verification of a realistic compiler", Communications of the ACM 52(7), July 2009.

[LER 10] Leroy X., CA formally verified compiler back-end", ACM Transaction on Programming Languages and Systems, 2010.

[MOU 04] de Moura L., Bjørner N., "Z3, An Efficient SMT Solver", www.microsoft.com/projects/z3, 2004.

[MOY 09] Moy Y., Automatic Modular Static Safety Checking for C Programs, PhD thesis, www.lri.fr/~marche/moy09phd.pdf, Paris-Sud University, 2009.

[PAR 10] Pariente D., Ledinot E., "Formal Verification of Industrial C Code using Frama-C: a Case Study", Proceedings of First International Conference on Formal Verification of Object-Oriented Software (FoVeOOS'10), June 2010.

[PRE 10] Prevosto V., "ACSL Tutorial", www.frama-c.com/download/acsl-tutorial.pdf, 2010.

[RTC 92] DO-178B/ED-12B, Software Considerations in Airborne Systems and Equipment Certification, RTCA Inc., 1992.

[RTC 11] RTCA EUROCAE DO-178/ED-12 version C, Aspects logiciels de la certification des systèmes et équipements aéronautiques, 2011.

[RUS 05] RUSTAN K., LEINO M., "Efficient weakest preconditions", *Inf. Processing Letter,* 93(6): p. 281–288, 2005.

[SIG 09a] SIGNOLES J., CORRENSON L., PREVOSTO V., "Frama-C Plug-in Development Guide", frama-c.com/download/plugin-developer-Boron-20100401.pdf, 2009.

[SIG 09b] SIGNOLES S., " Foncteurs impératifs et composés: la notion de projets dans Frama-C.", HERMANN (ed.) JFLA 09, *Actes des vingtièmes Journées Francophones des Langages Applicatifs 2009*, vol. 7.2, p. 245–280, *Studia Informatica Universalis*, June 2009.

Chapter 7

Efficient Method Developed by Thales for Safety Evaluation of Real-to-Integer Discretization and Overflows in SIL4 Software

7.1. Introduction

In the context of Thales' developments in the railway sector, the safety level of control-command software must be in compliance with the development process described by the CENELEC EN 50128 standard [CEN 01]. In order to verify the absence of (i) critical scenarios and (ii) possible design and programming errors, this development process is accompanied by different analysis techniques allowing us to evaluate the safety level of the software at each phase of its lifecycle, as well as tracing, refining and verifying the safety requirements of the upstream phases towards the downstream phases.

The safety analysis techniques used in the phases of requirements and architecture requirement are generally based on functional analysis, whereas those used during detailed component design phases often use static analyses or the critical rereading of code.

In parallel, the dynamic analysis of software by tests and simulation (during integration and validation phases) is carried out to debug the software. Formal methods can also be used in addition to tests and simulation.

Chapter written by Anthony BAÏOTTO, Fateh KAAKAÏ, Rafael MARCANO and Daniel DRAGO.

In this chapter we put forward a static analysis approach based on the arithmetic of intervals in order to allow firstly verification of the absence of errors linked to the discretization of the arithmetic algorithm (uncertainties due to the passage of real numbers to integers) during their implementation on a safety platform only supporting the *integer* type, and secondly, the absence of risk of arithmetic overflow (and divisions by zero).

In our code production chain, complex arithmetic functions are fully described by detailed functional requirements, then their design is done in a high-level language (SCADE®)[1], to finally automatically generate their implementation in C code. In the proposed method, real-to-integer discretization and overflows analysis is carried out in parallel to the verification of the design. The verification of design is thus facilitated because additional verifications in the generated code are avoided. In addition, owing to this approach it is possible to avoid the use of additional tools which are often used for the verification of arithmetic overflows.

The chapter is structured as follows:

– section 7.2 presents the issue linked to discretization errors (uncertainties) in the context of our code production chain;

– section 7.3 presents the modeling approach of the creation and propagation of uncertainties;

– section 7.4 presents the principles enabling us to make the proposed method applicable the to the context of our code production chain;

– section 7.5 presents the analysis of arithmetic overflows and divisions by zero;

– section 7.6 presents an application of the methodology for a train speed control software component;

The demonstration supplements are presented in section 7.8.

7.2. Discretization errors in the embedded code production chain

7.2.1. *Presentation of the issue*

The 2oo3 (2 out of 3) safety platform used in Thales requires the use of signed and coded integer numbers on 32 bits for the implementation of variables and software constants. This implementation constraint leads to a loss of precision in modeling of data and an accumulation of errors in numerical calculation chains, such as illustrated in Figure 7.1.

---

1 SCADE® is a product of EstereL-Technologies (see www.esterel-technologies.com).

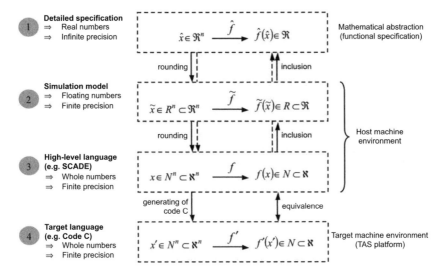

Figure 7.1. *Illustration of discretization errors*

It is possible to distinguish four levels of representation of a given processing.

Level 1

It corresponds to the detailed functional requirement of a processing represented in all or part of the set of real numbers, $\Re$. It is a mathematical abstraction of processing (even if the requirement is textual) established on the basis of a calculation precision which is presumed infinite.

Level 2

It corresponds to a simulation model developed in a machine (host) environment to represent the functional requirement of level 1. This simulation model is generally only justified for complex software components. In level 1, we consider the set of real numbers, $\Re$. In level 2, the corresponding set is a subset; $R \subset \Re$; of floating numbers (or number with floating comma) which can be represented on a machine by binary numbers. The subset R can be defined in base 2 as follows (see [IEE 85]):

$$R = \{0\} \cup \left\{ (-1)^s \cdot m \cdot 2^e \mid s, b_i \in \{0,1\}, \; m = 1 + \sum_{i=1}^{\ell} \frac{b_i}{2^i}, \; i, \ell \in \aleph^*, \; e \in \aleph \text{ and } E_{min} \le e \le E_{max} \right\} \quad [7.1]$$

where: m is the mantissa of the floating number; calculate m based on ℓ bits b_i of the fraction f of the binary number associated with the floating number (see Figure 7.2);

the size of the mantissa is by definition equal to $\ell+1$; e is the exponent of the floating number (as Figure 7.2 shows).

Figure 7.2. *Binary representation of a floating number*

Size of the binary number	Equiv. C ANSI	Size of s	Size of $f = \ell$	Size of e	E_{min}	E_{max}	Maj(ε_x)
32 bits (simple precision)	*float*	1 bit	23 bits	8 bits	-126	+127	$2^{-24} \approx 6.10^{-8}$
64 bits (double precision)	*double*	1 bit	52 bits	11 bits	1022-	+1023	$2^{-53} \approx 1.10^{-16}$

Table 7.1. *Size and precision of floating numbers*

Table 7.1 shows the size of different components (fraction, exponent, sign) of the binary representation of floating numbers on 32 and 64 bits. This table also specifies the value of an upper bound of the error relative to εr, which is by definition equal to:

$$\varepsilon_x = \left| \frac{\hat{x} - \tilde{x}}{\tilde{x}} \right| < 2^{-\ell} \qquad\qquad [7.2]$$

The upper bound $2^{-\ell}$ can be demonstrated by considering an upper bound of the weight of the smallest significant bit of the mantissa (*unit in last place* or *ulp*, see [LEF 04]).

It is also possible to demonstrate that errors relative to elementary arithmetic calculations are also bounded by the same upper bound (see [LEF 04]). Thus, if the functions $\hat{f}$ and $\tilde{f}$ represent an elementary arithmetic operation (+, -, /, ×), the error can be written as follows:

$$\varepsilon_f = \left| \frac{\hat{f} - \tilde{f}}{\tilde{f}} \right| < 2^{-\ell} \qquad\qquad [7.3]$$

Level 3

It corresponds to a design and an implementation of the detailed functional requirement with a high-level language that is data-flow oriented. In the rest of this chapter we will take the example of SCADE® language from Esterel Technologies[2] – where the only type used to represent numerical data is the integer type (or int) that is signed and coded on 32 bits (characteristic of the processor of the safety target platform).

According to input document levels, it is possible to envisage two types of transition to level 3:

1) direct passage from functional requirements (level 1) to SCADE® code (level 3) requires evaluating of error caused on the one hand by coding of real values $\hat{f}$ (of infinite precision) on integer numbers x signed and coded on 32 bits, as well as the approximation of real numeric functions $\hat{f}$ by integer numeric functions f (we can cite the well-known example of integer division which is an approximation of real division);

2) the passage from simulation model (level 2) to SCADE® code (level 3) requires evaluating the following approximations which depend on the characteristics of simulation models:

   - the passage of integer numbers on 32 bits of floating numbers initially coded on 32 or 64 bits: float 32 (or double 64) $\rightarrow$ int 32;

   - the real-to-integer discretization on 32 bits of integers numbers initially coded on 64 bits: int 64 $\rightarrow$ int 32;

   - the approximation of numerical functions with floating commas $\tilde{f}$ by us integer numerical functions f.

Level 4

This fourth and final level corresponds to embedded C code. If the certification of the code generator (KCG in the case of SCADE®) is proof that the generated C code truly represents the original code, in particular for arithmetic calculations (see the example in Figures 7.3 and 7.4 which illustrate the passage of "SCADE® $\rightarrow$ C" for elementary mathematical operations).

In theory there is no additional uncertainty to take into consideration for the generation of embedded code of software components' phase.

---

2 For more information, see www.esterel-technologies.com/.

Nonetheless, it is recommended to carry out boundry value analysis of the limits of the generated C code in target environment in order to verify that the extremal uncertainties determined during the theoretical analysis of models in level 3 were never exceeded.

7.2.2. *Objective of the analysis of the real-to-integer discretization*

The main objective of the present study was to evaluate this accumulation in terms of uncertainty in the software in order to respond to the following fundamental question: "Does the passage to integer preserve the restrictive nature of safety requirements?"

Or, in other words, "does it not make them more permissive?", which would be contrary to software safety and, on a larger scale, contrary to the safety of the system.

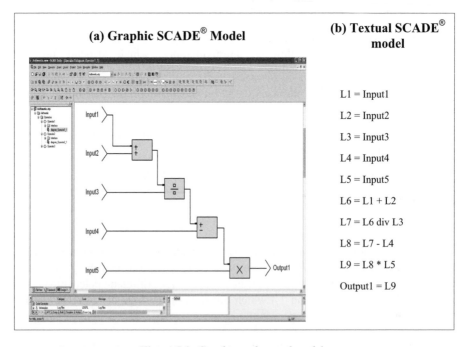

Figure 7.3. *Graphic and textual models*

(c) Code C generated without optimization (file *.c)	(d) Code C generated with level 3 optimization (f. *.c)
| ```c
#include "kcg_consts.h"
#include "kcg_sensors.h"
#include "Operator1.h"

void Operator1_reset(outC_Operator1
*outC)
{
}

/* Operator1 */
void Operator1(inC_Operator1 *inC,
outC_Operator1 *outC)
{
  /* Operator1::_L24 */ kcg_int _L24;
  /* Operator1::_L23 */ kcg_int _L23;
  /* Operator1::_L22 */ kcg_int _L22;
  /* Operator1::_L21 */ kcg_int _L21;
  /* Operator1::_L20 */ kcg_int _L20;
  /* Operator1::_L19 */ kcg_int _L19;
  /* Operator1::_L18 */ kcg_int _L18;
  /* Operator1::_L17 */ kcg_int _L17;
  /* Operator1::_L16 */ kcg_int _L16;

  _L16 = inC->Input1;
  _L17 = inC->Input2;
  _L18 = inC->Input3;
  _L19 = inC->Input4;
  _L20 = inC->Input5;
  _L21 = _L16 + _L17;
  _L22 = _L21 / _L18;
  _L23 = _L22 - _L19;
  _L24 = _L23 * _L20;
  outC->Output1 = _L24;
}
``` | ```c
#include "kcg_consts.h"
#include "kcg_sensors.h"
#include "Operator2.h"

void Operator2_reset(outC_Operator2
*outC)
{
}

/* Operator2 */
void Operator2(inC_Operator2 *inC,
outC_Operator2 *outC)
{
  outC->Output1 = ((inC->Input1 + inC-
>Input2) / inC->Input3 - inC->Input4) *
    inC->Input5;
}
``` |

Figure 7.4. *Generated code*

7.3. Modeling of the creation and propagation of uncertainties

7.3.1. *Creation of uncertainties*

We begin by presenting the basic hypotheses of this analysis before giving a few definitions and a summary of the proposed paradigm. Then we will explain how to construct an uncertainty propagation tree in software components as well as the methodological principles on which this analysis is based. We will finish with a didactic example that allows us to illustrate the notions seen throughout this section.

7.3.1.1. *Basic hypotheses of the analysis*

The present analysis of real-to-integer discretization of *applicative software* is based on the set of following hypotheses without which the results obtained could not be used for the demonstration of safety.

HYPOTHESIS 7.1.– The analysis of the real-to-integer discretization of applicative software is done at the components' level; there will therefore be as many analyses as there are software components (for components which do not use arithmetic calculations, these analyses will be trivial, and should therefore not be the subject of a particular development).

HYPOTHESIS 7.2.– The safety outputs of software components which provide inputs to the analyzed component are at least as restrictive as safety outputs corresponding to the associated level 1 models; this therefore implies that the real-to-integer discretization of these components has been previously analyzed.

As a consequence of the application of hypothesis 7.2, the inputs of the analyzed component are presumed correct.

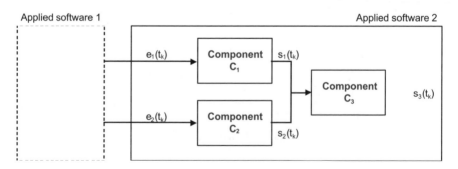

Figure 7.5. *Generated codes*

7.3.1.2. *Uncertainties computing: definitions and formalism*

DEFINITION 7.1.– *Absolute error.* The absolute error, marked $\varepsilon_x \in \mathfrak{R}$, between an exact value $\hat{x} \in \mathfrak{R}$ and an approached value $x \in \aleph$ is defined by: $\varepsilon_x = x - \hat{x}$, or also, which is the same, by: $x = \hat{x} + \varepsilon_x$.

We do not consider the absolute value of the absolute error, ε, as its sign is an important indication to determine the impact on the system safety of the real-to-integer discretization of the safety of the software.

Let us give a basic example. Consider a safety requirement which involves, for example that the functional output $\hat{x}$ must not be under-evaluated (case of the speed of a train). If the analysis of the discretization uncertainty related to $\hat{x}$ shows that $\varepsilon \geq 0$ ($\hat{x}$ is over evaluated), then all be it, it is possible to conclude there is no risk about the discretization of $\hat{x}$ in the software. However if $\varepsilon < 0$ ($\hat{x}$ is under-evaluated), it is possible to conclude in this case that the safety requirement mentioned above is not fulfilled and, thus that the hazard associated with this safety requirement is not covered in the software.

DEFINITION 7.2.– *Uncertainty interval.* An uncertainty interval associated with an ordered pair ($\hat{x} \in \mathfrak{R}$, $x \in \aleph$) is a compact interval (close and bounded) denoted by $\delta^x = [\delta^x_{min} \in \mathfrak{R}, \delta^x_{max} \in \mathfrak{R}]$, such as: $\delta^x_{min} \leq \varepsilon_x \leq \delta^x_{max}$ where ε_x is the absolute error (see above) associated with the ordered pair ($\hat{x} \in \mathfrak{R}, x \in \aleph$).

DEFINITION 7.3.– *Intrinsic uncertainty function* (QUF). Let $a \in Z$ and $b \in Z^*$ be two operands, $\lozenge$ a *real* mathematical binary operation which associates a result $\hat{c} = \lozenge(a,b) \in \mathfrak{R}$ with the ordered pair (a, b), and $\square$ the corresponding *integer* arithmetic binary operation ($\square \leftrightarrow \lozenge$) which associates a result $c = \square(a,b) \in Z$ with the ordered pair (a, b), the intrinsic uncertainty function $\delta^\square(a,b)$ of a integer arithmetic binary operation $\square$ is a function of a function which associates an uncertainty interval $\delta^\square(a, b) = \delta^c = [\delta^c_{min} \in \mathfrak{R}, \delta^c_{max} \in \mathfrak{R}]$ with an operation $\square(a, b) = c$ such as: $\delta^c_{min} \leq \varepsilon_c \leq \delta^c_{max}$, where ε_c is the absolute error (see above) associated with the ordered pair ($\hat{c} = \lozenge(a,b) \in \mathfrak{R}, c = \square(a, b) \in Z$).

DEFINITION 7.4.– *Integer division in* SCADE®. Let us call $a \in Z$, $b \in Z^*$, $q \in Z$ and $r \in Q$, we call "integer division of a by b" of the function $D(a, b)$, also written "÷", which, for all ordered pairs (a, b) associates a unique ordered pair (q, r) such as:

– the quotient q (also written $a \div b$) is the result of the integer division with:

- a/b is the division in $\mathfrak{R}$ (real division) of a by b;

- $q = 0$ if $a = 0$;

- $q = \max(n \in Z \mid n \le a/b)$ if $a \cdot b > 0$;

- $q = \min(n \in Z \mid n \ge a/b)$ if $a \cdot b < 0$;

– the rest r verifies the following property: $r = a/b-q$ and $|r| < 1/$

PROOF 7.1.– *Existence and unicity of integer division.* See section 7.8.

Let us note that integer division as it is defined above is not a Euclidean division because the rest of a Euclidean division is defined as positive or null. For example, the integer division of -7 by 2 gives: $-7 = -3 \times 2 - 1$; whereas for a Euclidean division we would have the following result: $-7 = -4 \times 2 + 1$.

PROPOSITION 7.1.– *Framing of the error of integer division.* Consider the absolute error (see definition above) of a integer division of $a \in Z$ by $b \in Z^*$, on the basis of definition 8.4, it is possible to find the bounds of this error as follows:

- $\varepsilon = 0$ if $a = 0$ or if a modulo $b = 0$

- $-1+1/ \mid \mid, b \le \varepsilon \le 0$ if $a \cdot b > 0$

- $0 \le \varepsilon \le 1-1/ \mid \mid, b$ if $a \cdot b < 0$

PROOF 7.2.– *Framing of the error of integer division.* See section 7.8.

Thus, on the basis of these definitions, it is possible to determine the QUF of basic arithmetic calculations of SCADE® language such as it is presented in Table 7.2.

In the code, QUFs are sometimes compensated for by constants called "uncertainty compensator terms", which are the subject of the following definition.

DEFINITION 7.5.– *Uncertainty compensator term* (UCT). An Uncertainty compensator term is translated in software by a constant $\chi \in Z$, which in general follows arithmetic operations whose QUF is not in the null interval, the UCT being able to be added or retracted, it will be introduced in the software design documents by the symbols $\oplus$ and $\ominus$, which will enable us to differentiate the additions and subtractions of functional terms (which do not compensate for uncertainty). The UCT has the effect of shifting the uncertainty interval to which it applies. In addition to this definition of the QUFs of arithmetic operators, we must specify that an uncertainty interval must naturally be modulated in a chain of arithmetic calculations: it can be amplified, reduced, or moved by mathematical operations on the intervals which are described in detail in what follows.

Operation	Operands	Notation	QUF		Condition
			Symbol	Uncertainty interval	
Addition	$a,b \in Z$	$a + b$	δ^+	$[0 , 0]$	N/A
Subtraction	$a,b \in Z$	$a - b$	δ^-	$[0 , 0]$	N/A
Multiplication	$a,b \in Z$	$a \times b$	$\delta^\times$	$[0 , 0]$	N/A
Real division	$(a,b) \in Z \times Z^*$	a / b	*This operator is not allowed in SCADE® models that are coded in int32*		
Integer division	$(a,b) \in Z \times Z^*$	$a \div b$	δ^+	$[0 , 0]$	$a = 0$
				$[0 , 0]$	a module b = 0
				$[-1+1/ \mid \ \mid,b \ , 0]$	$a \cdot b > 0$
				$[0 , 1-1/ \mid \ \mid,b]$	$a \cdot b < 0$
				$[-1+1/ \mid \ \mid,b \ , 1-1/ \mid \ \mid,b]$	Sign of $(a \cdot b)$ unknown
Modulo	$(a,b) \in Z \times Z^*$	$a \bmod b$	δ^{mod}	$[0 , 0]$	N/A

Table 7.2. *Intrinsic uncertainties of basic arithmetic operations of SCADE® language*

7.3.1.3. *Arithmetic of uncertainty intervals*

7.3.1.3.1. Calculation rules

Let us call a and b relative integer numbers, and $\delta^a = [\delta^a_{min} \in \Re, \delta^a_{max} \in \Re]$ $\delta^b = [\delta^b_{min} \in \Re, \delta^b_{max} \in \Re]$ be the corresponding uncertainty intervals.

The arithmetic of uncertainty intervals obeys the following calculation rules:

$$\delta^a + \delta^b = [\delta^a_{min} + \delta^b_{min}, \ \delta^a_{max} + \delta^b_{max}] \tag{7.4}$$

$$-\delta^b = [-\delta^b_{max}, \ -\delta^b_{min}] \tag{7.5}$$

$$\delta^a - \delta^b = \delta^a + (-\delta^b) = [\delta^a_{min} - \delta^b_{max}, \ \delta^a_{max} - \delta^b_{min}] \tag{7.6}$$

$$\delta^a \times \delta^b = \delta^a \cdot \delta^b = [\alpha, \beta], \text{ where:}$$

$$\begin{cases} \alpha = \min \ (\delta^a_{min} \cdot \delta^b_{min}, \ \delta^a_{min} \cdot \delta^b_{max}, \ \delta^a_{max} \cdot \delta^b_{min}, \ \delta^a_{max} \cdot \delta^b_{max}) \\ \beta = \max \ (\delta^a_{min} \cdot \delta^b_{min}, \ \delta^a_{min} \cdot \delta^b_{max}, \ \delta^a_{max} \cdot \delta^b_{min}, \ \delta^a_{max} \cdot \delta^b_{max}) \end{cases} \tag{7.7}$$

$$\delta^a \times c = \delta^a \times [c, c]$$

where $c \in Z$ is a constant or functional parameter; $\tag{7.8}$

$$(\delta^b)^{-1} = [(\delta^b_{max})^{-1}, \ (\delta^b_{min})^{-1}] \text{ if } 0 \notin \delta^b \tag{7.9}$$

$$\delta^a / \delta^b = \delta^a \times (\delta^b)^{-1} \tag{7.10}$$

$$\delta^a \div c = \delta^a \times [1/c, \ 1/c]$$

where $c \in Z^*$ is a constant or functional parameter; $\tag{7.11}$

$$\delta^a \div \delta^b = [\alpha, \beta], \text{ where:}$$

$$\begin{cases} \alpha = \min \ (\delta^a_{min} \div \delta^b_{min}, \ \delta^a_{min} \div \delta^b_{max}, \ \delta^a_{max} \div \delta^b_{min}, \ \delta^a_{max} \div \delta^b_{max}) \\ \beta = \max \ (\delta^a_{min} \div \delta^b_{min}, \ \delta^a_{min} \div \delta^b_{max}, \ \delta^a_{max} \div \delta^b_{min}, \ \delta^a_{max} \div \delta^b_{max}) \end{cases} \tag{7.12}$$

$$\min \ (\delta^a, \delta^b) = [\min(\delta^a_{min}, \delta^b_{min}), \ \min(\delta^a_{max}, \delta^b_{max})] \tag{7.13}$$

$$\max \ (\delta^a, \delta^b) = [\max(\delta^a_{min}, \delta^b_{min}), \ \max(\delta^a_{max}, \delta^b_{max})] \tag{7.14}$$

7.3.1.3.2. Properties of operations on intervals

In our study, all the calculated uncertainty intervals will not be relative to numbers; but to intervals.

NOTATION 7.1.– In the rest of the note, a capital letter signifies an interval, $A = [\underline{a}, \overline{a}]$ whereas the underlined letter $\underline{a} = \min (A)$ and the overlined letter $\overline{a} = \max (A)$ denote the extremities of the interval. This writing is quite intuitive and avoids all conflict with possible signs. For a scalar $x \in \Re$, we have: $x = X$ because $x = \underline{x} = \overline{x}$ by misuse of language.

Associativity

$$(A + B) + C = A + (B + C) \quad \text{and} \quad (A * B) * C = A * (B * C)$$

Commutability

$$A + B = B + A \quad \text{and} \quad A * B = B * A$$

Neutral element

$$0 + A = A + 0 = A \quad \text{and} \quad 1 * A = A * 1 = A$$

Sub-distributivity

$$A * (B + C) \subseteq (A * B) + (A * C)$$

Decorrelation of variables

Let us consider a variable $s1$ which varies in a functional range $[0,10]$. If we calculate $s2 = s1 - s1$, by relation [7.5] the arithmetic of intervals enables us to calculate its functional interval as follows:

$$s_2 = \left[0,10\right] - \left[0,10\right] = \left[-10,10\right]$$

However we know that $[0,0]$ frames the expected result.

This is an example where the calculation involves the same variable several times (here it is $s1$).

The arithmetic of intervals does not take into account the occurrence of this variable in the calculation, which gives too broad a result. We speak of *decorelation of variables*.

The decorelation of variable does not pose a safety problem as it induces a restrictive (englobing) calculation. Nonetheless, in certain cases it is necessary to refine the obtained results to be more relevant.

DEFINITION 7.6.– *QUF generalized to intervals* (GenQUF). Let us call $A \subset Z$ and $B \subset Z^*$ two intervals, $\Diamond$ a *real* mathematical operation which associates to the ordered pair (A, B) a result $\hat{C} = \Diamond(A,B) \subset \Re$, and $\square$ and the corresponding *integer* mathematical operation ($\square \leftrightarrow \Diamond$) which to the ordered pair (A, B) associates a result $C = \square(A,B) \subset Z$; the intrinsic arithmetic function $\Delta^{\square}(A,B)$ of a integer arithmetic operation $\square$ is a functional (function of a function) which to an operation $\square(A,B) = C$ associates an uncertainty interval $\Delta^{\square}(A, B) = \Delta^C = [\Delta^C_{min} \in \Re, \Delta^C_{max} \in \Re]$ such as: $\Delta^C_{min} \leq \varepsilon_C \leq \Delta^C_{max}$, where ε_C is the absolute error (see definition 7.1) generalized to the intervals associated to the ordered couple ($\hat{C} = \Diamond(A,B) \in \Re$, $C = \square(A,B) \in Z$).

As with operations on numbers, the only operation leading to a non-null GenQUF (noted Δ^+) in the case of arithmetic operators in SCADE® is integer division.

Let us call $A = [\underline{a}, \overline{a}] \subset Z$ and $B = [\underline{b}, \overline{b}] \subset Z^*$, we have: $\Delta^+ (A, B) = [\Delta^+_{min}, \Delta^+_{max}]$.

There are four cases:

– *case 1*, if B is a divider of A:

$$\begin{cases} \Delta^+_{min} = 0 \\ \\ \Delta^+_{max} = 0 \end{cases}$$

COMMENT 7.1.– We say that B is a divider of A if, and only if, $\forall b \in B, \forall a \in A, \exists n \in Z / a = n * b$;

– *case 2*, if $A*B < 0$:

$$\begin{cases} \Delta^+_{min} = 0 \\ \Delta^+_{max} = 1 + \dfrac{1}{\max(|\underline{b}|, |\overline{b}|)} \end{cases}$$

– *case 3*, if $A*B > 0$:

$$\begin{cases} \Delta^+_{min} = -1 + \dfrac{1}{\max(|\underline{b}|, |\overline{b}|)} \\ \Delta^+_{max} = 0 \end{cases}$$

– *case 4*, if $0 \in A$:

$$\begin{cases} \Delta^+_{min} = -1 + \dfrac{1}{\max(|\underline{b}|, |\overline{b}|)} \end{cases}$$

$$\Delta^+_{max} = 1 + \frac{1}{max(|\underline{b}|, |\overline{b}|)}$$

7.3.2. Propagation of uncertainties

NOTATION 7.2.– We can generalize the definition of uncertainty intervals defined by definition 7.4 to the notation 7.1 on intervals by:

$$\delta^A = [\delta_{min}{}^A, \delta_{max}{}^A]$$

with:

$$\begin{cases} \delta_{min}{}^A = \min_{a \in A}(\delta_{min}{}^a) \\ \delta_{max}{}^A = \max_{a \in A}(\delta_{max}{}^a) \end{cases}$$

we are sure that:

$$\forall a \in A, \delta^a \subset \delta^A$$

which guarantees the safety framing of uncertainties: when the software "sees" a variable to vary in a range A, the real corresponding variable will vary in the interval $A - \delta^A$.

7.3.2.1. Addition

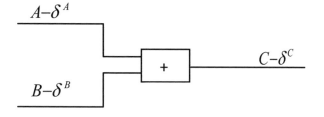

Figure 7.6. *Addition*

We have:

$$\delta^C = A + B - ((A - \delta^A) + (B - \delta^B))$$

$\delta^C = \delta^A + \delta^B$ given by [7.4]

The addition operation does not lead to a decorrelation issue of systematic variables.

7.3.2.2. Subtraction

We have:

$$\delta^C = (A - B) - (A - \delta^A) - (B - \delta^B)$$

$\delta^C = \delta^A - \delta^B$ given by [7.6]

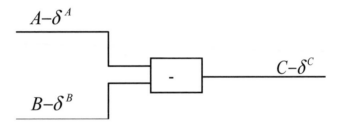

Figure 7.7. *Subtraction*

Subtraction can lead to problems of decorrelation of variables, as shown in section 7.3.1.3.2.

In some cases, it is possible to overload a bound of the interval calculated according to invariants found in variables in play (see section 7.3.1.3.2).

7.3.2.3. Multiplication

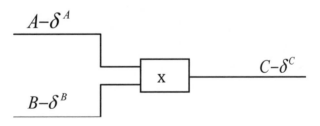

Figure 7.8. *Multiplication*

We have:

$$\delta^C = A*B - (A-\delta^A)*(B-\delta^B)$$

We can see that we cannot directly calculate δ^C according to δ^A and δ^B as the values of A and B directly intervene in the result. We are confronted with a problem of decorrelation of variables, which risks making the result too broad and therefore less relevant.

NOTE 7.1.– This was not the case with addition and subtraction operations as, for example in additions we have: $\delta^C = A+B - (A-\delta^A) + (B-\delta^B) = \delta^A + \delta^B$ which does not involve A and B in the calculation of δ^C (Same for subtraction).

In this case, it is possible to calculate a refinement of the interval. We have A, B, δ^A, δ^B which are intervals and can therefore be written:

$$\begin{cases} A = [\underline{a}, \overline{a}] \\ B = [\underline{b}, \overline{b}] \\ \delta^A = [\delta^A \min, \ \delta^A \max] \\ \delta^B = [\delta^B \min, \ \delta^B \max] \end{cases}$$

We distinguish here the notations of these intervals and those of ordered pairs of bound values:

$$\begin{cases} \{\underline{a}, \overline{a}\} \\ \{\underline{b}, \overline{b}\} \\ \{\delta^A \min, \ \delta^A \max\} \\ \{\delta^B \min, \ \delta^B \max\} \end{cases}$$

We set f:

$$\{\underline{a}, \overline{a}\} \times \{\underline{b}, \overline{b}\} \times \{\delta^A \min, \ \delta^A \max\} \times \{\delta^B \min, \ \delta^B \max\} \to \Re$$

$$(\alpha, \beta, \delta^\alpha, \delta^\beta) \to f(\alpha, \beta, \delta^\alpha, \delta^\beta) = \alpha\beta - (\alpha - \delta^\alpha)*(\beta - \delta^\beta)$$

We then have $\delta^C = [\delta^C \text{min}, \delta^C \text{max}]$ with:

$$
\begin{cases}
\delta^C \text{min} = \min_{\substack{\alpha \in \{\underline{a},\overline{a}\} \\ \beta \in \{\underline{b},\overline{b}\} \\ \delta^\alpha \in \{\delta^A_{\min}, \delta^A_{\max}\} \\ \delta^\beta \in \{\delta^B_{\min}, \delta^B_{\max}\}}} (f(\alpha,\beta,\delta^\alpha,\delta^\beta)) \\[3em]
\delta^C \text{max} = \max_{\substack{\alpha \in \{\underline{a},\overline{a}\} \\ \beta \in \{\underline{b},\overline{b}\} \\ \delta^\alpha \in \{\delta^A_{\min}, \delta^A_{\max}\} \\ \delta^\beta \in \{\delta^B_{\min}, \delta^B_{\max}\}}} (f(\alpha,\beta,\delta^\alpha,\delta^\beta))
\end{cases}
$$

PROOF 7.2.– Proof of the framing of uncertainties which come from a product: see section 7.8.

7.3.2.4. *Division*

General scenarios:

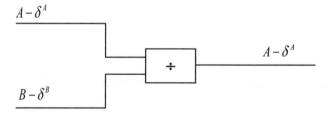

Figure 7.9. *Division*

Based on the example in Figure 7.8, the expression of the uncertainty interval on C is given by:

$$\delta^C = (A \div B) - (A - \delta^A)/(B - \delta^B)$$

We can see that (as for multiplication) we cannot directly calculate δ^C according to δ^A and δ^B. The values of A and B are involved in the calculation, which induces a possibility of decorrelation of variables.

For the propagation of uncertainties in divisions we will distinguish two cases.

– *First case:* $\delta^B = 0$ *(case where the divider interval does not propagate any uncertainty).*

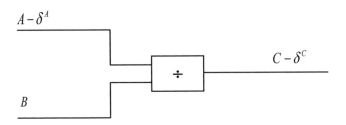

Figure 7.10. *First case*

We have:

$$\delta^C = (A \div B) - (A - \delta^A)/B$$

which is translated by:

$$\delta^C \subseteq (A \div B) - ((A/B) - (\delta^A/B))$$

We can note a loss of precision at this stage due to the subdistributivity of operations on intervals. This can be written:

$$\delta^C \subseteq \underbrace{(A \div B) - (A/B)}_{\text{First term}} + \underbrace{(\delta^A/B)}_{\text{Second term}}$$

The first term corresponds to a GenQUF defined in definition 7.6, where as the second is a simple division of intervals that we can calculate thanks to the relation [7.10].

– *Second case:* $\delta^B \neq 0$

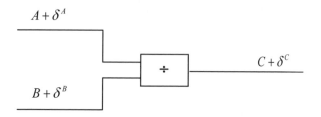

Figure 7.11. *Second case*

This case requires a matrix approach which is not the context of this chapter.

7.3.2.5. *Didactic example of propagated uncertainties*

Let us illustrate the concepts introduced in this section with the following simple example of Table 7.3 where:

– the inputs are scalars which are not polluted by uncertainties;

– the OK/NoK status is defined as follows: OK if $\varepsilon_{Si} \in [\delta^{Si}_{min}, \delta^{Si}_{max}]$, and NoK if not.

		Result of the processing $i \in \{1, 2, \ldots, 8\}$		Evaluation of passage to integer		OK/ NoK Status	Analysis
N°	Relation	$\hat{S}_i \in \Re$	$S_i \in Z$	Exact absolute error ε_{Si}	Uncertainty interval $[\delta^{Si}_{min}, \delta^{Si}_{max}]$		
R1	Input A	1	1	0	[0 , 0]	OK	No uncertainty on external inputs according to Hypothesis 7.2
R2	Input B	1000	1000	0	[0 , 0]	OK	No uncertainty on external inputs according to Hypothesis 7.2
R3	Input C	170	170	0	[0 , 0]	OK	No uncertainty on external inputs according to Hypothesis 7.2
R4	S1 = A/2	0.500	0	0.500	[0, 0.5]	OK	QUF Integer division: $\delta^{S1} = [0 , 1\text{-}1/2]$ (see Table 7.2)

R5	S2 = -100 * S1	-50	0	-50	[-50, 0]	OK	Amplification of uncertainty interval (QUF null for multiplication) $\delta^{S2} = -100 \times \delta^{S1}$ (see relation [7.8])
R6	S3 = S2 + B	950	1000	-50	[-50, 0]	OK	$\delta^{S3} = \delta^{S2}$ (QUF null for the addition)
R7	S4 = S3/C	5.588	5	0.588	[-0.294, 0.994]	OK	QUF Integer division + Reduction of uncertainty interval: $\delta^{S4} = \delta^{+}(S3,C) + \delta^{S3} / C$ (see Table 7.2 and relation [7.11])
R8	S5 = 17 * S4	95	85	10	[-5, 16.9]	OK	Amplification of the uncertainty interval (QUF null for multiplication) $\delta^{S5} = 17 \times \delta^{S4}$ (see relation [7.8])
R9	S6 = B/30	33.333	33	0.333	[0, 0.966]	OK	QUF Integer division : $\delta^{S6} = [0 , 1-1/30]$ (see Table 7.2)
R10	S7 = -7 * S6	-233.333	-231	-2.333	[-6.766 , 0]	OK	Amplification of uncertainty interval (QUF null for multiplication) $\delta^{S7} = -7 \times \delta^{S6}$ (see relation [7.8])

Table 7.3. *Example of propagated uncertainty calculation*

7.4. Good practice of an analysis of real-to-integer discretization

The example looked at in the previous section shows that analysis of real-to-integer discretization can be be complex to manage when there are numerous relations with several variables to study. This problem of complexity will also arise when it is necessary to manage conditional structures and iterative loops. With the aim of rigorously organizing and facilitating the analysis of the real-to-integer discretization, we have elaborated the following methodological principles which become essential when the processing under study becomes complex. Hereafter we illustrate this methodological principles while considering SCADE® code.

7.4.1. *Code extraction*

First of all, it is necessary to extract "useful" code in its context when the latter is not impacted by the real-to-integer.

For example, if an arithmetic processing is preceded by numerous pre-processing of data handling (transposing of a vector, sorting the number of variables, etc.) and followed by other similar post-processing, it is then pointless to study the whole chain {pre-processing → arithmetic processing → post-processing}, but it is better to extract the arithmetic processing from its context.

In the context of SCADE® language, the extraction is done by means of the function *convert to textual* applied to the considered operator. If an operator is already written textually, we will directly take this code.

Let us note that SCADE® authorizes two textual breakdowns for a same module. This is not ultimately a problem as it alternates the two possible breakdowns between two uses of the function *convert to textual*.

When the component uses a function (defined by another operator), we extract the SCADE® code of this function and we insert it after the instruction calling it.

7.4.2. *Functional code reorganisation*

In the case of synchronous languages such as SCADE®, code lines which come from the previous stage, can be in any order, and therefore not usable to do a propagation of uncertainties step-by-step.

Consequently it is necessary to reorganize this code by respecting the "any variable used in an instruction must be calculated upstream".

Let us note that this reorganization can be equipped (the tool needing to be qualified) and that if the module is coded textually, it is generally useless.

7.4.3. *Algorithmic breakdown in basic arithmetic relations*

Once the code is reorganized, it is necessary to carry out algorithmic breakdown. This stage consists in breaking down code lines in basic SCADE® instructions.

Here again, this activity can be automated (by a qualified tool) while respecting the following rules:

– the order of priority of basic SCADE® operations must be respected to guarantee the coherence of algorithmic breakdown and the effective sequence of calculations during the execution of the target embedded software;

– for the issue of the real-to-integer discretization, it is only necessary to break down arithmetic instructions, that is to say the following basic operations: "ˆ , + , − , (unary), * , / , mod , div";

– the code lines will be broken down until we obtain so-called *basic instructions*. A basic instruction calculates an output according to two inputs and a basic operator, mentioned above.

7.4.4. *Computation of uncertainties*

The propogation of uncertainties (see section 7.3.2) that propagate the uncertainties of variables, we must know the range of these variables and associated uncertainties ($\delta^C = f(A, B, \delta^A, \delta^B)$).

At this stage, we have:

– the algorithmic breakdown of the component code;

– the functional ranges and uncertainty intervals on the inputs of the component.

We are therefore able to carry out the study of the calculation and propagation of uncertainties in the code of the component. To do this we begin by calculating the functional ranges and uncertainty intervals associated to lines of code which involve the inputs of components. These calculations are done thanks to the rules of calculation and propagation of uncertainties defined in the previous section (section 7.3) which are highly recommended to automate in the form of qualified macros, ideally with an interface of ergonomic capture (indeed, these macros will be called times, which is likely to favor inattention mistakes). The results obtained will then be able to be regrouped in a table (see Table 7.4) where:

– the *instruction* column assigns a unique identifier to each basic instruction;

– the *algorithmic breakdown* column presents the extracted, reorganized and broken down code;

– the *uncertainty range* columns group together the lower and upper bounds of functional values which enable us to maximize uncertainties (coupling uncertainty/functional range). We place the lower bound in the left column and the upper bound in the right one;

– the *uncertainty intervals* columns group together the results of uncertainty calculation of the considered algorithmic breakdown line. The result interval is also designated by its lower bound in the left column and its upper bound in the right column. In view of simplifying filling in these two columns, it is recommended to automate, with the help of macros, all the calculations on intervals presented in previous section (section 7.3).

Instruction	Algorithmic breakdown	Uncertainty range		Uncertainty Interval		Comments
R54.14.01	A = Max(Q1, L2)	0	120	0.00	0.00	In order to refine the framing of this variable, it would be necessary to have a characterization of path
R54.14.02	B = Min(T1, L3)	120	120	0.00	0.00	
R54.14.03	C = A – L2	0	120	0.00	0.00	Overload of the bound inferior to 0
R54.14.04	D = C **div** 10	0	12	0.00	0.90	Creation of uncertainty
R54.14.05	E = L3 – A	-120	120	0.00	0.00	
R54.14.06	S = E **div** 10	0	12	0.00	0.90	Creation of uncertainty

Table 7.4. *Example of results*

It is possible to overload the bounds of this *uncertainty range* to be able to limit certain effects of variable decorrelation, as it is illustrated the example of Table 7.5.

This work is then reproduced on each instruction by using the previously calculated results to the outputs of the studied module (propagation of uncertainties step-by-step).

Instruction	Uncertainty range calculated with the arithmetic of interval		Real uncertainty range with overload bounds		Comment
	Lower bound	Upper bound	Lower bound	Upper bound	
L1 = a	-10	10	-10	10	OK
L2 =L1*L1	-100	100	0	100	Overload of lower bound as square is always positive

Table 7.5. *Example of limitation of decorrelation effects*

7.5. Arithmetic overflow and division by zero

The breakdown of arithmetic processing in basic instructions allows carrying out in parallel the study of the impacts of the real-to-integer discretization and the risk of arithmetic overflow and division by zero.

It is thus possible to obtain an integrated methodology which enables us to cover the main aspects of static analysis of code for highly arithmetic processing.

7.5.1. *Analysis of arithmetic overflow risk*

We consider in this section that the set of software variables, parameters and constants of signed integer type (int), will be coded on words of 32 bits.

Let us call x a variable calculated in the studied component:

– there is arithmetic overflow of x if and only if:

$$\exists i \in \langle 1,2,3....n \rangle / |x_i| > 2^{31} - 1 = \text{MAX\_INT}$$

– there is a risk of arithmetic overflow of x if and only if:

$$\exists j \in \langle 1,2,3....n \rangle / |x_j| > MAX\_INT - \varepsilon_{m \arg e}$$

In our study, the set of x_i and x_j are framed by the functional range of values.

We look at all the functional values which frame the values that software outputs can take and verify that their bounds do not go over 2^{31} - 1 in absolute value.

We will be able to consider that a software component does not have a risk of arithmetic overflow if it does not have processing which involves an arithmetic operation.

As components only make comparisons, logical processing or assignments are not impacted by this issue.

We will insert in to the table of the study of real-to-integer discretization two *Range Overflow* columns enabling us to calculate the functional ranges of software values (with the help of interval arithmetic), maximizing the risk of arithmetic overflow.

We will also insert an *Overflow* column which enables us to test if the values contained in *Range Overflow* are superior in absolute value to 2^{31} - 1.

Algorithmic breakdown	Range Overflow		Overflow
L1 = a	0	3,000,000,000	NoK
L2 = b	- 2,500,000,000	0	NoK
L3 = c	- 1,900,000,000	500,000	OK

7.5.2. *Analysis of the risk of division by zero*

The principle of this analysis is to verify that the set of values authorized (Range Overflow in the table above) for the denominators of integer divisions and to ensure that none of them is null.

We verify for each occurrence of the integer division function that the range authorized for the denominator does not contain zero.

If it does contain zero, we emit a *warning* which will lead either to a more subtle study of the risk of division by zero, or to the safety requirements of a software safeguard (defensive modeling).

7.6. Application to a rail signalling example

7.6.1. *General presentation of the communication-based train controller system*

As described by the IEEE (*Institute of Electrical and Electronics Engineers*) body and its standard IEEE 1474 [IEE 04], a CBTC (*communication-based train controller*) is:

"A set of embedded and on-the-ground calculators to process control and states data in order to implement three main functions:

– *Automatic Train Protection (ATP)*;

– *Automatic Train Operating (ATO)*;

– *Automatic Train Supervision (ATS)*".

Let us consider in this section the ATP function which can be seen as a processing chain carrying out among other things: the acquisition in safety of the speed of the train; the localization in safety of the cabins of the train; the evaluation of the ability of the train to stop upstream at a given point to protect on the line or to respect a given speed constraint.

The safety of train movements is ensured first of all by a broadband communication between:

– The subsystem SOL, which calculates and sends to each BORD subsystem its authorization of movement (zone of the track in which the considered train can move without a risk of collision or loss of itinerary). This zone is mainly calculated according to:

- the state of the track;

- the itineraries asked for by trains;

- the localizations of trains on the track;

– The BORD subsystem embedded in trains (one per train communicating with the SOL subsystem), which takes into account the authorized movement zone sent by the SOL and guarantees a respect of inscription of the train only in this zone. The BORD subsystem guarantees the respect of the zone by processing a speed control algorithm according to:

- the speed of the train;

- the localization of the train on the track;

- the end of the movement zone sent by the SOL subsystem;

- Static data of the track and rolling hardware.

In the following, we will focus on the software component which carries out the *speed control algorithm* embedded in the BORD subsystem.

7.6.2. *Example of analysis of the behavior of speed control*

We begin this example of analysis by presenting a simplified algorithm of the speed control. Then we develop the analysis methodology of real-to-integer discretization presented. Finally, we comment on some numerical results obtained by simulating the analyzed algorithm.

7.6.2.1. *Simplified speed control algorithm*

The inputs of the algorithm are integers signed and coded on 32 bits safely acquired by the SOL subsystem and communicated to the BORD subsystem or directly acquired by the BORD subsystem:

_v the instantaneous speed of the train;

_ x_t the abscissae of "the front of the train on the track";

_ x_{PAP} the abscissea of "Protected Point A" on the track;

_ z_t the altitude of the "front of the train";

_ z_{PAP} the altitude of "Protected Point A".

Which corresponds graphically to Figure 7.11.

According to inputs, the algorithm determines a Boolean "RespectZone" corresponding to the emergency breaking command of the train.

When "RespectZone" turns false, the system sets off an emergency breaking of the train (maximal deceleration) until the complete halt of the train.

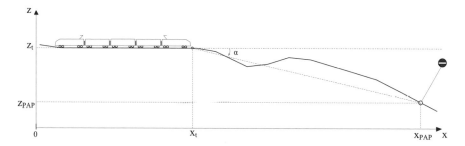

Figure 7.12. *Speed control use case example*

We presume that the train undergoes a constant $a_{train/fr}$ acceleration (deceleration) during emergency breaking due to:

– the average slope between the train and the point to protect α ;

– the guaranteed deceleration of emergency breaking of the train, γ_{FU} :

$$a_{train/fr} = a_{slope} + \gamma_{FU}$$

where γ_{FU} is a parameter measured on the rolling stock, whereas the slope a_{slope} is computed as follows:

$$a_{slope} = -\alpha g$$

We then make two approximations:

– approximation of small angles on the track as if the slope on rail tracks are weak, we then have: $\alpha \cong \tan(\alpha) = \dfrac{z_{PAP} - z_t}{x_{PAP} - x_t}$;

– the gravity acceleration g, is presumed constant during the deceleration phase of the train.

The stopping distance of the train is given by:

$$D_{stop} = -\frac{1}{2} * \frac{v^2}{a_{train/fr}}$$ with v and $a_{train/fr}$ defined above.

The train stops before the PAP if and only if:

$$D_{stop} \leq s_{PAP} - s_t$$

to guarantee the safety of the latter control:

$$\text{RespectZone} = D_{stop} + \text{margin} \geq s_{PAP} - s_t \text{ with margin} > 0 \qquad [7.15]$$

which can be written: $\text{RespectZone} = V_{\text{limit}} >^2 v^2$ where:

$$V_{\lim it}^2 = -2(\gamma_{FU} + g\left(\frac{z_{PAP} - z_t}{x_{PAP} - x_t}\right)) * [x_{PAP} - x_t + \text{magin}]$$

A pseudo code of the algorithm described is presented in Table 7.6.

RespectZone = false;	Initialization
RemainingDistance_cm = x_PAP_cm - x_T_cm;	Calculation of the distance between the front and PAP in cm
DifferenceAltitude_cm = z_PAP_cm - z_T_cm;	Computation of the difference in altitude between the train train and the PAP in cm
Alpha_1/1000 = $\dfrac{\text{corr1000*DifferenceAltitude\_cm}}{\text{DistanceRemaining\_cm}}$;	Computation of the slope in 1/1000
AccSlope_cmps2 = - $\dfrac{\text{Alpha\_1p1000* g\_cmps}}{\text{corr1000}}$;	Computation of the acceleration due to the slope in cm/s²
AccBrake_cmps2 = - GammaFU_cmps2 + AccSlope_cmps2;	Computation of the acceleration of the train during the breaking phase in cm/s²
Dsecu_cm = DistanceRemaining_cm + Margin_cm;	Calculation of the increased distance between the localization of the head of the train and the PAP in cm
Vlimit_cm2ps2 = - (AccBrake_cmps2 * Dsecu_cm)*2 ;	Calculation of the speed limit squared in cm²/s²

IF Vlimit_cm2ps2 < V²
    RespectZone = true;
 IF NOT
    RespectZone = false;
 ENDIF
	Test of setting off the alarm

Table 7.6. *Simplified algorithm of speed control*

With GammaFU_cmps2 = emergency breaking deceleration guaranteed in cm/s² measured on the rolling stock, here 100 cm/s². We will note emerging coefficients (corr1000) in relation to the requirement. These coefficients are the direct consequence of the implementation in integer of a requirement of infinite precision

Décomposition du code :	Range inf	Range sup	Incertitude inf	Incertitude sup	Range overflow inf	Range overflow sup
% Calcul des distances et des DiffAlt						
DistanceRestante_cm = xPAP_cm - xT_cm;		50 000	0,000	0,000	1	50 000
DifferenceAltitude_cm = zPAP_cm - zT_cm;	-5 000	5 000	0,000	0,000	-5 000	5 000
% Calcul de la pente en 1/1000						
Alpha1_p1000cm = 1000 * DifferenceAltitude_cm;	-5 000 000	5 000 000	0,000	0,000	-5 000 000	5 000 000
Alpha_1p1000 = Alpha1_1000cm DIV DistanceRestante_cm;	-1 000	1 000	-1,000	1,000	-1 000	1 000
% Calcul de l'ACC due pente en cm/s2						
AccPente_1000cmps2 = Alpha_1p1000 * g_cmps2 ;	-981 000	981 000	-980,980	980,980	-981 000	981 000
-AccPente_cmps2 = - AccPente_1000cmps2 * DIV 1000 ;	-981	981	-1,980	1,980	-981	981
%Calcul de l'ACC train pendant le freinage :						
AccFrein_cmps2 = GammaFU_cmps2 - AccPente_cmps2;	-1 081	881	-1,980	1,980	-1 081	881
% Calcul de la distance de sécurité entre T et PAP						
Dsecu_cm = DistanceRestante_cm + marge_cm;	201	50 200	0,000	0,000	201	50 200
% Calcul de la vitesse limite :						
DemiVlimite_cmps = AccFrein_cmps2 * Dsecu_cm ;	-54 266 200	44 226 200	-99395,015	99395,015	-54 266 200	44 226 200
Vlimite_cm2ps2 =-DemiVlimite_cmps * 2;	108 532 400	-88 452 400	-198790,030	198790,030	108 532 400	-88 452 400
% Contrôle du respect du Point						
Vcarre_cm2ps2 = V* V;	0	1 600 000 000	0,000	0,000	0	1 600 000 000
RespectZone = Vcarre_cm2ps2 < Vlimite_cm2ps2;	N/A	N/A	—	—	N/A	N/A

Table 7.7. *Result of the code analysis*

In our example (Table 7.6), the slope (Alpha_1/1000) was chosen in this unit (1/1000) as a slope in 1/1 is not usable in integer. By considering:

– DifferenceAltitude_cm =15671;

– RemainingDistance_cm = 198741;

a code without coefficient in front of the division would have given:

$$\frac{\text{DifferenceAltitude\_cm}}{\text{RemainingDistance\_cm}} = 0.07885137 = 0 \text{ in integer,}$$

which is not usable for the rest of the processing as the slope is non-null and non-negligible (7% in this case). The more bigger the coefficient, the more we will conserve significant numbers on this calculation for the rest of the processing. We then see a correlation between the precision of expected results and the risk of overflow associated with the code.

7.6.2.2. Static analysis of code

In Table 7.7 the overloaded cells are lines 7 and 12; the maximum slope on the track is equal to 10%. Let us also note that in this example the ranges which give the worst cases of uncertainty are also the ranges which give the worst cases for overflows. The code proposed in Table 7.8 is not for safety: the uncertainties on V_limite_cm2ps2 can be positive or negative, which means that the associated amount calculated in real can be overestimated or underestimated, depending on the individual case. The RespectZone alarm must not be wrongly true.

RespectZone = false;	Initialization
SI $x_{PAP} > x_T$	Avoids division by zero
RemainingDistance_cm = x_{PAP}_cm - x_T_cm;	Calculation of the distance between the front and the PAP
DifferenceAltitude_cm = z_{PAP}_cm - z_T_cm;	Calculation of the difference in train/PAP altitude
Alpha_1/1000 = $\dfrac{\text{corr1000*DifferenceAltitude\_cm}}{\text{DistanceRemaining\_cm}}$ -1;	Calculation of the slope
AccSlope_cmps2 = $-\dfrac{\text{Alpha\_1p1000* g\_cmps}}{\text{corr1000}}$ + 1;	Calculation of the acceleration due to the slope
AccBrake_cmps2 = - GammaFU_cmps2 + AccSlope_cmps2;	Calculation of the acceleration of the train during the breaking phase
Dsecu_cm = RemainingDistance_cm + Margin_cm;	Calculation of the increased distance between the front and PAP

Vlimit_cm2ps2 = - (AccBrake_cmps2 * Dsecu_cm)*2;	Calculation of limit speed squared in cm²/s²

IF Vlimit_cm2ps2 < V²
　　　　RespectZone = true ;
IF NOT
　　　　RespectZone = false ;
END IF
IF NOT
　　Continue
END IF
	Test setting off the alarm

Table 7.8. *Algorithm of corrected speed control*

To guarantee the safety of the calculation of this Boolean, V_limit_cm2ps2 must be systematically underestimated, which is not guaranteed by this code, which therefore needs to be corrected (see Table 7.8).

In the case where RemainingDistance_cm is null, there is a division by zero during the instruction: "Alpha_1p1000 = Alpha1_1000cm DIV RemainingDistance_cm;", the negative or null amounts of RemainingDistance_cm are not to be considered. The corrections to be added to the code are noted in bold in Table 7.8. Let us note that the coefficient corr1000 (=1000) had previously been sized in this example to cause arithmetic overflows while keeping good precision. The calculation table of uncertainties and ranges can nonetheless serve to calculate an optimal parameter to manage the risk/performance relation.

7.6.2.3. *Numerical application*

The following results were obtained by a Matlab®[3] simulation, the abscissea of the front of the train is given in cm whereas the breaking command corresponds to the ascending front of the command curve.

---

3 www.mathworks.com/products/matlab.

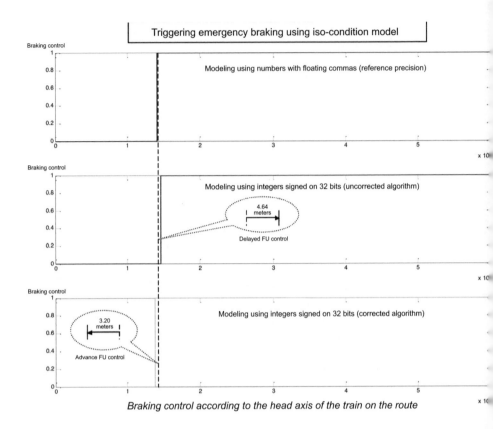

Figure 7.13. *Presentation of results*

These results show that the initial model in integers (Figure 7.12, central frame) leads to a setting off of FU (emergency braking) 4.64 meters late (in relation to the real world, Figure 7.12, top frame).

With the corrected model following our static analysis (Figure 7.12, low frame), we set off the FU in advance of 3.20 meters (still in relation to the real world top frame), which contributes to the safety of the software, allowing the train stopping before the protected point.

7.6.3. Industrial scale view: a few numbers

The previous example of this simple application had the objective of illustrating in a didactic way the different notions introduced throughout this chapter.

The passage to industrial scale of the proposed method of analysis was carried out with success at Thales for SIL4 rail applications characterized on average, for the following metrics:

– 200 analyzed SCADE® boards;

– propagation of uncertainties on 2,500 basic instructions;

– human resources: 15 to 20 man-days depending on the arithmetic complexity of the analyzed component;

– specific material resources: SCADE® license.

Finally, let us note, that the proposed method of analysis can also be served by software engineering teams during the detailed design, the implementation and debugging of software components to IVVQ teams and in safety assurance for activities of verification and validation of code.

7.7. Conclusion

We have presented an approach based on the use of the arithmetic of intervals [HAN 03] to carry out static analysis in the SCADE® design models, with the aim of processing uncertainties induced for calculations of integers signed on 32 bits in relation to the same calculations described in functional requirements and carried out in infinite precision [LEF 04], thus ensuring the conformity of the code generated.

The approach required the formalization of mathematical functions, enabling us to model the creation of uncertainties in the chains of arithmetic processing, then the establishment of propagation rules of these uncertainties on the outputs to be analyzed.

These functions must be applied to a breakdown of basic instructions of the model to be analyzed, as the order of priority of basic arithmetic operations counts in the evaluation of uncertainties.

Then, the uncertainty results propagated at the outputs of the software components are confronted with safety constraints emitted during the analysis of functional requirement (safety rules imposing the prohibition of overestimating or underestimating the real output). It then becomes possible to speak about the safety of implementation in integers signed on 32 bits of upstream functional requirements.

The methodology this developed enables us, in parallel, to analyze uncertainties – thanks to the arithmetic of intervals – arithmetic overflow risks on each basic operation.

In order to evaluate the relevance of the analysis method and to demonstrate its ability to be applied on an industrial scale, application was carried out on the speed control function [IEE 04], implemented by a software component of the highest safety level (SIL4) required in rail systems.

This application then led us to equip and integrate the approach in our embedded code production chain which uses modeling in SCADE®. However, the principle presented is independent of the language and cannot be extended to other high-level modeling languages.

The application of this method also enabled us to highlight the complementarity of the static analysis of component tests, and also as a debugging tool.

Indeed, our approach facilitates the detection of gaps between physical models of functional requirements and their initial implementation in integers.

The algorithmic errors highlighted in turn enabled us to refine the tests by producing scenarios corresponding to exceptions found (remarkable values or cases at the limits which could give rise to gaps).

A future direction for our work will consist in using affine forms in parallel with arithmetic of intervals to improve the precision of results which can be too englobing (too broad) due to the problem of decorrelation of variables.

7.8. Annexe: proof supplements

7.8.1. *Proof 1: existence and unicity of integer division*

Let us call $\in Z$, $b \in Z^*$, $q \in Z$ and $r \in Q$, let us show the existence and unicity of the ordered pair (q,r) associated with (a,b) such as:

– the quotient q (also marked $a \div b$) is the result of the integer division with:

  - a/b is the division in $\Re$ (real division) of a by b;

  - $q = 0$ if $a = 0$;

  - $q = \max (n \in Z \mid n \leq a/b)$ if $a \cdot b > 0$;

  - $q = \min (n \in Z \mid n \geq a/b)$ if $a \cdot b < 0$;

– the rest r verifies the following property: $r = a/b - q$ and $|r| < 1$.

Demonstration of the existence

Let us distinguish three cases:

– $a = 0$;

– $a.b > 0$;

– $a.b < 0$.

Study of case a = 0

– if $a = 0$ then $q = 0$, according to the definition;

– so $a/b - q = 0$;

– as $r = a/b - q$, we obtain $r = 0$.

Which proves the existence of (q,r) in this case.

Study of case a.b > 0

Let us consider the set $E_1 = \{n \in Z \mid n \leq a/b)\}$:

– we have $0 \in E_1$ because $a/b > 0$ in this case;

– so $E_1 \neq \varnothing$.

Let us set $d \in Z$ such as $d \geq E (a/b)+1$ with $E: \Re \rightarrow Z, X \rightarrow E(X)$ the integer part of X:

– by definition we have: $d \geq E(a/b)+1 > a/b$;

– so $d \notin E_1$ and d is an upper bound of E_1;

– as $E_1 \subset Z$, we have E_1 which has a maximum.

Which proves the existence of q in this case.

As $q = \max (E_1)$ we have $1+q > a/b$:

– that is to say $1 > a/b - q$;

– and as $a/b = q + r$, we get $r < 1$;

– furthermore, we have $q \in E_1$ so $q \leq a/b$, *that is to say a/b − q ≥ 0 is the same* as $r \geq 0$;

– then $0 \leq r < 1$ we therefore indeed have $|r| < 1$.

We have demonstrated the existence of the ordered pair (q,r) in this case.

Study of case a.b < 0:

Let us consider the set $E_2 = \{n \in Z \mid n \geq a/b)\}$:

– we have $0 \in E_2$ as $a/b < 0$ in this case;

– so $E_2 \neq \emptyset$.

Let us set $d \in Z$ such as $d \leq E(a/b)$ with $E: \Re \rightarrow Z$, $X \rightarrow E(X)$ the integer part of X:

– we then have by definition: $d \leq E(a/b) < a/b$ by definition of the function E in $\Re^-$;

– so $d \notin E_1$ and d is a lower bound of E_2;

– as $E_2 \subset Z$, we have E_2, which has a minimum.

Which proves the existence of q in this case.

As $q = \min(E_2)$ we have $q - 1 < a/b$.

That is to say $-1 < a/b - q$;

– and as $a/b = q + r$, we get $r > -1$;

– furthermore, we have $q \in E_2$ so $q \geq a/b$, *that is to say a/b − q ≤ 0 is the same* as $r \leq 0$;

– then $-1 < r \leq 0$ we indeed have $|r| < 1$.

We have demonstrated the existence of the ordered pair (q,r) in this case. This shows the existence of the ordered pair (q,r) in all cases.

Let us now show the unicity of (q,r).

Let us call (q,r) and (q',r') verify the properties of the quotient and rest of the integer division of a by b. We have:

$$- a = b.q + b.r \qquad (1) \qquad \text{we set } R = b.r;$$

$$- a = b.q' + b.r' \qquad (2) \qquad \text{we set } R' = b.r'.$$

First case: $a = 0$

By definition $q = q' = 0$ and as b is necessarily different from 0, $r = r' = 0$.

Second case: $a.b > 0$

In this case, q is defined as $q = \max (n \in Z \mid n \leq a/b)$.

As q' is also meant to verify the properties of the quotient of integer division of a by b, we have:

$- q' = \max (n \in Z \mid n \leq a/b)$;

– we have q and q' which are therefore maximums of the same non-empty part of Z.

We can conclude that $q = q'$ by unicity of the maximum.

Furthermore:

– $(1) - (2)$ gives: $0 = q + r - q' - r'$ which is equivalent to $q - q' = r' - r$ (3);

– as $q = q'$, according to (3) we have $r - r' = 0$, which proves that $r = r'$;

– so $r = r'$ and $q = q'$, which proves unicity in this case.

Third case: $a.b < 0$

in this case, q is defined as $q = \min (n \in Z \mid n \geq a/b)$. As q' is also supposed to verify the properties of the quotient of integer division of a by b, we have:

$- q = \min (n \in Z \mid n \geq a/b)$;

– we have q and q', which are therefore minimums of the same non-empty part of Z. We conclude that $q = q'$ by unicity of the minimum;

– furthermore, $(1) - (2)$ gives: $0 = q + r - q' - r'$;

– which is equivalent to $q - q' = r' - r$. (3);

– as $q = q'$, according to (3) we have $r - r' = 0$, which proves that $r = r'$;

– so $r = r'$ and $q = q'$, which proves unicity in this case.

Which proves the unicity of the couple in all cases and concludes the demonstration.

7.8.2. Proof 2: framing the error of integer division

Let us call $a \in Z$, $b \in Z^*$, $q \in Z$ and $r \in Q$ with (q, r) defined by definition 1. Let us call: $S = a / b \in \Re$.   We   have   the   error   of   the   integer   division: $\varepsilon = (a \div b) - (a/b) = -r$ by definition.

We can distinguish five cases:

– $a = 0$;

– $a > 0$ and $b > 0$;

– $a < 0$ and $b > 0$;

– $a < 0$ and $b < 0$;

– $a > 0$ and $b < 0$.

Case a = 0

Nothing to demonstrate, we have by definition, $r = 0$.

Case ab > 0

Case $a > 0$ and $b > 0$:

– we have $0 \leq r < 1$; so

$0 \leq r.b < b$;

– then, as r.b$\in$ Z, we have $r.b \in \{0,1,2,...,b-1\}$; so

$-0 \leq r.b \leq b - 1$; that is to say

$-0 \leq r \leq 1 - 1/b$;

– in this case, $r \in [0, 1 - \dfrac{1}{b}]$.

Case a < 0 and b < 0:

– we have $0 \leq r < 1$; so

– $b < r.b \leq 0$;

– then as $r.b \in$ Z, we have $r.b \in \{b+1, b+2, ..., 0\}$; so

$-b+1 \leq r.b \leq 0$; that is to say

$-0 \leq r \leq 1+1/b$; or

$-b = -|b|$ as $b < 0$;

– in this case, $r \in [0, 1-\dfrac{1}{|b|}]$.

Summary of case $ab > 0$ to summarize the first two cases:

– if $a.b > 0$, $r \in [0, 1-\dfrac{1}{|b|}]$;

– which means that $\varepsilon \in [-1+\dfrac{1}{|b|}, 0]$.

Case a.b < 0

Case $a > 0$ and $b < 0$:

– we have $-1 < r \leq 0$; so

– $0 \leq r.b < -b$;

– then as $r.b \in Z$, we have $r.b \in \{0, 1, 2, ..., -b-1\}$; so

– $0 \leq r.b \leq -1 - b$; that is to say

– $-1/b - 1 \leq r \leq 0$.

Case a < 0 and b > 0:

– we have $-1 < r \leq 0$; so

– $0 \leq r.b < -b$; then as

$-r.b \in Z$, on a $r.b \in \{0, 1, 2, ..., -b-1\}$; so

$-0 \leq r.b \leq -1 - b$; that is to say

$-1/b - 1 \leq r \leq 0$;

– in this case, $r \in [-1+\dfrac{1}{|b|}, 0]$.

Synthesis of the case $a.b < 0$. To summarize the last two cases:

$-$ if $a.b<0$: $r\in [-1+\dfrac{1}{|b|},0]$;

$-$ which means that $\varepsilon \in [0,1-\dfrac{1}{|b|}]$.

We indeed have the framings for r specified in proposition 7.1 of the present chapter.

7.8.3. Proof 3: rules of the arithmetic of uncertainty intervals

See Chapter 2 of *Global Optimization Using Interval Analysis* [HAN 03].

7.8.4. Proof 4: framing of uncertainties from a product

Let us consider $A = [\underline{a},\overline{a}] \subset Z$ and $B = [\underline{b},\overline{b}] \subset Z$ with $\delta^A = [\delta^A_{min},\delta^A_{max}] \subset \Re$ and $\delta^B = [\delta^B_{min},\delta^B_{max}] \subset \Re$ their associated uncertainty intervals defined in notation 2.

We wish to calculate:

$$\delta^C \supseteq [\delta^C_{min},\delta^C_{max}] = AB - (A+\delta^A)*(B+\delta^B) \tag{1}$$

We are confronted in this case with a problem of decorrelation of variables. The result of δ^C calculated with the arithmetic of interval is too vague.

The idea to refine the result of the calculation is to consider variables $x\in A$ and $y\in B$ and to look at the behavior of the frame.

If we develop (1):

$$\delta^C \supseteq AB - (A-\delta^A)*(B-\delta^B);$$

$$\delta^C \supseteq AB - (A - [\delta^A_{min},\delta^A_{max}])*(B-[\delta^B_{min},\delta^B_{max}]);$$

$$[\delta^C_{min},\delta^C_{max}] \supseteq AB - (A - [\delta^A_{min},\delta^A_{max}])*(B-[\delta^B_{min},\delta^B_{max}]) \tag{2}$$

$\forall x \in A$ and $\forall y \in B$, x and y verify (2), we can therefore write:

$$xy - (x - [\delta_{min}^A, \delta_{max}^A]) * (y - [\delta_{min}^B, \delta_{max}^B]) \subset \delta^C$$

According to rules of arithmetic on intervals:

$$xy - [x - \delta_{max}^A, x - \delta_{min}^A] * [y - \delta_{max}^B, y - \delta_{min}^B] \subset \delta^C \tag{3}$$

In our case, we presumed that the uncertainty intervals were independent of the functional values of A and B. Which is translated here by the fact that: $\delta_{min}^A, \delta_{max}^A$, $\delta_{min}^B, \delta_{max}^B$ do not depend on the values of x and y.

If we reconsider the writing of $\delta^C = [\delta_{min}^C, \delta_{max}^C]$ in expression (3), we can then deduce that:

δ_{min}^C is the minimum of a function which depends on x and y (as $\delta_{min}^A, \delta_{max}^A, \delta_{min}^B, \delta_{max}^B$ are independent of x and y);

δ_{max}^C is the maximum of a function that depends on x and y (as $\delta_{min}^A, \delta_{max}^A, \delta_{min}^B, \delta_{max}^B$ are independent of x and y).

We can therefore write:

$$\delta_{min}^C = \min\left(f_m(x,y)\right) \qquad \delta_{max}^C = \max\left(f_M(x,y)\right)$$

According to (3) and the rule of product of two intervals (see [8.7]) we have:

f_m and f_M of the same form of f such as:

$$\Re \times \Re \longrightarrow \Re$$
$$(x,y) \longrightarrow f(x,y) = xy - (x - \#_a) * (y - \#_b)$$
with $\#_a \in \left\{\delta_{min}^A, \delta_{max}^A\right\}$ and $\#_b \in \left\{\delta_{min}^B, \delta_{max}^B\right\}$

The goal is now to access the maximum and minimum of functions f_m and f_M to calculate δ^C.

This work corresponds to a research of extremums of functions with two variables. It is clear that if these two functions do not admit local extremums, we can find their maximums and minimums sought by monotony on the bounds of the sets of function range.

Let us calculate the partial derivations of functions f. Let us call $(x, y) \in \Re \times \Re$, we have:

$$f(x, y) = xy - (x - \#_a)*(y - \#_b)$$

$$f(x, y) = x*\#_b + y*\#_a - \#_a*\#_b \tag{4}$$

We therefore have:

$$\begin{cases} \dfrac{\partial f(x, y)}{\partial x} = \#_b \\ \\ \dfrac{\partial f(x, y)}{\partial y} = \#_a \end{cases} \tag{5}$$

the condition necessary for f to accept a local extremum:

$$\frac{\partial f(x, y)}{\partial x} = \frac{\partial f(x, y)}{\partial y} = 0$$

This condition interpreted in system (5) is translated by:

$$\#_a = \#_b = 0 \tag{6}$$

Let us consider that (6) is verified. We see in (4) that in this case:

$$\forall (x, y) \in \Re \times \Re, f(x, y) = 0$$

In this case, it is clear that f does not admit a local extremum. In all other cases: $\forall (x, y) \in \Re \times \Re$

$$\begin{cases} \dfrac{\partial f\left(x,y\right)}{\partial x} \neq 0 \\[2mm] \dfrac{\partial f\left(x,y\right)}{\partial y} \neq 0 \end{cases}$$

which proves that f does not admit local extremums.

Therefore f_m, and f_M are strictly monotonous functions on $\Re \times \Re$. So we can recuperate the minimum of f_m and the maximum of f_M by reasoning on the bounds of the intervals of definition.

In our case:

$$\begin{cases} \underline{a} \leq x \leq \overline{a} \\[2mm] \underline{b} \leq y \leq \overline{b} \end{cases}$$

Then finally, $\delta^C = [\,\delta^C\,\text{min},\ \delta^C\,\text{max}]$, where:

$$\begin{cases} \delta^C \text{ min} = \min_{\substack{\alpha \in \{\underline{a},\overline{a}\} \\ \beta \in \{\underline{b},\overline{b}\} \\ \delta^\alpha \in \{\delta^A_{\min},\delta^A_{\max}\} \\ \delta^\beta \in \{\delta^B_{\min},\delta^B_{\max}\}}} \left(\alpha\beta - (\alpha - \delta^\alpha)*(\beta - \delta^\beta)\right) \\[10mm] \delta^C \text{ max} = \max_{\substack{\alpha \in \{\underline{a},\overline{a}\} \\ \beta \in \{\underline{b},\overline{b}\} \\ \delta^\alpha \in \{\delta^A_{\min},\delta^A_{\max}\} \\ \delta^\beta \in \{\delta^B_{\min},\delta^B_{\max}\}}} \left(\alpha\beta - (\alpha - \delta^\alpha)*(\beta - \delta^\beta)\right) \end{cases}$$

7.9. Bibliography

[CEN 01] CENELEC, NF EN 50128, Applications Ferroviaires. Système de signalisation, de télécommunication et de traitement – Logiciel pour système de commande et de protection ferroviaire, CENELEC, July 2001.

[HAN 03] HANSEN E.R., WALSTER G.W., *Global Optimization Using Interval Analysis*, (2nd edition), Marcel Dekker, New York, 2003.

[IEE 04] IEEE, Standard for Communications-Based Train Control (CBTC) Performance and Functional Requirements, IEEE, 2004.

[IEE 85] IEEE, Norme IEEE 754: Standard for Binary Floating-Point Arithmetic, IEEE, 1985.

[LEF 04] Lefèvre V., Zimmermann P., Arithmétique flottante, Rapport de recherche, INRIA, N° 5105, INRIA, Paris, January 2004.

Conclusion and Viewpoints

Introduction

The objective of this chapter is to propose a summary of what has been presented in this book.

Problematic

The development of a certifiable software application (see definition 1.1) is constrained by standards associated with each domain (aeronautics [ARI 92], automotive [ISO 09], railway [CEN 01a], nuclear [IEC 06] and generic [IEC 98]).

It is to be noted that these different standards define the notion of the "safety level to attain": (DAL in aeronautics, SIL for the generic standard, SSIL for rail and ASIL for automotive). The safety level is generally linked to an implementation, which can be linked to an objective to be attained (aeronautics) or to a means of implementation (automotive, rail or generic).

The applicable standards recommend the implementation of a quality assurance (section 1.4.2) that is based on the implementation of a "V cycle"-type development process (see section 1.4.1 and more specifically Figure 1.3), which is based on verification and validation activities based on carrying out tests (UT, IT and FT[1]).

The implementation of test activities has several problems, which are:

− the cost and burden of test activities;

Conclusion written Jean-Louis BOULANGER.
1 UT for unit tests, IT for integration tests and FT for functional tests.

– the late detection of faults;

– the difficulty in carrying out all the tests in the allocated time;

– etc.

This is why it is necessary to implement other practices that must enable us to detect the software application faults as early and as widely as possible, all the while offering similar guarantees for the types of faults detected.

One of the possible orientations consists of implementing formal methods (for example method B [ABR 96], SCADE® [DOR 08], Vienna Development Model [JON 90], Z [SPI 89], etc.), which on the basis of a model and set of properties, enables us to demonstrate that the product verifies the said properties.

It can be interesting, using classic development languages (such as C), to explore the behaviors of the program and demonstrate that it verifies a certain number of properties. Demonstration is only possible via the addition of annotations describing local conditions (pre-condition, post-condition, invariant) and a propagation and/or proof mechanism.

In Chapters 2 to 7, we presented examples of static code analysis techniques based on:

– abstract interpretation [COU 00]: Chapters 2, 3, 4 and 6;

– program proof [HOA 69]: Chapters 2, 5 and 6;

– static analysis of code: Chapters 2, 5, 6 and 7.

It is worth noting that one of the difficulties in implementing these industrial example techniques lies in the absence of recognition of these techniques within current standards. Indeed, certain standards (automotive [ISO 09], rail [CEN 01a] and generic [IEC 98]) recommend the implementation of formal methods but they do not mention the notion of abstract interpretation (or derived methods).

Viewpoints

This first volume presented examples of the implementation of formal techniques used in the context of the static analysis of code. These examples are a first set of contributions that enable us to show the viability of the implementation of abstract interpretation and program proof as techniques of code verification.

It is worth noting that the abstract interpretation tools such as Polyspace® or Astrée are not new but their efficiency has evolved a great deal. We have moved on from tools that, 15 years ago, could require a week's worth of calculations to analyze a code, to tools that require only tens of minutes to arrive at a result.

Concerning viewpoints, it is necessary to better define which formal techniques are within standards (to introduce the notion of abstract interpretation, for example) and to authorize the verification of the behavior of a software application to not only be carried out via test activities but to also be a combination of formal and test techniques.

Conclusion

This book is part of a series of four books that cover different aspects of formal techniques: static analysis of code; B method; and formal methods.

Thus, this first volume concerns industrial examples of the implementation of formal techniques based on static analysis, such as the abstract interpretation and proof of program. There are examples of use of Astrée tools (Chapter 2), Caveat (Chapter 2), CodePeer (Chapter 5), Frama-C (Chapters 2 and 6) and Polsypace® (Chapters 3 and 4), as well as an example of generated C code analysis (Chapter 7).

One of the more delicate points regarding the implementation of different tools resides in the demonstration that the tool is usable for the targeted safety level. Indeed, it is then necessary to implement a qualification activity that can be based on:

– a certificate: there are certificates for certain tools, such as compilers and code generators (for example the C-code generator based on the SCADE® model is certified SSIL3-4 for the rail standard CENELEC EN 50128 [CEN 01a]);

– feedback: it is possible to construct an argument justifying feedback (list of projects, example of applications, number of hours of use, etc.); and/or

– a demonstration that the software can be used for the given safety level (it can be based on a safety demonstration, a validation campaign, etc.).

Bibliography

[ABR 96] ABRIAL J., *The B Book – Assigning Programs to Meanings*, Cambridge University Press, Cambridge, August 1996.

[ARI 92] ARINC, Software Considerations in Airborne Systems and Equipment Certification, DO 178B and EUROCAE, No. ED12, Edition B, ARINC, 1992.

[CEN 01a] CENELEC, NF EN 50128, Applications Ferroviaires. Système de Signalisation, de Télécommunication et de Traitement – Logiciel pour Système de Commande et de Protection Ferroviaire, CENELEC, July 2001.

[COU 00] COUSOT P., "Interprétation abstraite", *TSI*, vol. 19, no. 1-2-3, www.di.ens.fr/~cousot/COUSOTpapers/TSI00.shtml, 2000.

[DOR 08] DORMOY F.X., "Scade 6 a model based solution for safety critical software development", *Embedded Real-time Systems Conference*, 2008.

[HOA 69] HOARE C.,"An axiomatic basis for computer programming", *Communications of the ACM*, vol. 12, no. 10, pp. 576-580, 583, 1969.

[IEC 06] IEC, IEC 60880 – Nuclear power plants – instrumentation and control systems important to safety – software aspects for computer based systems performing category A functions. International Standards, IEEE, 2006.

[ISO 00] ISO, ISO 9000:2000 – Systèmes de Management de la Qualité – Principes Essentiels et Vocabulaire, ISO 2000.

[ISO 04] ISO, ISO 90003 – Ingénierie du Logiciel – Lignes Directrices pour l'Application de l'ISO 9001:2000 aux Logiciels Informatiques, ISO, 2004.

[ISO 08] ISO, ISO 9001:2008 – Systèmes de Management de la Qualité – exigence, ISO, December 2008.

[ISO 09] ISO, ISO/CD-26262, Road Vehicles – Functional Safety, ISO, 2009 (unpublished).

[JON 90] JONES C.B., *Systematic Software Development using VDM* (2nd edition), Prentice Hall International, Upper Saddle River, USA, 1990.

[SPI 89] SPIVEY J.M., *The Z Notation – a Reference Manual*, Prentice Hall International, Upper Saddle River, USA, 1989.

Glossary

Abbreviations	Terms	Chapter(s)
ACG	Automatic code generator	2
ACSL	ANSI/ISO-C Specification Language	6
ADU	To be defined later	7
AEEL	See SEEA	1
AMC	Acceptable mean of compliance	6
AMDE	Analysis of failure modes and their effects	1
AMDEC	See FMECA	1
API	Application programming interface	4, 6
ASA	Automata and structured analysis	1
ASIL	Automotive safety integrity level	1, 8
ATO	Automatic train operating	7
ATP	Automatic train protection	7
ATS	Automatic train supervision	7
BDD	Binary decision diagram	1
CBTC	Communication-based train controller	7
CDVE	Electric flight commands	2
CEM	Electromagnetic compatibility	1

Abbreviations	Terms	Chapter(s)
CENELEC[1]	*European Committee of Electrotechnical Standardization*	1, 4, 8
CFG	Control flow graph	2
CPU	Central processing unit	2
DAL	Development assurance level	1, 2, 6, 8
EASA	European Aviation Safety Agency	6
EB	Emergency breaking	7
E/E/PES	Electric/electronic/programmable electronics	4
FAA	Federal Aviation Administration	6
FDA	US Food and Drug Administration	3
FIQGEN	FIQ generalized to interval (see IUF for FIQ)	7
FMEA	Failure modes and effects analysis	1
FMEAC	Failure modes and effects analysis and criticity	1
FS	French standard	4
FT	Functional tests	1, 8
FU	Emergency breaking	7
FWS	Flight warning system	2
GUI	Graphical user interface	3
GVN	Global value numbering	5
HLR	High-level requirements	2, 6
HMI	Human−machine interface	2, 5, 6
IDE	Integrated development environment	5
IEC[2]	International Electrotechnical Commission	1, 4, 8
IEEE	Institute of Electrical and Electronic Engineers	7
IMA	Integrated modular avionic	2, 6
IPSN	Institute of Nuclear Protection and Safety/Institut de Protection et de Sûreté Nucléaire	3

---

1 See www.cenelec.eu/Cenelec/homepage.htm.
2 See www.iec.ch.

Abbreviations	Terms	Chapter(s)
IPT	Interactive predicate transformer	2
IPT	Inspection points	4
IRSN	Institute of Radioprotection and Nuclear Safety/ Institut de Radioprotection et de sûreté nucléaire	3
ISA	Independent safety assessor	4
ISO	International Organization for Standardization[3]	1, 8
ISSE	International Symposium on Software Reliability Engineering	3
IT	Integration tests	1, 8
IUF	Intrinsic uncertainty function	7
LLR	Low-level requirement	2, 6
MAGGALY	Large scale metro of the Lyon agglomeration/Métro Automatique á Grand Gabarit de l'Agglomération Lyonnaise	1
QAM	Quality assurance manual	1
MC/DC	Multiple condition/decision coverage	6
METEOR	Rapid East–West metro	1, 4
MISRA	Motor Industry Software Reliability Association	3
NHMO	NATO HAWK Management Office	3
ObjID	Identification object	5
OMG	Object Management Group[4]	1
OPRI	Office for Protection Against Ionizing Rays	3
PA	Automatic pilot	2
PAP	Point to protect	
AQP	Assurance quality plan	1
SQAP	Software quality assurance plan	1
SAP	Safety assurance plan	1
PGC	Configuration management plan	1
PSC	Coded safety processor	1

---

3 See www.iso.org/iso/fr/home.htm.
4 See www.omg.org.

Abbreviations	Terms	Chapter(s)
PVP	Propagation of possible values	5
PVV	Verification and validation plan	1
ROM	*Read-only memory*	3
RTE	*Run-time error*	4
SACEM	System to Aid Driving, Operation and Maintenance/ Système d'Aide à la Conduite à l'Exploitation et à la Maintenance	4
SADT	Structured Analysis and Design Technic	1
SAET	System for automation of train operation/Système d'automatisation de l'Exploitation des trains	1,4
SEEA	Software effects errors analysis	1
SI	International system of units (m, s, kg)	7
SIL	Safety integrity level	1, 4, 6, 7, 8
SSA	Static single assignment	5
SSIL	Software safety integrity level	1, 4, 8
STMF	Formal methods supplement technique/ Supplément techniques methods formalles	6
TCI	Uncertainty compensator term	7
TVM	Train vital management	4
ULP	Unit in last place	7
UML	Unified Modeling Language	1
UT	Unitary test	1, 8
VC	Verification condition	6
VHF	Very high frequency	2
VT	Validation test	1, 8
V&V	Verification and validation	1, 3
WCET	Worst case execution time	2
WP	Weakest precondition	3, 6
XML	eXtensible Markup Language	5

List of Authors

Samy AïT KACI
Paris
France

Antony BAïOTTO
Thales Security Solutions & Services
Vélizy-Villacoublay
France

Steve BAIRD
ADACORE
Paris
France

Jean-Louis BOULANGER
CERTIFER
Anzin
France

Arnaud CHARLET
ADACORE
Paris
France

David DELMAS
Airbus Operations SAS
Toulouse
France

Daniel DRAGO
INEXIA
La Plaine Saint-Denis
France

Stéphane DUPRAT
Atos Origin Integration
Toulouse
France

Christèle FAURE
SAFERIVER
Paris
France

Fateh KAAKAï
Thales Security Solutions & Services
Vélizy-Villacoublay
France

Emmanuel LEDINOT
Dassault Aviation
Saint Cloud
France

Rafael MARCANO
Thales Security Solutions & Services,
Vélizy-Villacoublay
France

Yannick MOY
ADACORE
Paris
France

Patrick MUNIER
MathWorks SAS
Paris
France

Dillon PARIENTE
Dassault Aviation
Saint Cloud
France

Jean SOUYRIS
Airbus Operations SAS
Toulouse
France

Tucker TAFT
SofCheck
Burlington
USA

Index